CORNOVIA

ANCIENT SITES OF
CORNWALL & SCILLY

CORNOVIA

Ancient Sites of Cornwall and Scilly

Craig Weatherhill

Bard *Delynyer Hendhyscans* of the Gorsedd of Cornwall

ALISON HODGE

ACKNOWLEDGEMENTS

To write a book of this kind is a demanding task, and it would not have been achieved without the help of others. For the provision of aerial photographs I am indebted to the Royal Commission on Historical Monuments (England), for the photographs on pages 29, 58, 63 and 69 (Crown copyright reserved); Professor Barri Jones of the University of Manchester, for the photograph on page 86 (copyright reserved); the Cambridge University Collection, for the photographs on pages 48, 87, 94, 95, 108 and 120 (copyright reserved); and to the Ministry of Defence, for the photographs on pages 30, 31, 34, 70, 84, 116 and 120 (Crown copyright reserved). Further invaluable help with photographs was given by David Clarke, Peter Marshall, Peter Pascoe and Ander Gunn.

For help, encouragement and advice, my thanks are due to the staff of the Cornwall Committee for Rescue Archaeology, the Royal Institution of Cornwall and the Cornwall Archaeological Society. I am also grateful to Professor Charles Thomas, Peter and Audrey Pool, Vivien Russell, Nick Johnson, Peter Rose, Tony Blackman and Alison Hodge.

Finally I should like to extend my heartfelt thanks to all the people in Cornwall and the Isles of Scilly who made me so welcome wherever I went.

First published in 1985 by Alison Hodge, Bosulval Farmhouse, Newmill, Penzance, Cornwall.

ISBN 0 906720 12 5

Designer: Stuart Hamilton

Typesetting and origination by TNR Productions Ltd, 19 Westbourne Road, London N7.

Printed and bound by Dowrick Design and Print Ltd, St Ives, Cornwall.

DEDICATION

This book is dedicated to the memory of a great and courageous man, who saw the start of the project but, sadly, did not live to see its completion: Lieutenant Arthur W. Weatherhill, RN (1909–1982), my father.

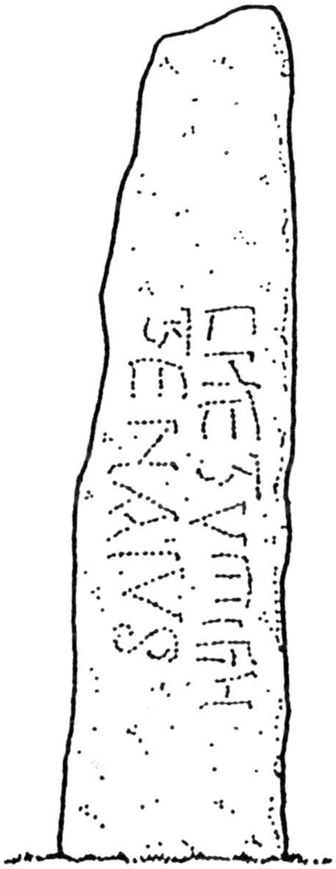

CONTENTS

Introduction

In her book *When I Set Out For Lyonesse . . .* (Alison Hodge, 1984), Judith Cook says that in Cornwall 'you feel you are in the presence of something very old indeed'. To take just some of the walks she outlines will bring you face to face with that very timelessness: Cornwall is famous for its wealth and diversity of ancient sites. Turn a corner in a lonely lane and you may be confronted by a massive standing stone, or a stone circle looking for all the world like frozen dancers. Another corner may bring you to one of the great megalithic tombs, or the burial mound of a Bronze Age chieftain. A walk to the top of a hill could take you to the huge ditches and ramparts of an Iron Age fortress. In what at first glance seems featureless moorland, the discerning eye will detect the foundations and outlines of houses and fields abandoned thousands of years ago.

Cornwall is special; its archaeological richness is second to none. At the time of writing, the Sites and Monuments Record of the Cornwall Committee for Rescue Archaeology holds approximately 40,000 records. Yet strangely, no comprehensive field guide to Cornwall's best and most interesting sites has ever been produced. This has prompted the writing of the present book, which features no less than 200 prehistoric and pre-Norman sites in Cornwall and the Isles of Scilly.

Cornovia is not intended to supercede my previous book, *Belerion: Ancient Sites of Land's End* (Alison Hodge, 1981), which should be regarded as a companion volume. In *Belerion* I wrote at some length about people and their way of life through the ages. In *Cornovia* the monuments themselves receive that attention. The presentation too is different. In *Belerion* I grouped the sites according to their ages – neolithic, Bronze Age, Iron Age and Dark Age/Early Christian. In *Cornovia* this is not possible, for with sites like King Arthur's Hall, their age and purpose are unknown. Instead, I have divided the gazetteer into districts, using the local government districts created in 1974. These were preferred to the old Cornish hundreds for two reasons: first, the new districts have become known and accepted by most folk in Cornwall; and secondly in the hope that the local authorities themselves might recognize the importance of Cornish archaeology and play their part more fully in the preservation and safeguarding of their heritage.

For visitors to Cornwall, these districts are as follows:

Caradon covers the south-east of Cornwall, including the southern reaches of Bodmin Moor. Its principal towns are Liskeard, Saltash, Torpoint, Looe and Callington.

Carrick stretches from the south coast to the north, and could be described as western mid-Cornwall. The principal towns are Truro, Falmouth and Perranporth.

Kerrier adjoins Carrick on the west and includes the entire Lizard peninsula as well as the granite hills of the Wendron moors and the coast to the north of Camborne and Redruth. Its other principal town is Helston.

North Cornwall, the largest of the districts, covers north-east Cornwall, including the greater part of the archaeologically rich Bodmin Moor. Curiously, its south-western limit is a few miles south and south-west of the Camel estuary, rather than the estuary itself. North Cornwall's most important towns are Bodmin, Camelford, Bude, Launceston, Wadebridge and Padstow.

Penwith, which virtually preserves the ancient hundred of Penwith, is the far western tip of Cornwall, and its incredible wealth of ancient sites is second to none. Principal towns are Penzance, St Ives, St Just and Hayle.

Restormel, named after the magnificent medieval castle to the north of Lostwithiel, covers eastern mid-

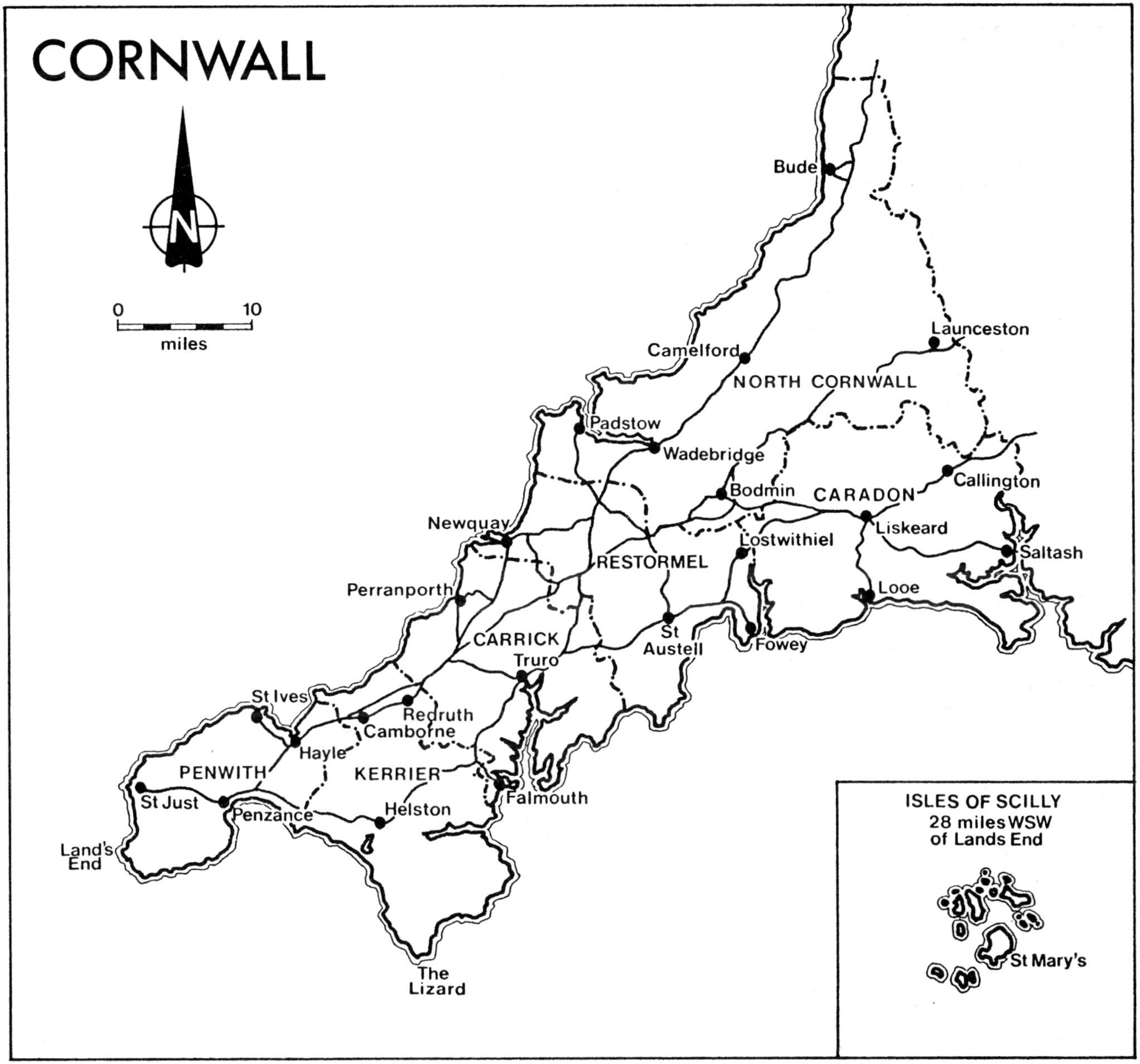
CORNWALL
N
0
10
miles
Bude
Launceston
Camelford
NORTH CORNWALL
Padstow
Wadebridge
Bodmin
CARADON
Callington
Newquay
Liskeard
Lostwithiel
Saltash
RESTORMEL
Perranporth
Looe
St
Austell
Fowey
CARRICK
Truro
St Ives
Redruth
Camborne
Hayle
PENWITH
KERRIER
Falmouth
St Just
Penzance
Helston
Land's
End
The
Lizard
ISLES OF SCILLY
28 miles WSW
of Lands End
St Mary's

Cornwall, with coastlines to north and south. Its principal towns are St Austell, Fowey, Lostwithiel and Newquay.

The Isles of Scilly, the beautiful granite archipelago twenty-eight miles to the south-west of Land's End, are also extraordinarily rich in ancient remains, especially megalithic tombs. As recently as Roman times Scilly consisted of one major island which included what are now the islands of St Mary's, St Martin's, Tresco, Bryher, Samson and the Eastern Isles, with a smaller island (St Agnes, Gugh and Annet) just offshore to the south-west. To the Romans Scilly was *Sylina Insula* (note the singular tense). Over the years the islands have been slowly sinking, and a great deal of their archaeology now lies beneath the sea. Many prehistoric huts and fields have been detected under the water between the islands; some are visible at low water, especially on the east side of Samson. The stretch of water known as Crow Sound has been navigable only since Tudor times, and its lack of depth explains why the RMV *Scillonian* is so shallow draughted. The principal island is St Mary's, and the other inhabited islands – Tresco, Bryher, St Martin's and St Agnes – are all served by regular boat services from Hugh Town, St Mary's.

Ancient sites and the law

1984, when most of this book was written, was British Heritage Year, but for Cornish archaeology it was a disaster. A large part of the Iron Age village of Chysauster's well preserved field system was bulldozed away and there was an orgy of dreadful damage to over forty ancient sites resulting from commercially inspired national treasure hunts.

The vast majority of ancient sites featured in this book are Scheduled Ancient Monuments; in other words, they are protected under the law. To damage or tamper with them in any way is a criminal offence which carries a heavy penalty. The law is designed to protect these sites against the indiscriminate treasure-seeker and the irresponsible minority of metal-detector operators.

Our ancient sites must be left alone and undamaged, not only for our own enjoyment and education, but for future generations. Without a past to learn from, how can we hope to have a future? We still have much to learn about the peoples of the past and the diverse structures they built.

A number of the sites described here are on private land, and it is essential to seek the owner's permission to visit them. In almost every case, the response will be cordial and helpful. Always close gates behind you, keep to footpaths, or at the very least to the edges of cultivated fields. Leave no litter, and please don't let dogs loose among livestock. If you keep to these simple guidelines you can enjoy the Cornish countryside and its ancient sites, and Cornwall will enjoy having you.

Finally, should you see an ancient monument being damaged, or if you find fresh damage, please notify the Cornwall Committee for Rescue Archaeology, Rooms 3 and 4, Old County Hall, Truro, telephone Truro (0872) 74282, extensions 328 and 330.

Dating

Only a few Cornish archaeological sites have been dated by scientific methods; the majority of dates have been deduced from pottery finds analogous to those sites which have undergone radio-carbon dating. This method, also known as C14 dating, is based on the fact that all living organisms absorb radioactive carbon from the atmosphere, but cease to absorb it once they have died. Then the carbon 14 decays and can be measured against the absorbed amount of carbon 12, which does not decay. When the C 14 has decayed to half the original amount, this is known as the 'half-life', which has been variously interpreted as 5,568 years and 5,730 years. In certain circumstances the C 14 does not decay at the average rate, so radio-carbon dates are expressed as, say, 1500bc plus or minus 100, ie. 1600bc to 1400bc. There is a 66 per cent probability that the actual date falls between these two dates.

Until a few years ago it was assumed that C 14 decays at a uniform rate, but checking by means of counting and then C 14 testing the rings of the Bristlecone pine, a long-living American tree, showed that this is not so. In fact there was more C 14 in the atmosphere at some times than at others, so the radio-carbon dates for those periods are too young. Calibration curves (that of Clark, 1975, is the most widely used) have been produced to provide the true years. In general terms, C 14 dates of 3000bc are about 800 years too recent; 2000bc is 500 years too young, and 1000bc about 250 years too recent. Therefore, radio-carbon dates are expressed as years bc; the recalibrated dates are shown as years BC. For example, 1250bc (1550 BC).

A selection of Cornish radio-carbon and recalibrated dates is given at the end of the book.

Maps

The recommended maps, which cover the whole of Cornwall and Scilly, are the Ordnance Survey 1:50,000 Landranger Series, sheets 200 (Newquay and Bodmin), 190 (Bude and Clovelly), 201 (Plymouth and Launceston), 203 (Land's End, the Lizard and the Isles of Scilly) and 204 (Truro and Falmouth).

The British National Grid Reference system, used throughout this book, is clearly and simply explained on each Ordnance Survey map. The system applies to all Ordnance Survey maps, regardless of scale.

Abbrevations

The abbrevations NT and DE will be found in the gazetteer. These indicate monuments under the guardianship of either the National Trust or the Department of the Environment.

Measurement

With reluctance I have bowed to metrication. Linear measurements are given in metres (m) and centimetres (cm), areas in hectares (ha) and weights in tonnes, which for the purposes of this book may be closely equated with imperial tons. However, I have kept to miles for greater distances.

For many people, metric measurements are hard to visualize, and the following tables may prove helpful. They are simple to use: the figures in the central columns may be read as either the metric or the imperial measure. For example: 1 inch = 2.5 centimetres; or 1 centimetre = 0.4 inches (I have taken these figures to the first decimal place only for simplicity's sake).

centimetres		inches	metres		feet	metres		feet
2.5	1	0.4	0.3	1	3.3	30.5	100	328.1
5.1	2	0.8	0.6	2	6.6	60.1	200	656.2
7.6	3	1.2	0.9	3	9.8	91.4	300	984.2
10.2	4	1.6	1.2	4	13.1	121.9	400	1312.3
12.7	5	2.0	1.5	5	16.4	152.4	500	1640.4
15.2	6	2.4	1.8	6	19.7	182.9	600	1968.5
17.8	7	2.8	2.1	7	23.0	213.3	700	2296.6
20.3	8	3.2	2.4	8	26.3	243.7	800	2624.6
22.9	9	3.5	2.7	9	29.5	274.2	900	2952.7
25.4	10	3.9	3.1	10	32.8	304.7	1000	3280.8
27.9	11	4.3	6.1	20	65.6	459.1	1500	4921.2
30.5	12	4.7	15.2	50	164.0	609.4	2000	6561.6

metres		yards	hectares		acres
0.9	1	1.1	0.4	1	2.5
1.8	2	2.2	0.8	2	4.9
2.7	3	3.3	1.2	3	7.4
3.7	4	4.4	1.6	4	9.9
4.6	5	5.5	2.0	5	12.4
5.5	6	6.6	4.0	10	24.7
6.4	7	7.7	8.1	20	49.4
7.3	8	8.8	12.1	30	74.1
8.2	9	9.8	16.2	40	98.8
9.1	10	10.9	20.2	50	123.6
91.4	100	109.4	30.4	75	185.3
457.2	500	547.0	40.5	100	247.1

An outline of Cornish archaeology

The Stone Age

From the earliest traces of human presence in Britain to about 8000 BC is known as the palaeolithic era (Old Stone Age). The last of the glaciers had retreated and small numbers of nomadic hunters, gatherers and fishermen drifted into Britain from the Continent, over the land bridge which was finally inundated at the end of the palaeolithic period. A few axeheads dating from this time have been found in Cornwall.

The gradual improvement in the climate encouraged further groups of industrious people to settle in Britain, so beginning the mesolithic era (Middle Stone Age). Cornish evidence suggests that these folk inhabited various inland sites, notably Dozmary Pool on Bodmin Moor, but wintered on the coast. Their mode of life was similar to that of their palaeolithic predecessors: hunting, gathering and fishing; but as the sea has risen about thirty-six metres since then, many mesolithic sites are presumably under water. Nevertheless, traces of their flint-working sites can be found all along the north coast of Cornwall, especially at Land's End and Trevose Head, where their tiny *microliths*, used for points, barbs and cutting edges, are often turned up in freshly ploughed fields.

The earliest monuments to survive to this day date from the succeeding neolithic (New Stone Age) period, which began around 4500 BC. The new peoples who arrived in Britain at the beginning of this period brought with them the knowledge of agriculture. They were the first to found permanent settlements, mainly of timber-built houses whose traces have sometimes been found by accident. Some settlements were sited on rocky uplands within *tor enclosures* such as the recently excavated example on Carn Brea which may date from as early as 3900 BC, one of the oldest known settlements in Britain.

The fine craftsmanship of the neolithic era produced polished stone axes and exquisite leaf-shaped arrowheads, once fearfully known as 'elf-bolts'. The first pottery appeared at this time; in Cornwall the usual finds are of undecorated, round-bottomed, hand-made ware known as the *Western* type, but decorated and moulded types are known.

The Cornish neolithic period is typified by the great *chamber tombs*, of which two main types occur: the Penwith tombs, variants of the portal dolmen and better known as 'quoits', and the Scillonian tombs, or 'entrance graves', of passage-grave type. Doubt has recently been cast on the presumed funerary function of these monuments. The burial practice of the time was inhumation, but as the neolithic period drew to a close, cremation became more common.

A further type of neolithic tomb, the *long barrow*, is rare in Cornwall and ritual practice in the later neolithic era is shown by the appearance of *henges*. There is much evidence of trade, especially the manufacture and transportation of Cornish axes to many parts of southern Britain along established routes by land, along *ridgeways*, and by sea along inshore routes.

Towards the close of the neolithic period, *circa* 2500 BC, numbers of *Beaker* folk (so-called from the characteristic ware often found accompanying their burials) settled in Britain. These dynamic people adapted and developed the henge monuments and began the erection of *stone circles*, *menhirs* and *stone alignments*. They tended to use

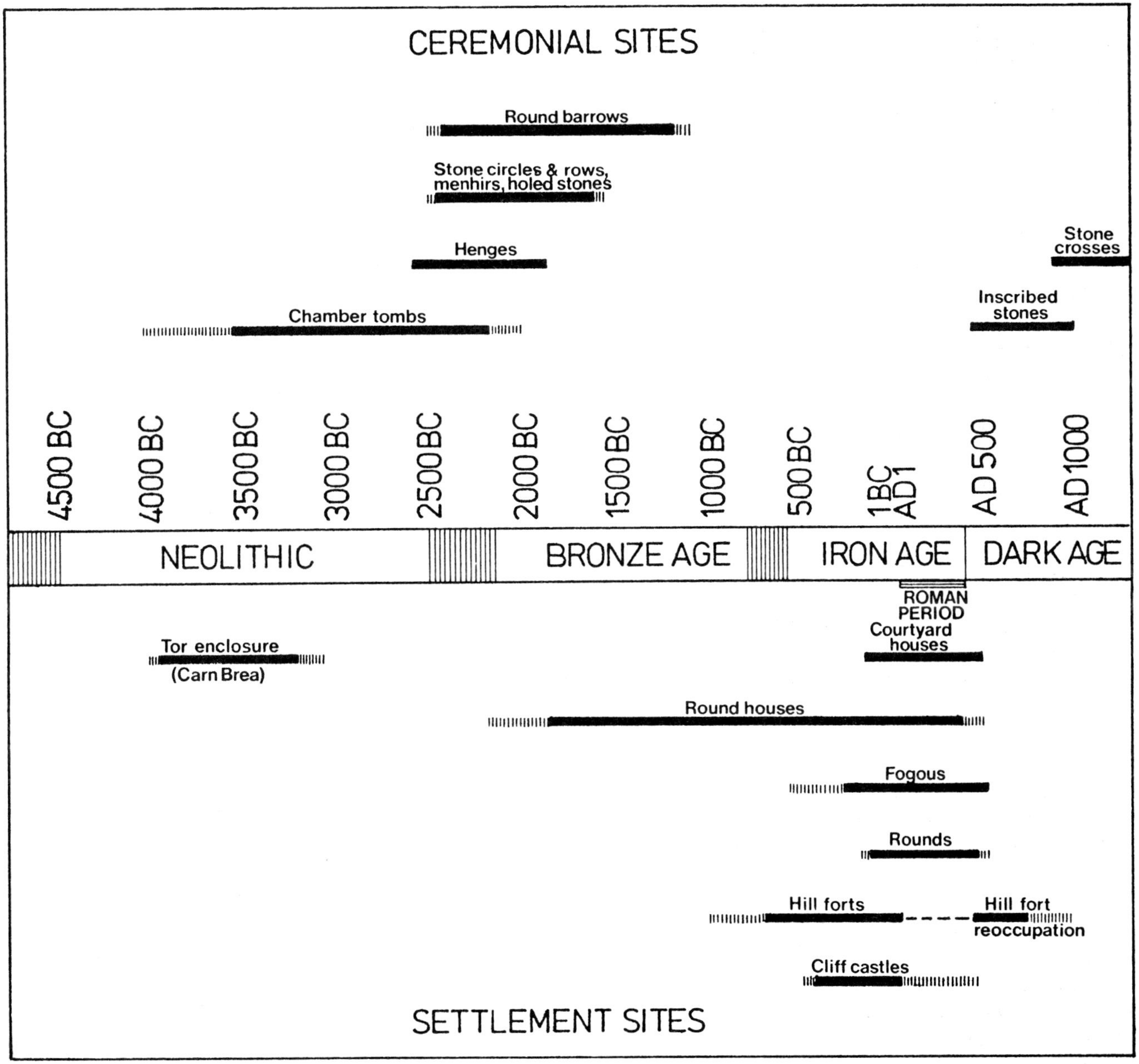

CEREMONIAL SITES
Round barrows
Stone circles & rows, menhirs, holed stones
Henges
Chamber tombs
Stone crosses
Inscribed stones
4500 BC
4000 BC
3500 BC
3000 BC
2500 BC
2000 BC
1500 BC
1000 BC
500 BC
1BC AD1
AD 500
AD 1000
NEOLITHIC
BRONZE AGE
IRON AGE
DARK AGE
ROMAN PERIOD
Courtyard houses
Tor enclosure
(Carn Brea)
Round houses
Fogous
Rounds
Hill forts
Hill fort reoccupation
Cliff castles
SETTLEMENT SITES

the existing chamber tombs for burial, as well as their own fashion of single inhumation in pits, or in *cists* under simple *round barrows*.

The Bronze Age

Bronze Age cultures began to take shape around 2200 BC, with new ideas spreading from the Continent to the existing population. The most dominant of these may have been spread by the class-structured warriors and tin merchants then resident in Brittany. Cornish tin and copper began to be exploited, thus originating the Cornish tin-trade with the Continent with the shipment of the smelted ores to Brittany, and thence to Mediterranean customers. Bronze, the alloy of tin and copper, became the standard metal for weapons and tools, and beautiful jewellery and decorative ware, often of gold, became the hallmark of what has been called the *Wessex culture*.

The erection and use of *stone circles*, *menhirs*, *stone alignments* and *holed stones* continued, and the *round barrow* of the Beaker folk was developed into a series of different architectural types. Cremation was now the usual burial practice, and sophisticated styles of pottery, such as *collared urns* and *food vessels* became commonplace.

By 1400 BC a social decline had set in, perhaps partly due to the deterioration in climate; the full reasons have yet to be determined. The stone circles and other ceremonial sites were abandoned as though the old gods were being discarded in favour of new ones. Standards of craftsmanship fell, and there is some evidence of emigration to the Low Countries. The sophisticated pottery of the Early Bronze Age gave way to inferior ware such as the *Deveral-Rimbury* type, and the characteristically Cornish *Trevisker* ware.

To date, little has been found of settlement remains prior to 1500 BC, but many of the *round house settlements* and *field systems* common on Bodmin Moor and in West Penwith date from the Later Bronze Age. The inhabitants of these settlements carried out subsistence farming on a ranch-like principle.

A sudden boom in metalcraft occurred after about 1000 BC, with new items, notably advanced types of spearheads, appearing. Some early *hill forts*, usually of univallate (single defence) type were already being built, possibly by advance parties of *Celts*.

The Iron Age

The arrival of ideas from Celtic north-western Europe after 800 BC heralded the start of the Iron Age. Like the earlier Wessex culture, the Celts lived in a structured society headed by a warrior aristocracy. Skilled mariners, warriors, craftsmen, farmers, builders and metalworkers, they spoke the *Brythonic* tongue, forerunner of the Cornish, Welsh and Breton languages. Their use of iron was mainly restricted to edged tools and weapons; for utensils and decorative ware they continued to use copper, bronze and gold. The style of life was similar to that of the preceding Later Bronze Age, with farms of *round houses* and *field systems* and univallate *hill forts*.

Further waves of Celtic immigration in the fourth or fifth century BC began a golden age of hill fort building, these largely consisting of multiple defences. The long range weapon of the time was the slingshot: the bows and arrows common in the neolithic and Bronze Ages do not seem to have been part of the Celtic arsenal.

Cornwall's flagging tin trade was revived, probably by the Veneti tribe of southern Brittany, many of whom settled in Cornwall. Their massive ships were used to transport the ingots across the channel to their homeland, and thence overland by the old route through the Carcassone Gap for sale at the then Greek colony of Massilia (Marseilles). The mining, smelting and transportation of tin from west Cornwall was described by Pytheas of Massilia *circa* 325 BC, who was quoted by Diodorus Siculus two centuries later. The people of west Cornwall were described as 'civilized and courteous'. The district itself was known as *Belerion* – possibly from the Cornish *paloryon*: (place of) diggers.

Many of the *cliff castles* have been ascribed to the Veneti, or to Venetic influence. These are prominent headlands with defences thrown up across the neck of land connecting them to the mainland.

The Celtic *round houses* were generally larger and more substantially built than their Bronze Age predecessors. In upland areas they were built of stone; the timber-built variants of lower, less stony regions are found only by excavation. In most of Cornwall, like the rest of Britain, the round house was the standard dwelling type throughout the Iron Age and the Roman period. In the Land's End peninsula, though, a much larger and improved design, the *courtyard house*, appeared during the first century BC. But strangely these large, oval structures did not supercede the round houses, nor did they spread to other upland areas of the south-west.

Enclosed settlements, known in Cornwall as *rounds*, appeared throughout the region at about the same time as the courtyard house. Associated with both types of site west of the Fal are the enigmatic structures known as *fogous*.

The Celts divided Britain into a series of kingdoms. Cornwall formed the westernmost part of the kingdom of *Dumnonia* which also covered Devon and parts of Dorset and Somerset. Cornwall itself was known as *Cernyw* (*Kernow* in modern Cornish), which was later latinized to *Cornovia*. This word seems to mean 'place of promontory-dwellers', probably alluding to the large number of cliff castles around the coast. Dumnonia was ruled by a high king with a number of lesser kings or chieftains of smaller regions which, in Cornwall, may have been the forerunners of the old 'hundreds'.

The Roman period

The impact of the Claudian invasion of AD 43 and the following four centuries of Roman rule was felt less in Cornwall than in most of occupied Britain. Although integrated into the Roman system, Cornwall was still more or less autonomous, and the nearest Roman city and administrative centre was Exeter (*Isca Dumnoniorum*), from which no Roman road led westward. It seems that the Romans may have intended a road through Cornwall, perhaps to exploit Cornish tin, for *milestones* were set up to mark the route during the third century AD. Five of them survive, but the road was never built.

Cornwall has just one *Roman fort*, near Bodmin, dating from the first century AD, but it was extremely short-lived. Roman objects were recovered from a ritual shaft within an earlier enclosure at Bosence, St Hilary; and a *Roman villa*, possibly native-built, was found to the north of Camborne, but there is nothing to be seen of this today. Finds of Roman coins have been common and widespread, indicative of strong trading links between the Cornu-Britons and the Romans, but life in general remained unaffected by Roman rule. In reality, Cornish Iron Age cultures continued, so that here the Roman period is better described as the *Roman Iron Age*, or *Romano-British period*.

Native occupation of courtyard houses and enclosed settlements continued throughout the period, but the hill forts and cliff castles largely fell into disuse. A degree of late Roman influence is shown by the appearance of red *Samian ware* on some settlement sites. But it seems that although Dumnonia had become a Roman province, the native kings continued to rule.

The final withdrawal of the Romans from Britain was in AD 410, by which time they had ceased to be looked on as enemies, and were felt to be friends and protectors. By then a significant change was beginning to take place among the native population. Christianity and the Celtic church had arrived.

The Dark Ages (post-Roman or Early Christian period)

By AD410 the last of the Roman forces had left Britain in a desperate bid to foil barbarian advances on the shrinking empire. They were never to return. In Cornwall, though, this had little effect. Some of the *courtyard houses* and *enclosed settlements* were still in occupation, but they were being abandoned in favour of more open farming settlements on lower ground.

No doubt word was reaching Cornwall of the Teutonic invasions, settlements and advances on the opposite side of Britain, which were repulsed and checked for a while by Romano-Celtic generals like Ambrosius Aurelianus and Artorius (Arthur) up to the early part of the sixth century. It was to be another two hundred years before Cornwall had to face the Anglo-Saxons. Nevertheless numbers of Cornishmen were migrating to Brittany.

In the sixth century, however, certain *hill forts* were reoccupied and refurbished, in common with a number of other forts in south-western Britain and south Wales; perhaps to meet an Irish threat. Buildings within these forts, and on other sites like Tintagel, show that rectangular designs were replacing the round and oval buildings of the past.

Inscribed stones, as memorials to the dead, were a Christian innovation of the fifth century, and were set up extensively during the following centuries. Six stones with bilingual inscriptions, in Latin and the strange Irish Ogam script, bear witness to a certain amount of Irish incursion, as do a number of plain Latin inscriptions with Irish names.

Two *linear earthworks*, assumed to be early post-Roman, can still be traced. The Giant's Hedge may mark the northern border of land ruled by a minor king; the purpose of the smaller Bolster Bank is not clear.

The proliferation of *stone crosses*, mostly waymarks on paths to churches, began in the ninth century.

Cornwall first faced the Anglo-Saxon advance when King Centwine won a battle in north Devon which resulted in the Saxon occupation of the north-east tip of Cornwall, apparent even today in the large number of Saxon place-names in that area. A second battle, at Linig (probably between the rivers Lynher and Tamar), resulted from King Gerent of Cornwall's refusal to allow the Celtic church to follow the call of the English church (which was perhaps as much as 300 years younger) to conform to the standards of Rome. The battle took place in 710 and was fought against the Wessex king Ine and his kinsman Nonna. No victor is named, but results indicate that Gerent was not successful.

At the battle of Hehil (probably Slaughter Bridge on the River Camel) in 722 the Cornish pushed back a Saxon offensive in north-east Cornwall. Further battles occurred in east Cornwall during the eighth century, but the victors are not recorded. It seems, though, that the Cornish held firm. King Egbert regained north-east Cornwall in 815, pushing as far west as St Breock. The battle of Gafalforda (probably Galford on the Devon side of the Tamar) took place ten years later; again the victor is not known.

The battle of Hengestsdun (Hingston Down, above Callington) in 838 effectively ended Cornish resistance to the Anglo-Saxons when Egbert defeated a Cornish army augmented by Danish Vikings who were apparently using Cornish havens as bases from which to harry the coast of Wessex. Many more Cornish folk migrated to Brittany.

However, the Saxons did not push on for total conquest, perhaps happy that any further resistance would be of a passive nature. Cornwall remained autonomous until the reign of Athelstan. In 926 he expelled the Cornish, last of the Dumnonians, from their ancient capital of Exeter, and agreed with Huwal, the last known Cornish king, that the left bank of the River Tamar be set as the border between Cornwall and England, and that the crown of Cornwall be subject to the crown of England. The true conquest of Cornwall was left to the Normans.

The present name of Cornwall is a hybrid: the old Celtic name for the land, *Cernyw* (*Kernow*), plus the Saxon word *wealas* (strangers, foreigners), the word from which Wales is also derived.

The Monuments

Chamber tombs

The great megalithic tombs of Cornwall and Scilly are among the earliest of all the surviving monuments. Two main types are to be found: the awesome Penwith chamber tombs, better known as 'quoits', and the Scillonian chamber tombs, or 'entrance graves', which are confined to the Isles of Scilly and the Land's End peninsula. These are less spectacular than the huge, gaunt quoits, but no less impressive and fascinating.

Penwith chamber tombs

These are variants of the *portal dolmen* which are also common in Wales and Ireland. Of the dozen surviving Cornish tombs, only three (Pawton Quoit, North Cornwall; Trethevy Quoit, Caradon, and Zennor Quoit, Penwith) are true portal dolmens. A few others were apparently simple, closed boxes, Chûn Quoit in Penwith being by far the best example. The rest are now so ruined or altered, as is Lanyon Quoit, Penwith, that their original form can no longer be determined. All the quoits comprised of large upright slabs forming a chamber roofed by a single, massive capstone many tonnes in weight. The size of each quoit and the skill that must have been put into their construction are staggering. While the heaviest capstone (estimated at 14.5 tonnes) tops the comparatively low dolmen of Pawton Quoit, the achievements of neolithic engineering are best appreciated at Zennor Quoit where a 9.5 tonne capstone, 5.5m long, was positioned on a chamber of granite slabs 2.4m high.

At both Zennor and Trethevy Quoits two of the side stones of the main chamber projected forward to form an antechamber fronted by a pair of façade slabs. At Pawton Quoit the portal effect was achieved by a series of slabs forming a wide frontal façade. There was no antechamber.

Even the 'closed box' tombs retain hints of a portal design. At Chûn Quoit, for example, the southern elevation is immediately the most impressive. A narrow, restricted gap affords the sole access to the chamber; the slightly tilted capstone is at its highest on this side, and also presents its thickest and most regular edge. There are signs of a possible approach passage from the south.

A number of these tombs retain vestiges of a surrounding circular or oval mound. At Chûn, for instance, some stones of the kerb or outer retaining wall of the mound remain. Until recently it was accepted that the mounds formerly covered the stone chambers, but it has been reasonably argued that they did not; that the chambers were so visually and architecturally impressive that at least part of them was meant to be seen. It is quite possible, therefore, that the capstone and façade of each tomb was left exposed, and that the approach was by a passage leading through the mound to the front of the tomb. Two large stones embedded in the mound on the south side of Chûn Quoit may be the remains of just such an approach.

All the mounds surrounding the quoits are round or oval. Until recently, Lanyon Quoit was assumed to stand at the north end of a long barrow; but what was taken for the barrow is now thought to represent the spread remains of two adjoining oval mounds, one containing the quoit, the other a number of stone cists, or small box-like structures.

To date, only one of the surviving tombs – Sperris in Penwith – has been excavated using modern techniques, with further small examinations at Lesquite, North

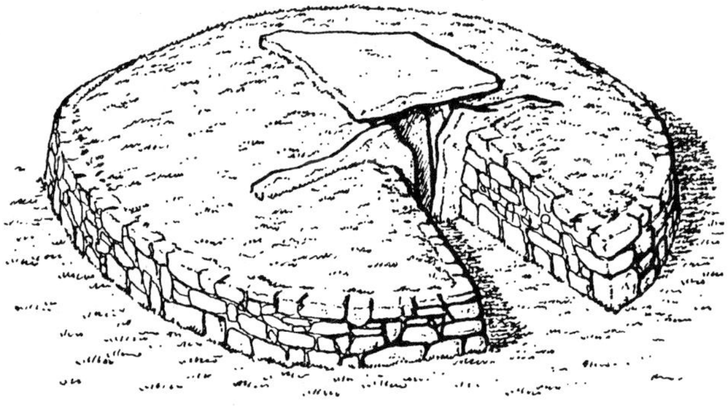

ZENNOR QUOIT, Penwith.

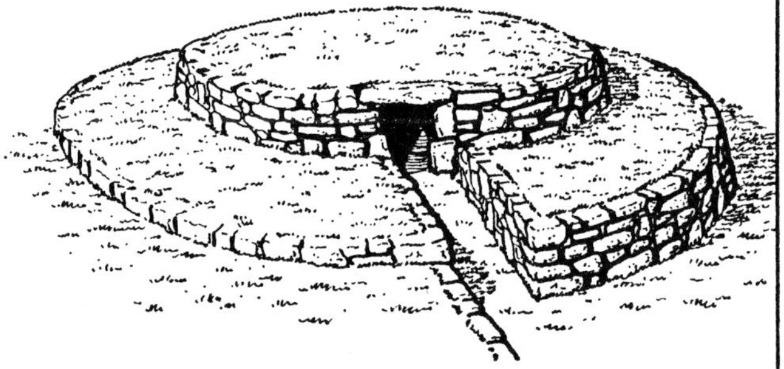

BANT'S CARN, Isles of Scilly.

BALLOWALL BARROW, Penwith.

Cornwall, and Devil's Coyt, Restormel. A number have suffered under the spade (or, like Zennor Quoit, explosives) during the last 250 years. Unfortunately, such grandiose structures have invited pillage throughout the ages and most recorded finds seem to date from secondary use of the tombs. These include cremated remains from a presumed antechamber at Sperris Quoit, and a perforated whetstone, tentatively dated to *circa* 1600-1500bc (1975-1835 BC), from the antechamber of Zennor Quoit. The positions of these secondary objects add weight to the argument that the front part of each tomb was always left exposed.

Inhumation burial seems to have been the usual practice when the quoits were built. Evidence of this came from the discovery of West Lanyon Quoit which was found in a collapsed state following the removal of its mound *circa* 1800. The chamber contained a large number of disturbed human bones, and it appears that it had been a virtual charnel house over a long period: as a body was placed in the tomb, so the bones of former interments were pushed aside to make room for it. Dr Borlase's eighteenth-century references to pits containing 'black, greasy loam' within the chambers of Lanyon and Mulfra Quoits might also be taken as possible evidence of inhumation.

Dating the quoits is difficult, owing to the lack of dateable finds from the earliest use of the tombs. However, it is reasonable to assume that they were built during the middle to late neolithic period, *circa* 3500-2500 BC. Recent results from the excavation of the Welsh portal dolmen of Dyffryn Ardudwy may push this dating back by as much as 500 years.

At the time of writing, the Cornwall Archaeological Society is proposing to conduct a thorough and detailed study, including survey and excavation, of all the Penwith chamber tombs.

Chamber tombs: suggested reconstructions.

Scillonian chamber tombs

In its simplest form, the Scillonian chamber tomb or entrance grave consists of a circular mound, usually between 6 and 12 metres across, retained by a heavy kerb of granite blocks. Within the mound is a passage-like chamber whose walls are large slabs on edge, or stone walling, which opens onto the side of the mound. The chamber, usually about a metre in both height and width, is roofed by a number of small capstones.

Several of these tombs show a second phase of construction, often in the form of a lower collar surrounding the original mound. This is best seen at Bant's Carn on St Mary's in the Isles of Scilly. Other second-phase alterations include the blocking of the outer end of the chamber, as at Tregiffian and Tregeseal, both on the mainland in Penwith. Grander forms of multi-phase construction are also to be found. The huge and unique Ballowall Barrow (or Carn Gloose), Penwith, presents a number of possibilities regarding the exact sequence of phases, but it is likely that a conventional entrance grave was built first, before the construction of the massive and complex structure into which it is incorporated. An apparent entrance grave on the summit of Chapel Carn Brea, Penwith, was later covered by a massive cairn incorporating a number of retaining walls and a large stone cist. Some aspects of entrance grave design in Scilly even suggest the existence of a specialist architect.

The chambers are seldom of a simple rectangular plan; usually a distinct bulge occurs near the inner end, resulting in a coffin-shaped plan. The entrances are often constricted, as at Porth Hellick Down, Scilly, where an upright slab reduces the entrance to less than half the width of the chamber and its approach passage.

The Isles of Scilly contain an astonishing number of these tombs: more than fifty still survive. On the mainland, where they are restricted to the Penwith peninsula, only a dozen or so have been identified.

Assigning a date to the entrance graves is no easier at present than dating the Penwith chamber tombs. Only a handful have been properly excavated, and very few contained human remains (cremation in almost all of the few cases). Charcoal from the Tregiffian tomb produced a carbon-14 date of *circa* 1540bc (1900 BC), which conflicts with the late neolithic pottery yielded by similar tombs. Such cremations must date from secondary use, and much doubt has been cast as to whether or not entrance graves were originally built as tombs at all. One theory is that they served as focal points for a cult concerned with soil fertility.

Recent fieldwork in the Isles of Scilly indicates that the island tombs derived from those on the mainland, and not vice versa as previously thought. As the islanders were not colonized until *circa* 2230 BC, by a farming group of Beaker successor people, it follows that the mainland tombs are older. It is likely that a date prior to 2500 BC should be considered for the origin of entrance grave design and construction.

Henges

These presumably ceremonial sites are to be found throughout lowland Britain; relatively few occur in upland areas. Only three Cornish examples survive in any degree of preservation.

A henge consists of a flat circular or oval area, sometimes featureless, sometimes containing a stone or timber circle, surrounded by a ditch and an external bank. This arrangement precludes any defensive function for these sites.

The Cornish henges belong to the Class I group, because they have a single entrance. The site at Castilly, Restormel, appears to have a pair of entrances directly opposite each other, but it has been shown that the southern opening dates from a medieval re-use.

Castilly and Castlewich, Caradon, show no signs of their central areas having been anything other than featureless, but the Stripple Stones, North Cornwall, which is slighter and more crudely built than either of the others, contains the ruin of a stone circle. Despite this, it is thought that the origin of henge-building belongs somewhere in the mid neolithic period, *circa* 3000 BC, somewhat earlier than the beginning of stone circle construction. Their use probably spanned the remainder of the neolithic and the Early Bronze Age.

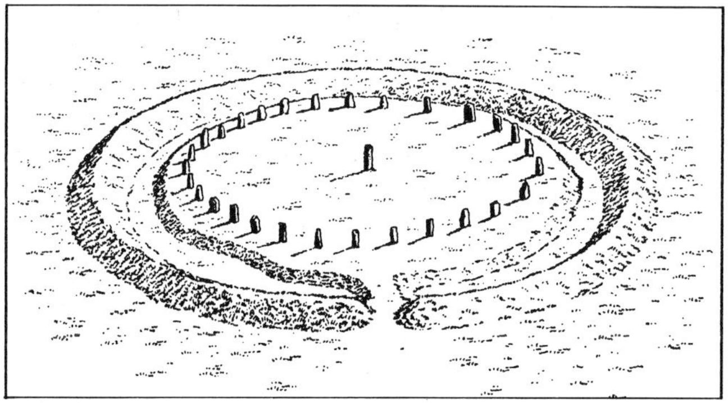

The Stripple Stones circle-henge: reconstruction.

Stone circles

Even in ruin, stone circles can be among the most inspiring and atmospheric of all prehistoric sites. Few have been excavated – in Cornwall, only the Stripple Stones henge-circle, North Cornwall, and the Hurlers, Caradon, have been partially examined – and there have been few dateable finds. It is generally accepted, however, that the Cornish circles date from the Early Bronze Age, *circa* 2500-1600 BC. Their exact purpose is obscure, although it is almost certain that they performed some ceremonial function. Cornwall has no less than twenty-five of these circles, four of which have been discovered only recently.

Much has been made of researches suggesting astronomical orientations of stone circles through alignments with outlying menhirs, barrows and natural features, but there is insufficient evidence to form any conclusion. At only six Cornish circles can any astronomical connections be shown; some on Bodmin Moor appear to be positioned in such a way that certain hilltops mark the position of midsummer, midwinter or Equinoctial sunrise or sunset. Similarly, some circles seem to have connections with nearby prominent peaks which may have had sacred significance for the Early Bronze Age folk.

Many stone circles do form the focal point of systems of outlying barrows, menhirs, and, in some cases, holed stones. The best example is the Merry Maidens, Penwith, where six menhirs, including two pairs, a number of barrows (one of which is the superb Tregiffian tomb, a chamber of the Scillonian type) and three holed stones occur within a radius of half a mile. The significance of such a system has yet to be fully understood.

Stone circles vary in shape. Some, like the Merry Maidens, are true geometric circles, probably laid out by means of a rope and a central peg. Others are elliptical, or egg-shaped like the central ring of the Hurlers. Another common shape is the flattened circle: half follows the arc of a true circle; half is curiously flattened. Arguments rage as to whether this is an intended design, or the product of laying out the site by eye; the shape seems to occur too often to be purely accidental.

The majority of Cornish circles are large, open rings, with stones about a metre or so in height. Diameters vary from 16 to 46 metres, the larger sizes occurring on Bodmin Moor. The exception is the little ovoid ring at Duloe, Caradon, with its abnormally large quartz stones and a mean diameter of just 9 metres. These open rings have stones of fairly regular size and spacing, which often present a flat, even face to the interior of the circle. Many have graded stones, with the smallest directly opposite the largest; the stones between being suitably graded in height. The original number of stones in these circles varies from fifteen to thirty-two, although Duloe has only nine.

Fernacre and Stannon, North Cornwall, and Treen Common, Penwith (if the latter can be said to fall into the category of stone circles) are radically different. All three are large, flattened rings with many stones of irregular spacing and size; both Fernacre and Stannon have in excess of seventy stones.

Two circles – Boscawen-ûn, Penwith, and the Stripple Stones – have a large pillar set just to the south, or south-west, of true centre. More doubtful central stones can be found at the middle ring of the Hurlers and the Nine Stones, North Cornwall.

Multiple circles also occur: a pair of circles can be seen on King Arthur's Downs, North Cornwall; there used to be another pair at the Wendron Nine Maidens, Kerrier. It seems too that the Merry Maidens is the survivor of a widely spaced pair. A line of three circles still survives at the Hurlers, while the remaining ring at Tregeseal, Penwith, was the easternmost of another line of three.

The colloquial name 'Nine Maidens' has been applied to a number of stone circles, although they may comprise more than nine stones. It is thought that 'maiden' may derive from *medn*, a late form of the Cornish *mên* (pl. *meyn*) – a stone. The origin of the word 'nine' in this context is less clear: some suggest it may be a corruption of *an ûn* (the downs). Christian movements were responsible for the common legends explaining stone circles as girls turned to stone for dancing on a Sunday. A similar story applied to the Hurlers, metamorphosed for playing the ancient Cornish sport of hurling on the sabbath.

Boskednan stone circle: reconstruction.

Stone alignments

Stone alignments, or stone rows, are common on Dartmoor but something of a rarity in Cornwall. Until recently it was believed that the Nine Maidens, Restormel, was the only Cornish example but others have been discovered at Greenbarrow, Trehudreth Downs, Cardinham Moor, Carneglos, Leskernick Hill, Bray Down and Fox Tor, all on Bodmin Moor. A further example near Lezant was no sooner discovered than it was destroyed.

The Dartmoor rows are often connected or aligned with an outlying feature such as a barrow or standing stone. The Nine Maidens were aligned on a menhir variously called the Fiddler, Old Man or Magi Stone, the shattered remains of which lie on higher ground 500 metres to the north-east. Whether or not the Bodmin Moor rows follow the same rule is not yet known; their discovery is too recent for sufficient research to have been carried out.

The Bodmin Moor examples are similar to the Dartmoor rows in that their stones are generally quite small, often less than 0.5 metres high. In contrast, the Nine Maidens contains much larger stones.

These stone rows are generally thought to be more or less contemporary with the stone circles, i.e. *circa* 2500-1600 BC, and their original purpose is equally obscure.

Menhirs

The word *menhir* is a Celtic one, and means literally 'longstone', by which name these Bronze Age standing stones are also known. A great many survive in Cornwall: the Penwith peninsula can still boast as many as forty-eight. Usually found singly, but occasionally in pairs, the stones range from about man-height to 4.6 metres tall, the tallest being the north-eastern stone of the pair known as the Pipers in Penwith. At one time even this would have been dwarfed by Mên Pearn near Constantine, Kerrier, which stood a colossal 7.3 metres high. It was torn down last century and split up into twenty gateposts.

Menhirs seem to have fulfilled a variety of functions. Some certainly marked burial sites; others may have marked tribal boundaries or trackways, or were perhaps a Bronze Age equivalent of the totem pole.

Evidence of burial has come to light at a number of stones, notably in the Penwith peninsula. Under a flat slab at the foot of the Tresvennack stone was a pair of large urns, one containing traces of cremation. Near the base of the Try menhir was a stone cist containing both burnt and unburnt bones, and a 'handled A' beaker which must date from *circa* 1800bc (2200 BC). At the close-set pair of stones at Higher Drift a rectangular pit, possibly a grave, was found in an off-line position between them.

An interesting sequence was discovered during the excavation of the Longstone in the china clay country north of St Austell. First a timber post had been erected, then this was replaced by a standing stone. This in turn was taken down and a new stone put up in its place. This stone survived until modern times and was recently moved to a new site at Roche in advance of the extension of china clay workings. There does not appear to have been an associated burial at the Longstone.

The ritual significance of the menhirs is apparent from the distances some were brought before their erection. The massive Dry Tree stone on Goonhilly Downs is two miles from the nearest natural occurrence of that sort of stone. A similar example is the menhir at Mount Charles, St Austell.

These stones date from about the same period as the stone circles, *circa* 2500-1600 BC. Many Cornish fields contain an upright stone; most were set up in recent times as rubbing posts for livestock, and it is often difficult to tell whether such a stone is modern or a genuine, but small, menhir. 'If it's higher than a cow's back' is a very rough guide, and it is fairly safe to say that if such a stone is under 1.5 metres high it is not a menhir. If it is over 1.8 metres high, then probably it is. With stones between these two heights it is difficult to tell!

Holed stones

A number of these curious objects occur in west Cornwall. They are upright slabs perforated by a circular hole, generally between 7 and 15 centimetres in diameter. There are two notable exceptions, both of which are featured in this book. The most famous is the Mên-an-tol, on the moors of West Penwith, which is pierced by a 46-centimetre diameter hole. The other is the Tolvan, near Gweek, at the head of the Helford River; the hole through this stone is 44 centimetres across. Both examples are countersunk on one side.

These holed stones are a complete mystery. They are tentatively assumed to be Bronze Age as many are apparently part of a stone circle's system of outliers, or are associated with other Bronze Age sites. They are often said to have been the porthole entrance slabs to long-vanished portal dolmens, but there is no evidence to support this theory, nor are there any Cornish parallels. Many people have suggested astronomical connections for the Mên-an-tol and its pair of flanking uprights, apparently in ignorance of the fact that at least one of the stones has been moved from its former position in recent times. Folk legends ascribe oracular and healing powers to the Mên-an-tol.

Long barrows

Although fairly common in the counties of Wessex, these monuments are rare in Cornwall, with just two known examples: the Woolley Barrow, north of Kilkhampton and close to the Cornish border, and the Brane long barrow near Sancreed at the opposite end of the Duchy, quite close to the well-known Scillonian chamber tomb.

These sub-rectangular mounds may be anything from 20 to 120 metres in length, wedge-shaped with one end higher than the other, and flanked by a pair of quarry ditches. Earthen long barrows contain no megalithic chambers and are considered older than the chambered long barrows. Both types are of the neolithic period, and date from the years *circa* 3700 BC to 2500 BC. At present it is not known whether the Brane and Woolley barrows are chambered, and it has to be said that there is some doubt concerning the true origin of the Brane site.

Until recent surveys the Penwith chamber tomb of Lanyon Quoit was considered to stand at the northern end of a long barrow. But what was taken for the barrow now appears to be a pair of badly damaged oval or circular mounds in juxtaposition.

Round barrows

The round barrows of the Bronze Age are the most common monuments in Britain, occupying hill- and ridge-tops as well as lowland and clifftop sites. Some stand alone, but many form groups; either strung out in linear cemeteries like that on Taphouse Ridge near Lostwithiel, or collected in concentrated groups, known as nuclear or nucleated cemeteries, of which the Pelynt group is a good example. Barrows, usually marked on the map as 'tumuli', are often found in association with stone circles and other ritual sites.

The earliest barrows are the small mounds erected by the Beaker people over burial cists, slab-lined and roofed boxes, dating from *circa* 2500 BC. During the Early Bronze Age the round barrows began to develop into a number of different styles. Bowl, bell, disc, saucer and pond barrows proliferated throughout southern Britain. In Cornwall, however, some of these styles are unknown. The bowl barrow, resembling an upturned bowl and surrounded by a quarry ditch, is by far the most common. The bell barrow – like the bowl barrow in form, except that its surrounding ditch stands at a distance from the base of the mound – occurs only rarely. Warren's Barrow, by the A 30 at Carland Cross, may be of this type, although its shape may have been due to alteration for use as an Armada beacon. A triple bell barrow, one of only three in

Britain, exists in the parish of Advent near Camelford.

Other types of barrow are to be found in Cornwall. The platform, or plate barrow, is a low, flat-topped mound, best seen at Botrea in West Penwith, where four such barrows form a linear group. In stony, upland areas the bowl barrow is represented by the stone cairn, another form of which is the ring cairn where the cairn forms a circle around an area which may be featureless, or may contain a prominent natural boulder or outcrop. Probably the most outstanding example of this type is on Showery Tor, the northern shoulder of Cornwall's second highest hill, Rough Tor. Retaining kerbs of large stones are common features of upland and clifftop barrows.

The dimensions of round barrows vary over a wide range: some are only 4 metres across; the largest is the colossal Carne Beacon near Veryan, 33 metres in diameter and 6.5 metres high.

Excavation of some of the few barrows not extensively robbed in antiquity has shown that most contained a centrally placed burial, usually cremation after the Beaker period, in either a pit or a stone cist. This was often surrounded by rings of stakes or stones, or a ring cairn before being covered by the turf mound. Recent excavation of barrows in the St Austell granite area revealed that for a time they were capped with bright yellow clay. Secondary burials are not uncommonly found, and Bronze Age folk were not averse to reusing neolithic chamber tombs. Evidence of a huge funeral pyre was found beneath one of the large bowl barrows on the clifftop north of Trevelgue Head, Newquay.

Grave goods have been unearthed in a number of round barrows, the most famous discovery being the Rillaton cup of corrugated sheet gold and its accompanying bronze dagger. Burials near Harlyn Bay (destroyed) produced the beautiful collars, or lunulae, of Irish gold which are prominently displayed in the County Museum, Truro, as is the dagger or short sword from one of the Pelynt group. Axeheads and barbed, tanged arrowheads are fairly common finds; so too are the large bi-conical,

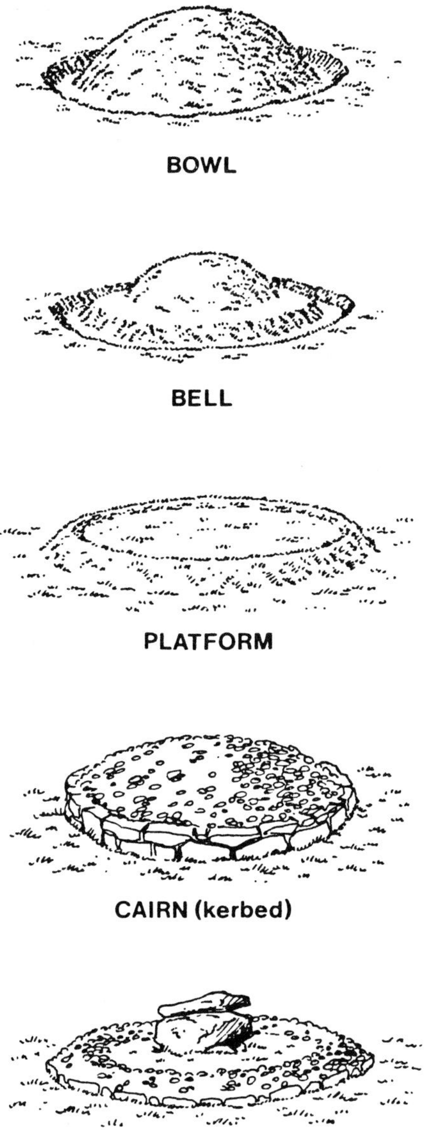

Cornish round barrow types.

ribbon-handled urns, known as Cornish urns or Trevisker ware.

During the Late Bronze Age, from *circa* 1200 BC, round barrows became increasingly rare, and it is possible that the flat cemeteries usual in the succeeding Iron Age were beginning to be the fashion.

Forts and enclosures

Tor enclosures

This term has been coined in recent years to describe those hilltop sites in which stone built defensive walls join rock outcrops to form irregular enclosures. Although formerly classified as hill forts of Late Bronze Age and Iron Age type, they have been tentatively placed apart in the light of excavated evidence from the enclosed eastern summit of Carn Brea, where the enclosure wall and the former settlement within were dated to the neolithic period and to the early fourth millenium BC.

A similar, unexcavated site on Helman Tor is very likely of the same period, as are other tor enclosures such as Rough Tor, Stowe's Pound, Berry Castle and Trencrom Castle. Apart from Carn Brea, only Trencrom has produced material. Although it may have early origins it was certainly used in the Iron Age and post-Roman period, and perhaps also during the second millenium BC.

Hill forts

The construction of hill forts began in the Late Bronze Age, after *circa* 1000 BC. The majority were univallate, consisting of a single rampart and external ditch; the rate of their building increased somewhat after the arrival of the Celts and the Iron Age. A great wave of hill fort building began in about the fourth century BC when multiple defences became the norm. The term 'bivallate' describes two concentric lines of defence; forts with more than two ramparts and ditches are known as 'multivallate' sites.

The majority of Cornish hill forts occupy the summits of hills and are round or oval in plan. Most employ 'glacis' or 'dump' ramparts of earth which in section resemble an inverted V. The top of at least the inner rampart probably carried a palisade or breastwork of timber or stone. In a few cases the defences were built entirely of stone, the best example being Chûn Castle.

In general the entrances of Cornish hill forts are of a simple straight-through type, sometimes accompanied by inturned rampart ends which formed a passage-like gateway. Chûn Castle is an exception: its staggered entrance replaced an earlier straight-through type, pobably during its post-Roman occupation.

Iron Age dwellings of the round house type are commonly found inside Cornish hill forts, and natural supplies of water usually occur either within or close to the fort. In a few, artifical dewponds have been found.

A number of forts, for reasons known only to their builders, are not on hill summits but on the slope, usually on the lee side, of the hill. Tregeare Rounds and Warbstow Bury are outstanding examples.

Most bivallate or multivallate forts have close-spaced ramparts, but a number have widely separated defences. These have been called 'multiple enclosure' forts. Excavation has revealed evidence of occupation sites between the ramparts, but not in the central enclosure which may have been reserved for livestock.

Annexed enclosures are fairly common, whether as secondary additions, as is probable at Caervallack and Kelly Rounds, or part of the original design as at Castle Dore, where the outer rampart runs close to the inner for two-thirds of the circuit, then bulges away on the east side to form a crescentic enclosure.

In comparison with some of the great British hill forts like Maiden Castle and Herefordshire Beacon, the Cornish forts are small, none being larger than 6 hectares in extent. Often, though, the ramparts reach an imposing height even today.

The evidence suggests that most of the Cornish hill

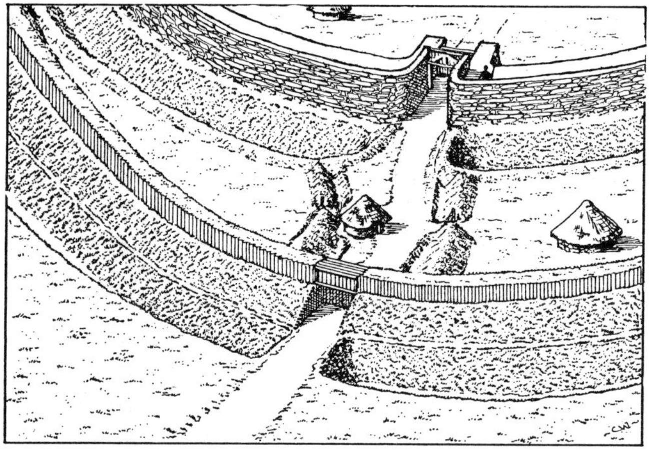

Castle Dore hill fort: suggested reconstruction of the entrance. Phase II.

forts fell into disuse during Roman times, but some have revealed proof of post-Roman occupation, notably Chûn Castle and Castle Dore.

Cliff castles

Cornwall and the Isles of Scilly have no less than thirty-three coastal headlands with Iron Age defences. These, in the form of earth or stone ramparts with external ditches, cross the base or neck of the headland, adequate defence on all other sides being provided by the cliffs and crags. As with the hill forts, univallate, bivallate and multivallate examples all occur, the most heavily defended site being the long-lived cliff castle of Trevelgue Head, Newquay, which has six major lines of defence.

Many cliff castles contain traces of round houses; some of the larger ones even have tiny field systems. The oldest known is the fourth century BC Maen Castle, a few hundred metres from Land's End. No sign of permanent occupation was found there, but a series of beautifully preserved Iron Age fields overlook the site.

The magnificent cliff castle at the Rumps, near Polzeath, was found to have housed a thriving community which perhaps had trading links with the Mediterranean

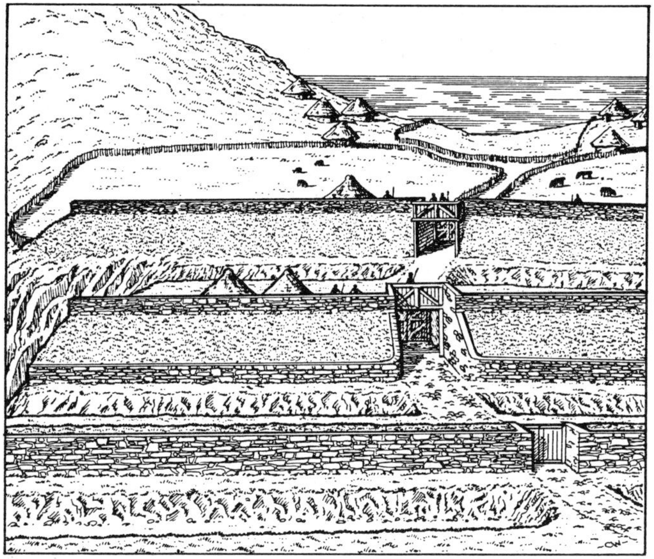

The Rumps cliff castle: reconstruction.

through the Breton tribe, the Veneti. It may be that the Veneti themselves built the Rumps and other cliff castles, notably Gurnard's Head which bears similarities to Breton cliff castles on the coast formerly inhabited by the Veneti. Julius Caesar's own account of the Gallic Wars tells how the Veneti would occupy one of their cliff castles, close the gates against the Roman forces and prepare for the inevitable siege. After the Roman expense of time, effort and lives, when the fort was close to falling to the Empire, the Veneti would whistle up one of their massive oak ships, descend the cliff and sail off to the next fort, to the utter frustration of Caesar and his army. So far, few of the Cornish cliff castles have been found to have lasted in use beyond the Roman period, although some, notably Trevelgue, produced evidence of desultory occupation.

Settlement enclosures (rounds)

Cornish rounds are generally small, univallate enclosures. Most contained small settlements, farmsteads of round houses sometimes built close to the encircling rampart to leave a useful farmyard in the centre. The farms were defensible, not purely defensive, rather like the medieval moated farms of eastern England. Their siting was based on agriculture rather than strategy. Two of the West Penwith rounds contain courtyard houses: at Goldherring the courtyard house was built inside an already existing round; at Porthmeor the round was a secondary structure.

Today few rounds contain visible traces of dwelling sites and, because they occur in both highland and lowland areas, ploughing has reduced a large number to low humps in a field, or to mere cropmarks visible only from the air.

Most of the Cornish settlement enclosures are oval or circular in plan, although some rectangular and sub-rectangular examples exist. Until a few years ago many of these were thought to have been Roman fortlets or marching camps. It is now known they were native-built.

Rounds are generally later than hill forts. Many appear to have been built during the final two centuries BC and the first century AD, with occupation continuing throughout the Roman period and, in some cases, beyond.

Miscellaneous enclosures

Cornish archaeology is seldom clear-cut. Some structures are hard to classify or to date without the benefit of proper excavation. Among these are the enigmatic, lonely King Arthur's Hall on Bodmin Moor near St Breward, and the Crowpound near St Neot. Suspicions and theories as to function and dating abound for both sites, as they do for the equally mysterious Bartinnê Castle in Penwith. They are classified in the gazetteer merely as 'enclosures'.

Settlement sites

Round houses

Visible remains of prehistoric settlement in Cornwall date back to at least *circa* 1500 BC, before the beginning of the Later Bronze Age. Settlement of earlier times has been found only by excavation. From the Later Bronze Age to the end of the Roman Iron Age the standard dwelling type was the round house, formerly called the hut circle. As the name implies, this was a circular structure with a conical roof of timber and thatch.

In the upland areas of Cornwall round houses were stone walled; in some of the early ones the walls are a single ring of stone blocks. Most, however, are double-walled: there is an inner and outer stone facing, the core filled with rubble. This produces a wall of at least a metre thick which would have stood to a height of between 1.2 and 1.5 metres. Often upright stone doorjambs remain. In less stony and lowland areas, round houses were timber-built with wattle and daub walls. These, of course, have disappeared from view, and are found only by excavation.

A round house settlement may consist of up to a hundred dwellings, as can be seen in several places on Bodmin Moor where an astonishing number of Bronze Age settlements survive. Some, like the Black Tor settlement, have their houses clustered closely together, the remains of their fields close by; those in the region of Rough Tor are spread out among vast field systems which include tracks and droveways. There are smaller, similar settlements on the moors of West Penwith.

Iron Age round houses, if not structurally different from, tend to be larger than those of the Bronze Age. Some are as much as 16 metres in overall diameter.

Courtyard houses

The round house was the standard dwelling in the Iron Age, but during the first century BC someone in West Penwith had a different idea: to include living quarters, workshop, stores and byre within a single self-contained unit. This was the courtyard house, which is peculiar to the Land's End peninsula. Best seen at Chysauster, these houses are huge structures, roughly oval in plan, and averaging 25 metres in length by 18 metres wide. A paved entrance passage, often turned away from the prevailing south-westerly winds, leads into a central, presumably unroofed courtyard, around which are a variety of rooms

ROUND HOUSE

partially built into the thickness of the massive exterior wall which was probably in the region of 2-2.5 metres high.

A typical courtyard house has a long recess on one side of the central yard, probably a stable or byre, and on the opposite side a long, narrow room, perhaps a workshop or store. Between the two, and directly across the courtyard from the house entrance, is the largest room, circular or oval in shape, which was set aside for the living, eating and sleeping needs of the family. There may be other rooms too, and some of the living rooms have a back door leading out of the house. Stone-lined and capped drains are a feature of these houses, as are stone hearths and a curious flat slab which bears a carved socket, perhaps to house the base of the main roof support post, if such a post was used.

Most of the courtyard house sites are village groups with, on average, four or five houses each. There may be round houses in addition, and it is a mystery why the improved house type did not supercede them. But it did not; neither did the courtyard house spread beyond Penwith, except for a late example in the Isles of Scilly, possibly founded by a settler from the mainland.

The courtyard house villages and their agricultural inhabitants flourished throughout the Romano-British period. They were peacefully and gradually abandoned between the second and sixth centuries AD.

COURTYARD HOUSE

Twenty-one recognized courtyard house settlements survive; a further nine structures are suspected of being of courtyard house type. Another ten sites have been destroyed during the last two centuries. Similar, but not identical house types, known as enclosed homesteads, are found in north-west Wales.

Post-Roman settlements

In the two centuries following the final Roman withdrawal from Britain in AD 410, the enclosed settlements and courtyard houses began to be abandoned in favour of a more open type of farming on lower ground, often on newly-cleared land. Often though, especially in West Penwith, some of the Iron Age fields continued in use as part of a new holding. Many of the new farms developed through the ages to become some of today's settlements. Among those that did not was the site at Gwithian which had seen almost continuous occupation since the meso-

Left: *Dark Age settlement, Tintagel Island: reconstruction.*

Far left: *round house and courtyard house: reconstructions.*

lithic era. Here the old style of round house continued in use until the seventh century. However, this type of architecture was being superceded by rectangular designs, forerunners of the medieval longhouses. One such building occurred in the final phase at Gwithian, continuing the occupation of the site from the seventh to the eleventh century.

At Mawgan Porth, Newquay, a site which is still visible, rectangular buildings of stone clustered around a central courtyard – almost an imitation in oblongs of the Late Iron Age courtyard houses. Four such clusters are known at Mawgan Porth, which seems to have been occupied from the ninth to the eleventh centuries.

Earlier than these – dating from the fifth or sixth century – are the clustered groups of buildings at Tintagel, which until recently were thought to have been an early monastery of the Celtic church. New appraisal of the evidence suggests that they were an important lay settlement.

Reddish bowls and dishes of Mediterranean origin (Tintagel A ware) and coarse, handled amphorae, also from the Mediterranean (Tintagel B ware), turned up in quantities at Tintagel, and at Gwithian and in the courtyard houses at Porthmeor (abandoned in the sixth century), Chûn Castle and other Dark Age sites in south-western Britain.

Chûn Castle, on the Penwith moors, was one of a number of Iron Age forts reoccupied between the fifth and seventh centuries. The foundations of sub-rectangular buildings of this period can still be seen backing onto the inside of the inner wall; they were found to overlie at least a dozen Iron Age round houses. The fortress entrance was probably altered to its present clever staggered design by its reoccupants, and a small outer hornwork was thrown up. It is not clear why such forts were reused; perhaps there was a sea-borne threat in the shape of pirates from Ireland.

Grass-marked pottery (whose bases bear the impressions of the chopped grass on which they stood before firing) found at sites like Gwithian and Chûn Castle may be Irish in origin, but this should not be assumed at present. Other pottery found on early post-Roman sites includes locally made pots and jars imitating late Roman styles, including large storage jars.

Castle Dore, Fowey, was another reoccupied Iron Age fort. Again, some refortification was carried out on a small scale, but the real find was of huge post holes which have been interpreted as belonging to a sixth-century chieftain's hall and palace.

Christianity made its mark with the foundation of small monasteries at Dinuurin (Bodmin) and Perranzabuloe. The recently reburied ninth-century St Piran's Oratory at Perranzabuloe may be the remains of one such monastery. There were others at St German's, Padstow, Probus and St Buryan. One which did not develop beyond the sixteenth century was the seventh- or eighth-century monastery on St Helen's in the Isles of Scilly.

Fogous

Despite a number of excavations, these structures remain enigmatic. Named from the Cornish word *fogo*, a cave, they are found only west of the Fal estuary and in association with either courtyard house villages or enclosed settlements. In general, fogous consist of stone-lined and roofed passages, often with subsidiary passages and chambers. Twelve sites exist today, although one of these, at North Treveneage, St Hilary, has been lost for a number of years, apparently covered rather than destroyed. Fogous are often described as underground structures; in fact four are truly underground, four semi-underground and the rest above ground. The theory that they were concealed refuges has been virtually discounted; opinion is split between those who interpret fogous as cold stores for meat and dairy produce, and those who see them as ritual structures. The latter have certain support in the form of a carving at the mouth of the Boleigh fogou near Lamorna Cove which depicts the upper parts of a human figure holding a staff or spear in one hand and what may be a snake in the other.

The magnificent fogou at Carn Euny, Sancreed, was found to have been built in a number of stages. The circular, corbelled chamber and its approach passage were built *circa* 500 BC, pre-dating the courtyard houses around it and the long passage constructed a couple of centuries later. Both ends of this were closed, and it seems that at this stage the only entry into the fogou was the tiny 'creep' passage, or possibly the entrance passage to the corbelled chamber. When the courtyard houses were built, during the first century BC, the north-eastern end of the long passage was opened; it appears that the opposite end of the passage remained closed until fairly recent times.

Pottery finds from other fogous indicate construction during the later stages of the pre-Roman Iron Age, although the Phase I stage of the Carn Euny fogou is echoed almost to the centimetre by the above ground structure at Bosporthennis. A similar, fifth-century BC date is therefore suggested by analogy.

The fogous of west Cornwall may be descended from the souterrains of Brittany which generally date from the early Iron Age. Similar structures in southern Scotland tend to be a few centuries later, while souterrains in Ireland were in use into the early medieval period.

With one exception, Piskey Hall, Constantine, the passage walls of the fogous are corbelled, and their plans reveal a curved shape to their design, usually a gentle curve.

Roman sites

Cornwall has few Roman sites: five milestones as markers for a projected Roman road which was apparently never built; one fort on the outskirts of Bodmin, and an unusual altar on the Isles of Scilly. A Roman-style villa was discovered at Magor, north of Camborne, in 1931 and was excavated then, but it is no longer visible. It was built in the mid second century AD, extended during its occupation, and abandoned about a century later. It was perhaps built by a native Celt who had been in Roman service, maybe in Exeter (Isca Dumnoniorum), and decided to build a Roman-style retirement home on his return. This theory is supported by the fact that there was not a right angle in the place, and the usual symmetry of Roman design was missing. The villa was also notably lacking in amenities.

The fort at Nanstallon, Bodmin, covering an area of 0.9 hectares, is typically Roman: rectangular with rounded corners and an entrance at the mid point of each side. Wooden barrack blocks were found, as well as the commandant's house. It is thought that the fort would have been occupied by an auxiliary detachment of mixed infantry and cavalry – perhaps 500 men. Founded *circa* AD 55, it was curiously short lived and was abandoned peacefully about twenty-five years later.

The milestones, two at Tintagel (one actually at Trethevey, just outside Tintagel), one near Gwennap Pit, and one each at Breage and St Hilary, are squared stones standing from 1.3 to 1.5 metres high. They are not milestones in the generally accepted sense of the word, but markstones erected along a routeway with inscriptions praising the emperors of the time, from which they can be dated. The earliest, at Gwennap, falls within the years AD 238 to AD 244; the latest is the St Hilary stone which dates from between AD 306 and 308.

There are a number of rectangular or rectilinear earthworks in Cornwall, for example Carvossa, Probus, and Merthen, Constantine, which were formerly believed to have been Roman camps. It is now accepted that they were native-built enclosures of the later and Roman Iron Age, and not necessarily imitations of Roman design, for a number pre-date the Roman occupation.

There have been many finds of Roman coins in Cornwall over the years which may well point to strong trading links with either the Romans themselves or coin-using Celtic tribes from southern Britain, perhaps the Durotriges from the Dorset area or the Atrebates from north-west Hampshire, west Berkshire and Wiltshire. The Dumnonii of Devon and Cornwall preferred a trade economy based on barter, but the finds of coins show that they did accept coinage, even though they had none of their own.

The Roman altar discovered at Hugh Town, St Mary's, in the Isles of Scilly and subsequently moved to the Abbey Gardens, Tresco, is a rare find and does not bear the usual inscription. Its presence in Scilly is a little mysterious; the Romans certainly knew the islands but no trace of Roman occupation has been found there.

Inscribed stones

Memorial stones giving us the earliest known names of Cornish folk began to appear early in the post-Roman period, perhaps as early at AD 450. Dating is difficult and is judged by the type of inscription and the lettering style in comparison with certain Welsh stones which have been accurately dated. The earliest inscriptions tend to be fairly long and carved in horizontal lines, but in the early sixth century the style of writing deteriorates, the lines crawl vertically down the stone, and the inscription itself becomes shorter and more terse. All are in a slightly misspelt Latin, even to the Celtic names becoming Latinized, and all are believed to be Christian monuments. Some certainly covered burials, but not all, and it is quite likely that some stones, like the Mên Scryfa on the Penwith moors and the Tristan Stone at Fowey, were Bronze Age menhirs before being put to a Christian use.

With few exceptions the inscriptions take three forms: first HIC IACET X (Here lies X), followed by the pride of ancestry displayed in X Y FILI (X son of Y). The third type combines the two: X HIC IACIT FILIUS Y (X lies here, the son of Y).

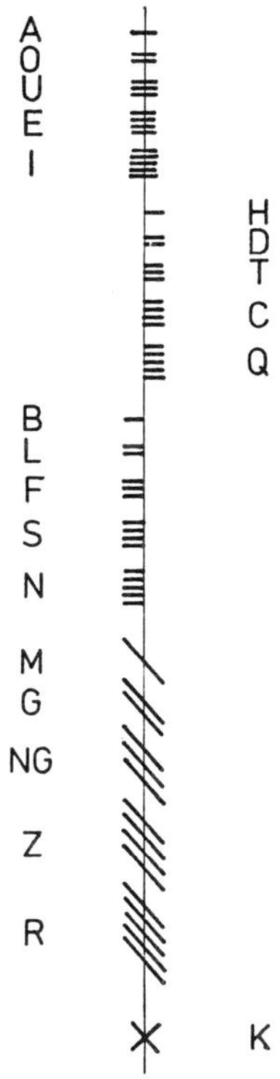

The Ogam alphabet

Evidence of an Irish incursion in the early post-Roman period is provided by certain stones bearing Irish names, and stones which bear not only a Latin inscription, but a repeated inscription in the curious Irish script known as Ogam, or Ogham. All are in north-east Cornwall, except the stone at St Clement, Truro.

That there was Anglo-Saxon settlement in north-east Cornwall by the tenth century is attested by the large number of Anglo-Saxon place names there. The stone at Lanteglos-by-Camelford bears an inscription in an early form of English.

Further evidence of Christianity appears on a few stones incised with various forms of the Chi-Rho monogram (the first two letters of the name of Christ in the Greek alphabet). Particularly good examples are the Selus Stone, St Just (Penwith), and the Brocagnus stone, St Endellion, which also bears inscriptions in both Latin and Ogam and a carved cross.

Cornish royalty has its memorial stones, notably the Mên Scryfa in Penwith, the Doniert Stone near St Cleer, and the Tristan stone at Fowey.

Linear earthworks

Two linear earthworks are known in Cornwall, apparently smaller versions of such Dark Age examples as the Wansdyke. The better known of the two, the Giant's Hedge, stretches from the upper reaches of the Fowey estuary to the mouth of the Looe, and may have been erected to protect the large area of land behind it from the threatened Irish incursion from the north.

The Bolster Bank at St Agnes cuts off St Agnes Beacon and the coast between Trevaunance Cove and Chapel Porth. The reason is far from clear; perhaps it protected an area of mineral richness. Neither earthwork has been accurately dated and it is assumed that both belong to the early post-Roman period. Both consist of a single high earth bank fronted by a ditch.

Stone crosses

Cornwall is famous for its wayside crosses which began to appear in the ninth century. There are so many they cannot all be included here, and this book seeks only to mention those which have some special interest such as an inscription.

The crosses probably marked paths to early churches, and the early date of some is attested by sites such as the King Doniert stone, a cross-base dated to *circa* 875, and St Piran's Cross on Penhale Sands, which was recorded in the year 960. The massive Green Market cross which now stands outside the Penlee House museum, Penzance, bears an inscription to King Ricatus which has been dated to the early tenth century.

Gazetteer

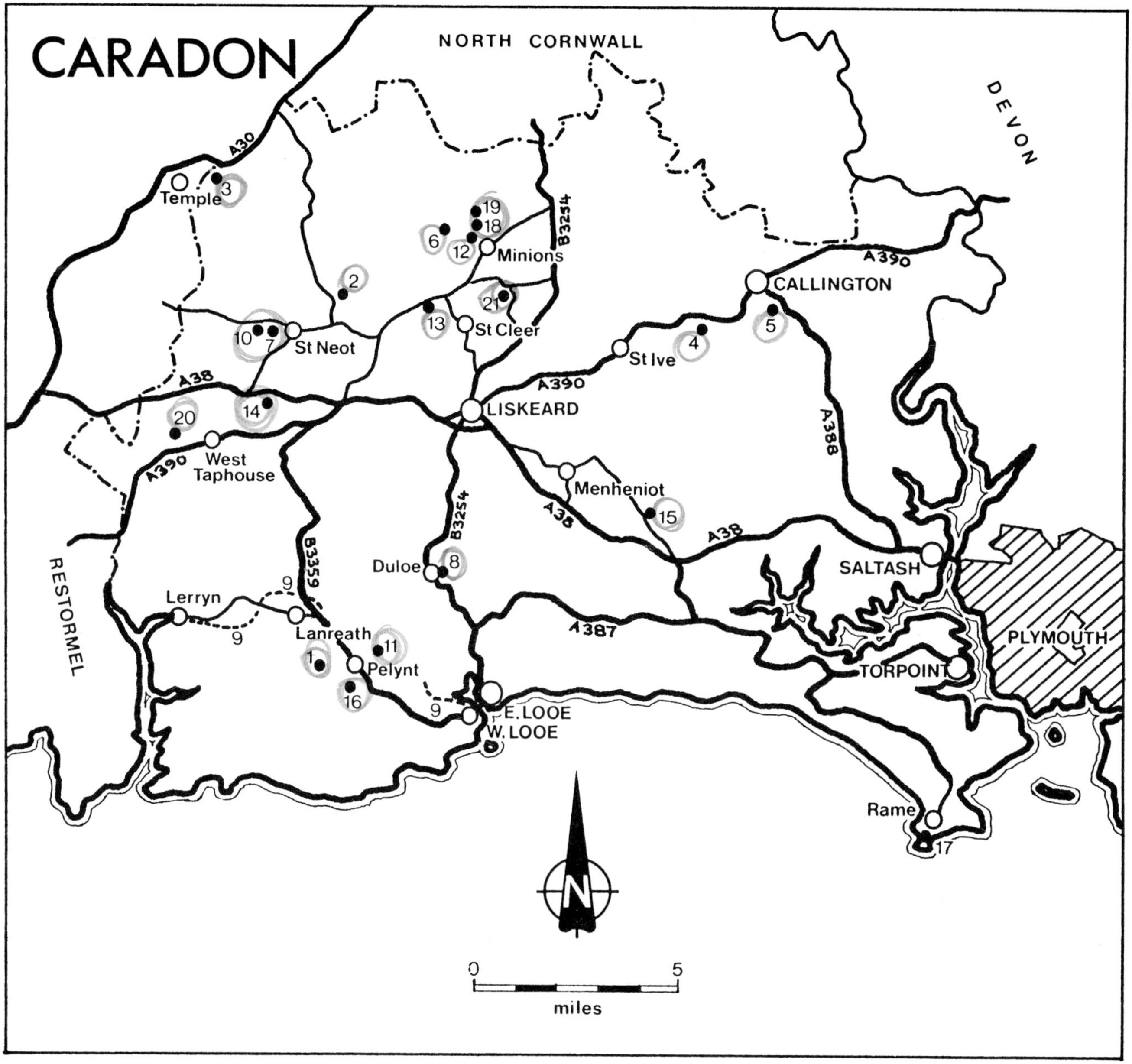
CARADON
NORTH CORNWALL
DEVON
RESTORMEL
A30
Temple
3
19
18
6
12
Minions
B3254
2
21
13
St Cleer
CALLINGTON
A390
10
7
St Neot
4
St Ive
5
A38
20
14
A390
LISKEARD
West Taphouse
A390
Menheniot
A388
B3254
15
A38
A38
B3359
8
Duloe
9
SALTASH
Lerryn
9
Lanreath
A387
PLYMOUTH
1
11
Pelynt
TORPOINT
16
9
E. LOOE
W. LOOE
Rame
17
N
0
5
miles

1 Bake Rings, settlement enclosure, Pelynt.

SX 187549.
On W side of minor road from the B3359 to Lansallos, 1 mile W of Pelynt.

This site consists of a circular rampart and outer ditch about 90m in diameter. Attached to its eastern side is a large rectilinear annexe with a probable south-eastern entrance protected by a short, curving outwork. The annexe, which is defined by a single bank and ditch, has been damaged by ploughing, but the circular enclosure is in fair condition, the rampart reaching a height of 1.0m. Bake Rings dates from the Iron Age/Romano-British period.

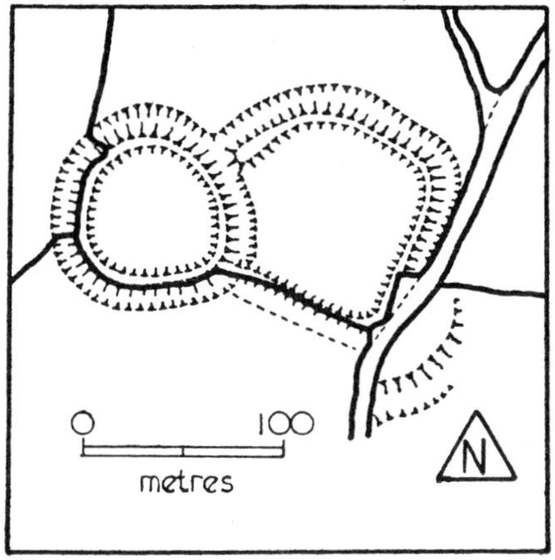

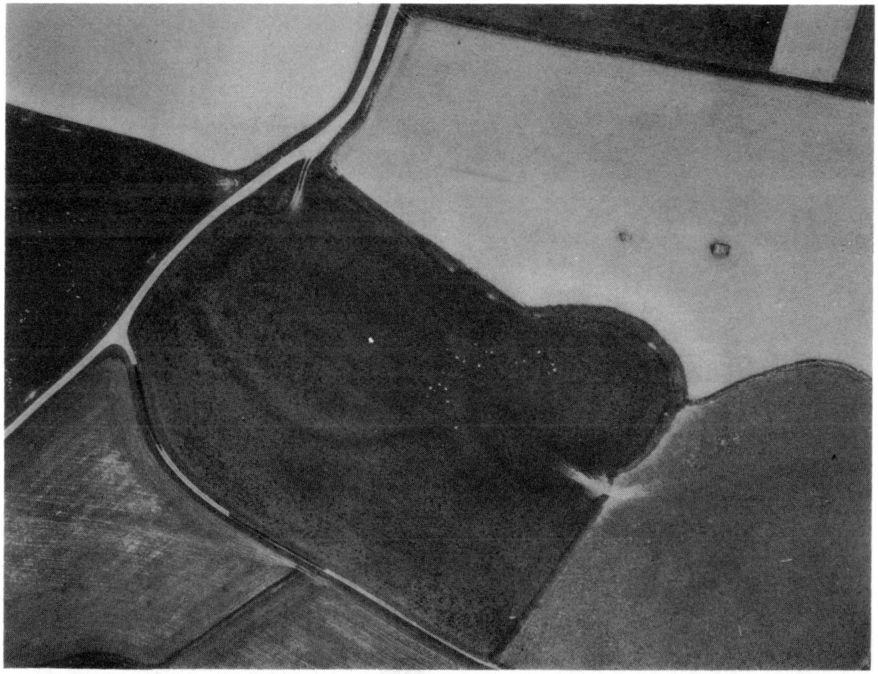

Bake Rings (1)

2 Berry Castle, tor enclosure, St Neot.

SX 197689.
On hilltop 1 mile NE of St Neot, easily reached by footpaths from lane leading N from Wenmouth Cross.

The main enclosure is rectilinear, 110m from north to south, by 82m, and consists of a tumbled, unditched stone and earth bank up to 1.5m high. It incorporates natural rock outcrops. Within the enclosure are the remains of eight round houses; a ninth lies just outside the north wall. These are between 8.0m and 14.0m in diameter, and most have south-east facing entrances. The southern side of the enclosure utilizes a natural rocky scarp to form a double defence pierced by an inturned entrance. A hollow way leads from this entrance through an incomplete annexe attached to the southern side of the enclosure. This is bounded by a stone and earth bank up to 1.0m high; its west side is missing. The enclosure is thought to be Bronze Age, but may even have neolithic origins.

Berry Castle (2)

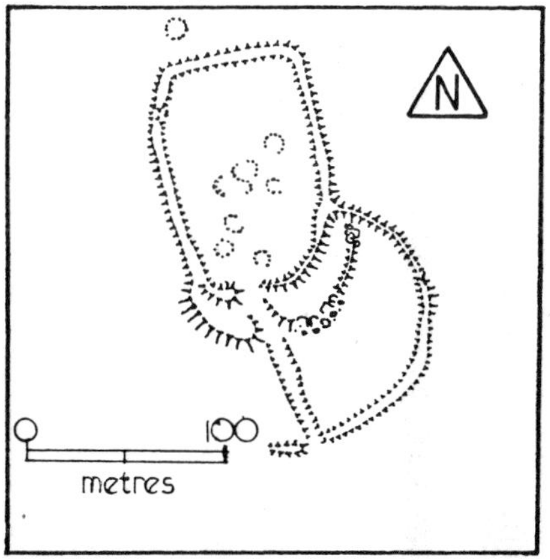

3 **Black Tor, round house settlement,** Temple.

SX 158733.
On open moorland immediately S of eastern junction of the A30 and lane to Temple.

A huge, open settlement, probably Bronze Age, containing about eighty round houses within an area of 4 ha. The huts are between 5.0m and 11.0m in diameter, with walls up to 1.0m high and 1.6m thick. Most have south to south-east facing entrances, often with upright jamb-stones in place. Some of the hut entrances have stone-lined approaches, and many huts either adjoin others or are linked by lengths of low walling. Most, however, are free-standing. Evidence of field enclosures is fragmentary, but best seen to the south-east of the settlement.

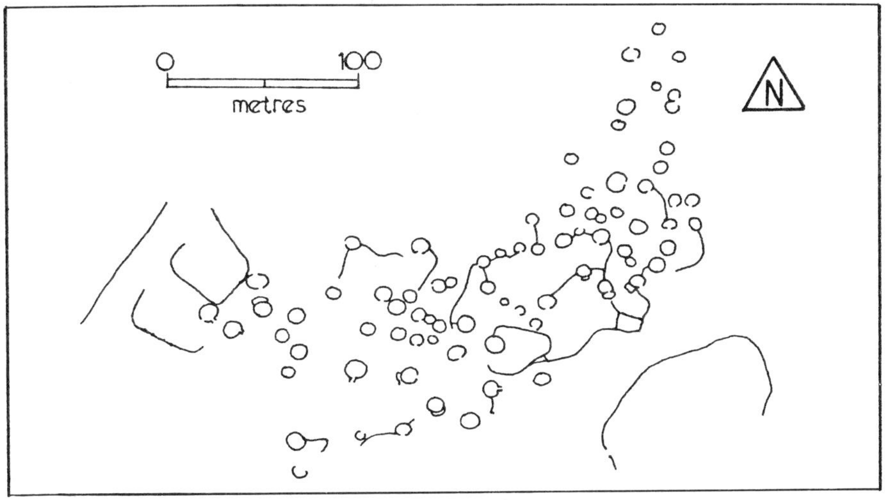

Black Tor (3)

4 **Cadson Bury, hill fort,** St Ive.

SX 343674. NT.
On hilltop ½ mile SE of Newbridge. Approached by footpath from the road running S from the A390 at Newbridge towards Crift.

This impressive Iron Age fort has a large single rampart describing an oval 275m from north to south, by 170m. The internal height of the rampart reaches 2.0m; the external height is much greater due to the sudden steepness of the hillside below. The southern half of the fort has an outer ditch which peters out to become a narrow terrace around the northern half. Two fine inturned entrances occur on the west and east sides, and a staggered breach in the southern defence may be an original feature. No dwelling sites are visible within the fort.

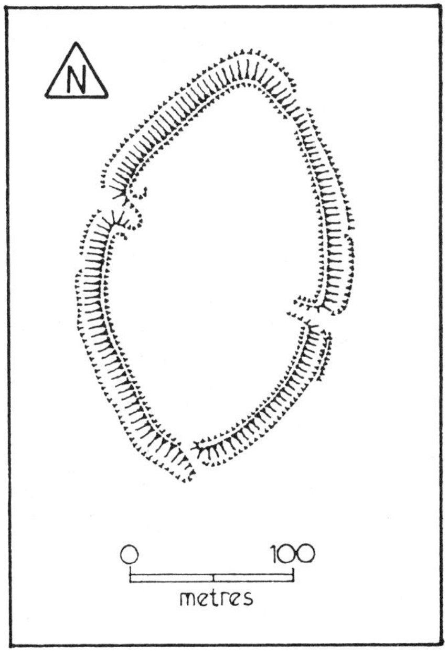

Cadson Bury (4)

Cadson Bury (4)

5 Castlewich, henge,
Callington.

SX 371685.

1 mile SE of Callington on the A388, from the S side of which a lane leads to Westcott. Site lies on hillside to NW.

First recognized as a neolithic henge in 1951, the somewhat ploughed down bank and internal ditch cover an area 90m in diameter. An indistinct entrance occurs on the south side, but there appears to be no corresponding causeway over the ditch. There is no visible evidence to suggest that there were any internal stone or timber settings. Like Cornwall's other two surviving henges – Castilly (Restormel) and the Stripple Stones (North Cornwall) – this site was positioned close to a major prehistoric trackway; trade may have played a part in the function of the henge. Balstone down, close by to the north, was the source of greenstone for the manufacture of neolithic axes. The bank of the henge reaches a height of 1.0m; the maximum depth of the ditch is 1.2m.

Castlewich (5)

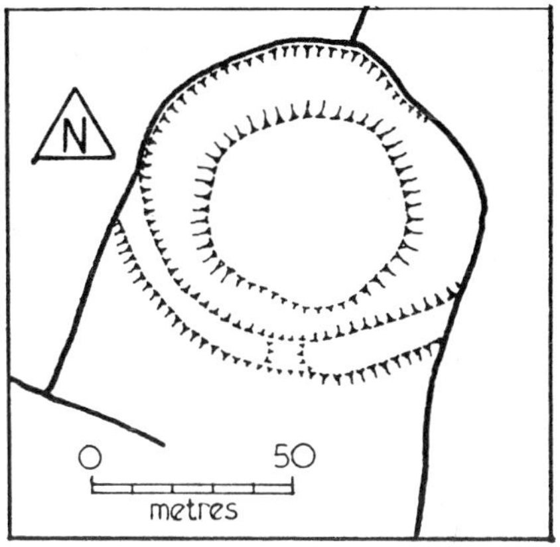

Castlewich (5)

6 Craddock Moor, stone circle,
Minions.

SX 249718.

¾ mile NW of the Hurlers (Site 12), and reached from there by a walk across open moorland.

This ruinous circle, discovered in 1923, is 39.3m in diameter. It now consists of seventeen stones: sixteen are prone, the other is a mere stump 0.3m high. The prostrate stones measure from 1.2m to 2.3m in length, and all are overgrown which makes the circle a little difficult to find. It appears to have been a true circle in plan, probably with twenty-seven or twenty-eight stones.

Craddock Moor (6)

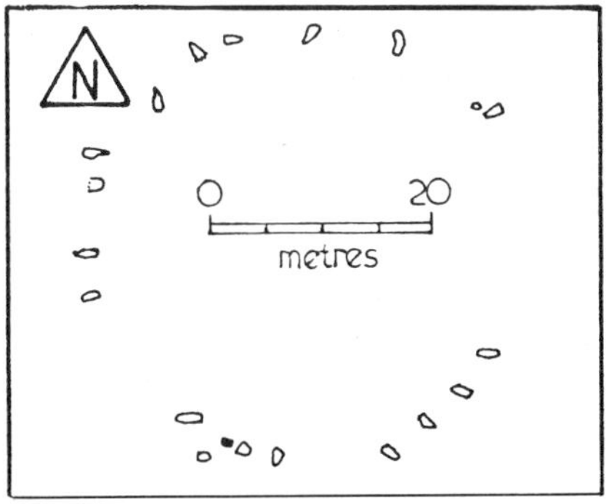

7 **Crowpound, enclosure,** St. Neot.

SX 174678.

Beside crossroads ½ mile due W of St Neot.

An enigmatic rectangular earthwork, 52m by 40m, formed by a bank 0.8m high with traces of an outer ditch. The original entrance faces south. In the centre of the enclosure is a circular bank 10m in diameter with a breach in its northern side, suggestive of a prehistoric round house. Without the benefit of excavation it is difficult to assign a date to the Crowpound; it could be of any date between the Romano-British and medieval periods.

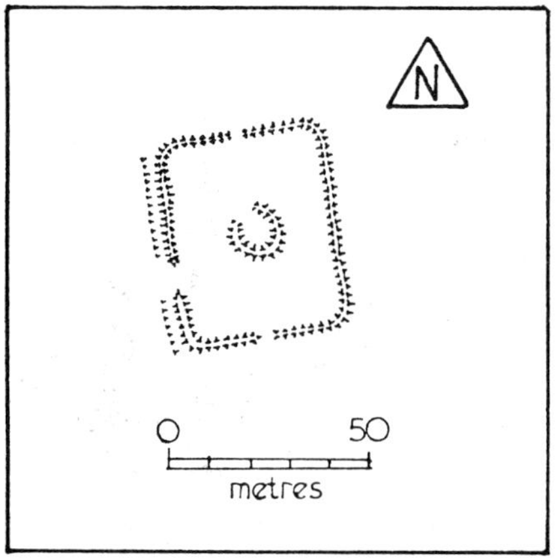

Crowpound (7)

8 **Duloe, stone circle,** Duloe.

SX 236583.

In Duloe village, reached by turning E off the B3254 just N of the church.

An unusually small example, this is an ovoid ring with diameters of 11.7m and 10.2m, yet its eight stones of white quartz are by far the largest of any Cornish circle, the tallest being 2.7m high. One stone has fallen. The circle was restored *c.* 1860 when a bisecting hedge was removed and at least one urn was found. It is remotely possibly that the stones retained a barrow, but they seem ridiculously large for this purpose. The site is Bronze Age.

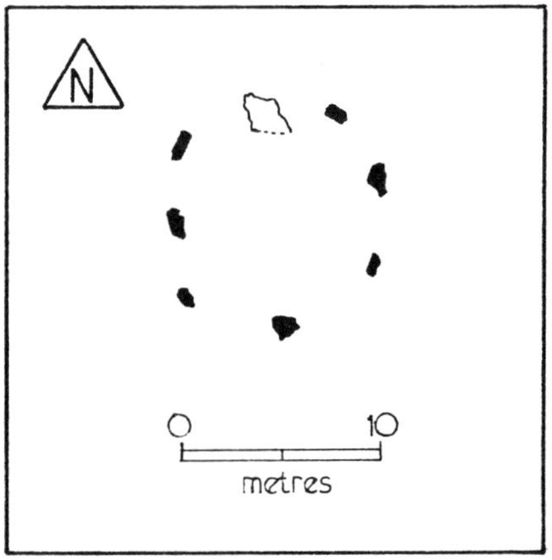

Duloe (8)

9 **The Giant's Hedge, linear earthwork,** Lerryn-Lanreath-Looe.

SX 141572 to SX 247536.

One day, the Devil, having nothing to do,
Built a great hedge from Lerryn to Looe.

So says an old rhyme, and much of this hedge remains, although tradition now ascribes it to a giant. The earthwork stretches from the tidal head of the Lerryn River, a creek of the Fowey estuary, to West Looe. It is generally agreed that the Giant's Hedge marks the northern boundary of a post-Roman petty kingdom.

The ravages of agriculture have split the hedge in two. The longest surviving stretch is 5½ miles, from the village of Lerryn at SX 141572 eastward to Muchlarnick at SX 217566. This length variously appears as a north-facing scarp between 2.0m and 5.0m high; as an extremely thick, stone-faced hedge bank, and as a high rampart. Traces of a ditch are visible here and there on its north side. The best preserved part of the Hedge is in Willake Wood (SX 153569) where it is seen as a rampart 3.5m wide, 1.0m high on the south side and 1.7m high on the north side. The ditch here is 3.0m wide and 0.8m deep.

After Muchlarnick there is a gap of 1¼ miles where the Hedge has been utterly destroyed. It reappears to the south-east in Kiln Wood, at SX 223547, and can be traced through Ten Acres and Kilminorth Woods where it follows the contours before finally vanishing on the outskirts of West Looe at SX 247536. In this south-eastern stretch the earthwork is largely represented by a scarp up to 2.5m high, stone-revetted in places and occasionally fronted by a ditch.

10 **Goonzion, settlement enclosure,** St Neot.

SX 171677.

On S side of road W from St Neot on Goonzion Downs, 300m W of the Crowpound (Site 7).

This small, square enclosure has sides measuring 60m in length. It consists of a ploughed down rampart 1.4m high with an external ditch 0.3m deep. The entrance faces south. Because of its shape, the enclosure was once thought to be exclusively Roman. It is now accepted that it was an enclosed settlement of Romano-British and post-Roman times, native-built and possibly in imitation of Roman design.

Goonzion (10)

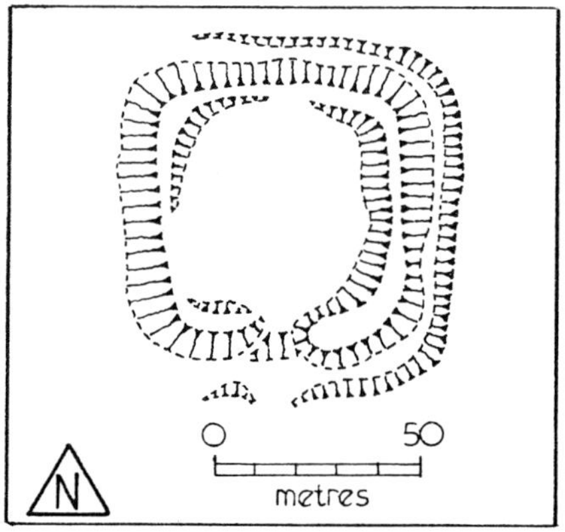

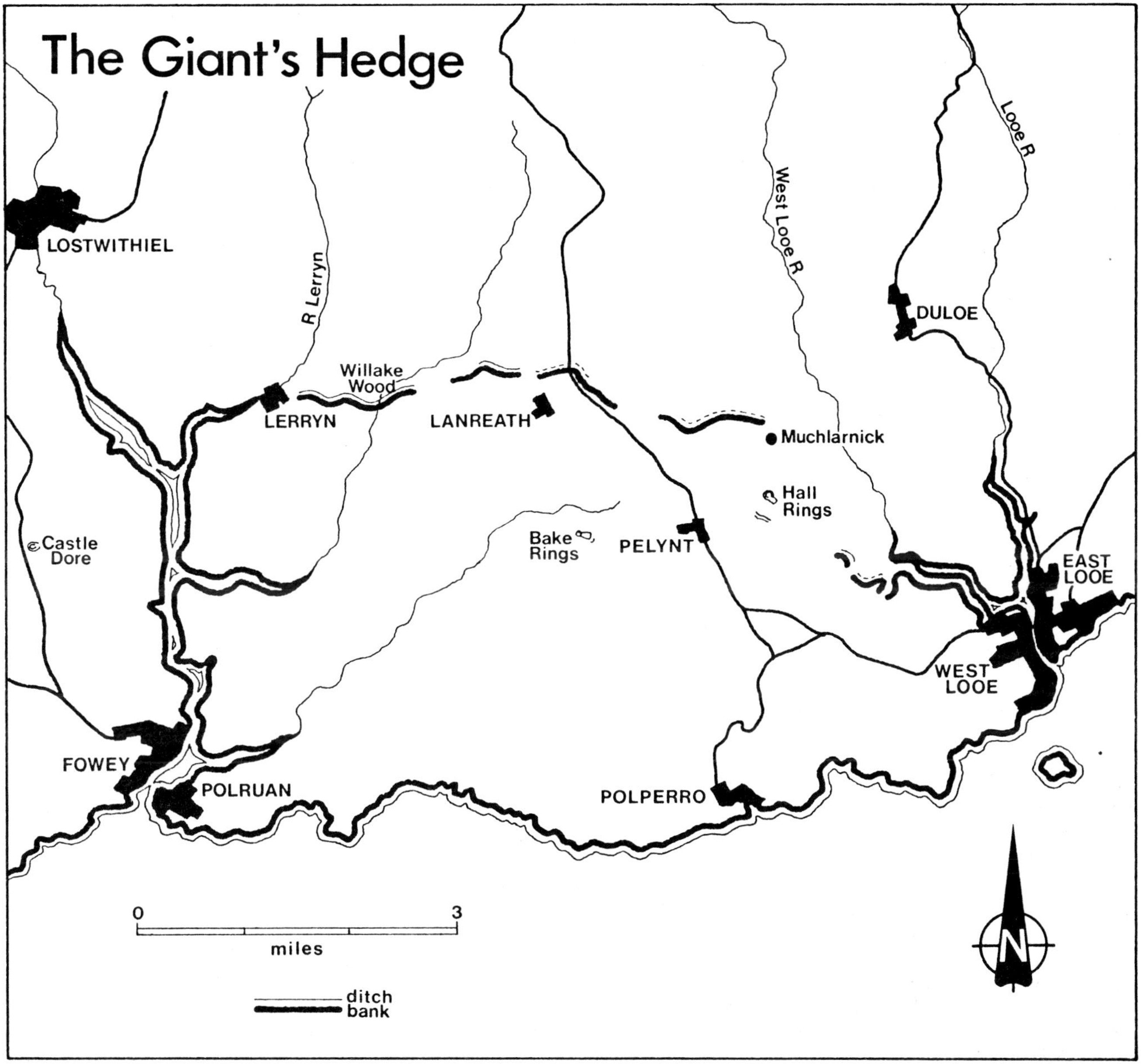
The Giant's Hedge
LOSTWITHIEL
R Lerryn
Willake Wood
LERRYN
LANREATH
West Looe R
Looe R
DULOE
Muchlarnick
Hall Rings
Castle Dore
Bake Rings
PELYNT
EAST LOOE
WEST LOOE
FOWEY
POLRUAN
POLPERRO
0
3
miles
ditch
bank
N

Hall Rings (11)

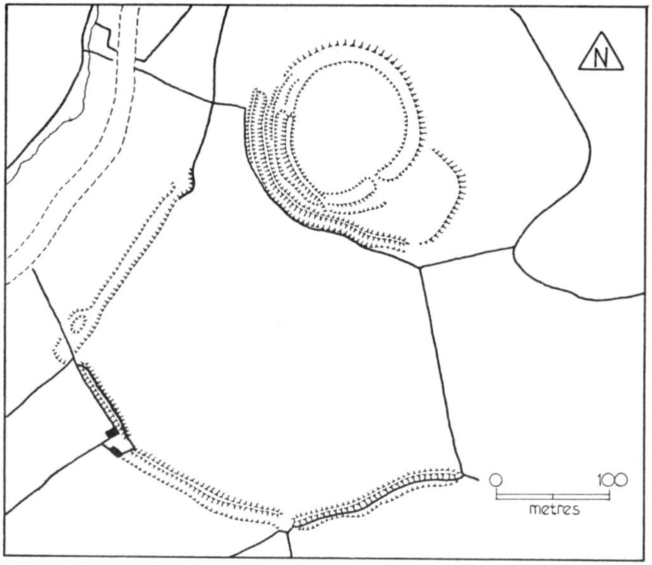

Hall Rings (11)

11 Hall Rings, hill fort.
Pelynt.

SX 214555.

¾ mile NE of Pelynt; reached by a track turning E off the B3359 just N of Pelynt church.

This Iron Age fort, situated on a spur overlooking a deep valley to the north, was badly damaged by agriculture during the Second World War. Only its south-west half remains intact. Two concentric banks and ditches describe a circle 145m in overall diameter, with an entrance on the south-east. The north-eastern halves of these defences have been ploughed into a single spread bank 1.7m high. In contrast, the western ramparts reach a height of 4.3m. The west side of the fort is additionally defended by a third rampart and heavily counterscarped ditch which bulges out to form an annexe on the south-east, through which passes the entrance. 250m to the south, across the flattish neck of the hill spur, is an outwork formed by a single bank up to 2.8m high and a deep outer ditch. This terminates at the head of the steep slope on the east side, but on the west it returns in the direction of the fort.

12 The Hurlers, stone circles,
Minions.

SX 258714. DE.

Immediately NW of Minions, on NE side of unfenced track leading NW from Upton Cross – Redgate road.

Three Bronze Age stone circles are arranged in a close row aligned roughly north-east to south-west. The northern circle has eleven stones standing and four fallen. Small marker stones indicate the sites of a further nine missing stones, and others may once have existed. This is a true circle 34.7m across and was connected to the central circle by a paved path 1.8m wide.

The central ring is slightly egg-shaped, with diameters of 43.4m and 41.7m. There are fourteen upright stones and fourteen markers. A small stone 0.8m high stands just south of centre. This circle probably contained twenty-nine stones, not including the central one.

The southern circle is the most ruinous. Apparently a true circle 32.8m across, it retains only nine stones from a probable original twenty-eight or twenty-nine. Two are still upright; a number of the fallen ones have become overgrown.

The stones of the three circles, many of which have been re-erected, are between 0.6m and 2.0m tall; they appear to have been roughly dressed before being positioned. Excavation in 1935 awarded a tentative date of 1850 BC to the circles. Just to the west are 'The Pipers', apparently a pair of outlying menhirs 2.0m tall and 3.0m apart, but there are doubts as to their antiquity.

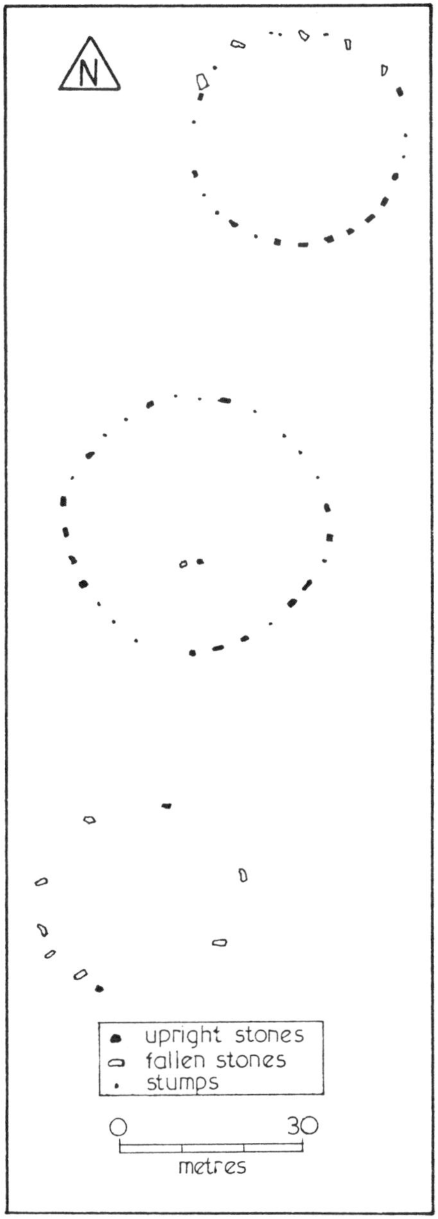

The Hurlers (12)

13 **King Doniert's Stone, inscribed stone,** St Cleer.

SX 236688. DE.
In a small enclosure adjoining S side of minor road between Redgate and Darite, ½ mile E of Redgate.

The enclosure contains two finely worked stones, one of which is a tall cross-shaft decorated with a panel of interlaced carving. Beside it is a squat cross-base, also with interlacing, which bears the clear inscription: DONIERT ROGAVIT PRO ANIMA: 'Doniert ordered (this memorial) for (the sake of) his soul'. Doniert is equated with the Cornish king Dunjarth whose tragic drowning *c.* AD 875, possibly in the nearby River Fowey, was recorded in the *Annales Cambriae.* The style of carving and lettering on the stone supports this date. Doniert is often said to have been the last of the Cornish kings, but two later monarchs are known.

King Doniert's Stone (13)

14 **Largin Castle, hill fort,**
West Taphouse.

SX 169646.

Within Largin Wood, reached by a track through Largin Farm, leaving N side of the A390 half-way between West and Middle Taphouse.

This Iron Age fort is built on a hillspur above the deep valley of the River Fowey. The triple ramparts and ditches surround an oval central enclosure 105m by 70m. The inner pair of defences, with ramparts up to 2.8m high, are concentric and pierced by a south-facing entrance. The outer rampart, which reaches a height of 3.5m, is surrounded by a ditch that is counterscarped on the north side of the fort. The rampart bulges to form a southern annexe to the fort. This has two entrances: one facing south-east, the other south-west. To the south of the fort, crossing the base of the hillspur, is a series of discontinuous outworks including a small rectangular enclosure which may date from the Civil War.

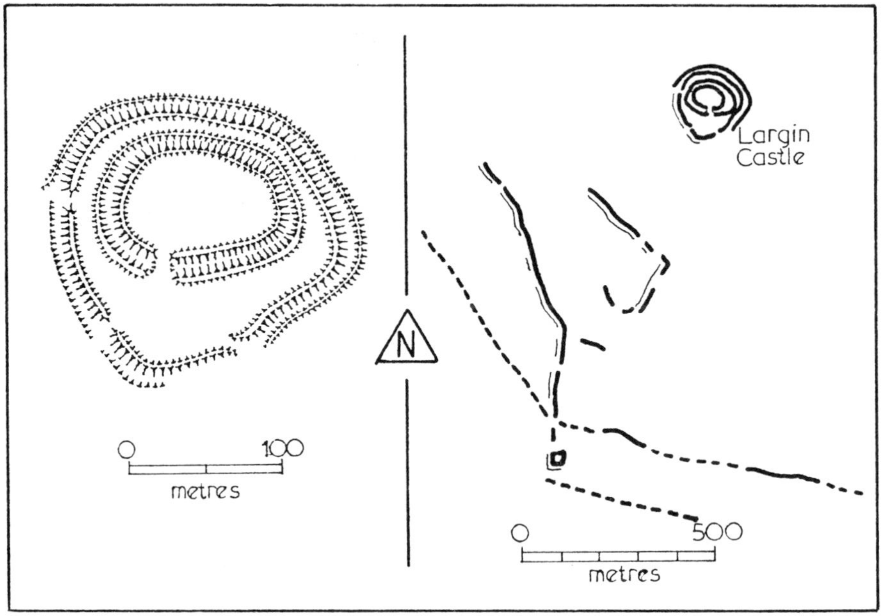

Largin Castle (14)

15 **Padderbury Top, hill fort,**
Menheniot.

SX 314611.

By E side of road leading SE from Doddycross to the A38.

Padderbury Top (15)

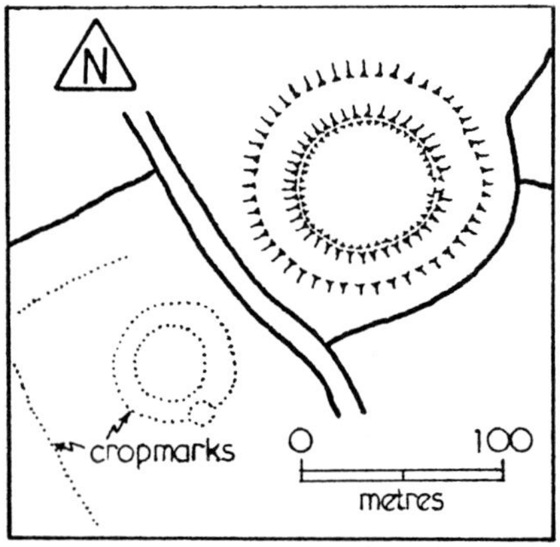

This Iron Age fort, 130m in diameter, appears to be bivallate, with an inner bank up to 3.0m high surrounded by a ploughed-down scarp 1.0m in height which is probably the remains of an outer rampart. No ditches are visible now, and the position of the entrance, probably on the east side, is far from obvious. Aerial photographs have revealed that the fort originally had four lines of defence: one between the two visible ramparts, and an outermost bank and ditch. Further cropmarks point to the former existence of a small bivallate enclosure, 60m in overall diameter, immediately to the south-west of the hill fort.

16 **Pelynt, round barrow cemetery,**
Pelynt.

SX 200544.

Minor road W from the B3359 at Pelynt church. Turn left after ½ mile; barrows lie on N side of road.

Pelynt (16)

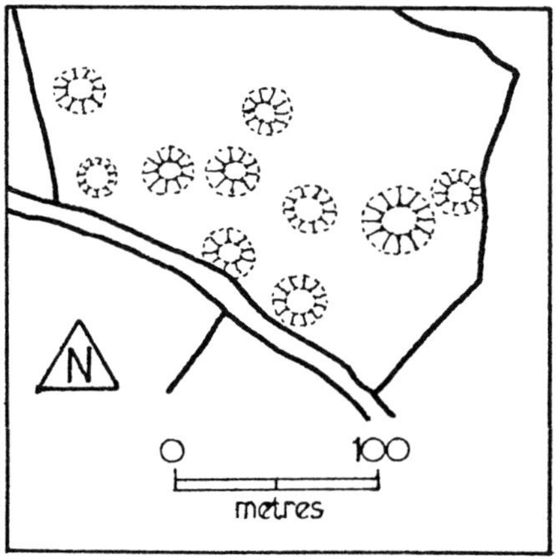

This is a nuclear cemetery of ten Bronze Age bowl barrows; the sites of more, destroyed by ploughing, have been detected from the air. The largest is 24m across, and their heights range from 0.3m to 1.5m. Some of the barrows were opened in 1830 and 1845 and yielded several important finds. These included urn cremations, one of which was accompanied by a locally made greenstone axe and an ogival bronze dagger. Another barrow contained a dagger of eastern Mediterranean, possibly Mycenaean, design, which was dated to 1400-1200bc (1710-1495 BC). Traces of funeral pyres were also found beneath the barrows.

17 Rame Head, cliff castle, Rame.

SX 418484.
B3247 S from Millbrook. Turn right on to minor road at Coombe Farm to Rame; from here a lane leads to the coastguard station at Rame Head.

The extremely narrow neck of this fine headland is crossed by a deep, well-defined Iron Age ditch with a central entrance causeway. Only vestiges of the rampart remain. The summit of the strikingly conical headland, beyond the prehistoric defence, is crowned by the ruins of the medieval chapel of St Michael.

Rame Head (17)

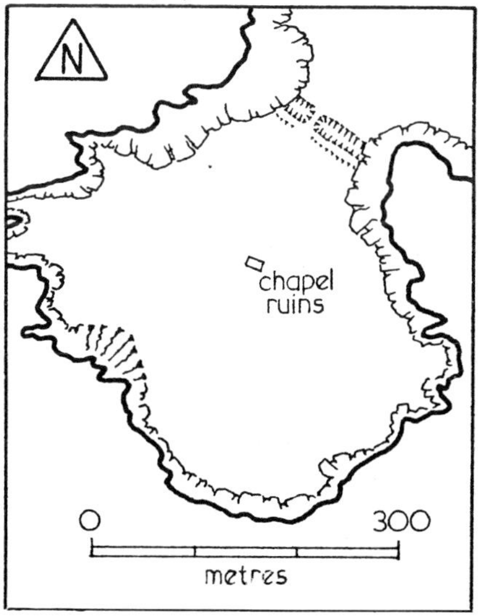

18 Rillaton, round barrow, Minions.

SX 260719.
On hilltop ½ mile NE of the Hurlers (Site 12).

A fine Bronze Age bowl barrow 37m in diameter and 2.4m high, with a grave-robber's pit in its top. Now exposed on the east side of the mound is a stone cist 2.3m long, 1.2m wide and 0.9m high which was opened in 1818. The cist contained a skeleton lying full length, accompanied by a bronze, grooved ogival dagger and the famous Rillaton cup. This is a handled beaker of corrugated sheet gold, similar in style to gold and silver vessels from Mycenae, Greece. The cup was lost for a number of years before being rediscovered in King George V's dressing room. Both cup and dagger are now in the British Museum, but an exact copy of the cup can be seen in the County Museum, Truro.

Rillaton (18)

19 Stowe's Pound, tor enclosure, Minions.

SX 258725.
Directions as for the Hurlers (Site 12) and the Rillaton barrow (Site 18). From the barrow, walk to the Cheesewring on prominent hilltop ¼ mile NW. The site lies just beyond this curious natural formation.

On the bleak summit of Stowe's Hill are two contiguous enclosures. The southernmost, adjacent to the Cheesewring, is pear-shaped, measuring 130m from north to south, by 80m. The single, unditched rampart is of tumbled stone up to 5.0m high externally, and 1.5m high on the inside. It seems that the original internal height of this wall was in the region of 3.0m. Its single entrance faced south-east, and is now virtually on the lip of the disused quarry. No hut sites are known within this enclosure which did not communicate with the larger enclosure adjoining its northern side.

Stowe's Pound (19)

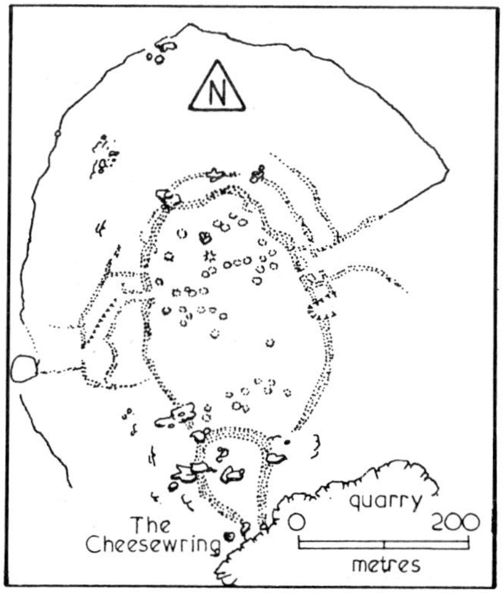

Stowe's Pound (19)

The northern enclosure measures 300m from north to south, by 200m, and is defined by an unditched, tumbled wall up to 1.5m high externally. Some coursing is visible on the west side. Here there is a well-defined entrance with a walled approach through a roughly rectangular annexe, and a hollow way into the main enclosure which contains no less than thirty-nine round houses. A simple entrance gap occurs on the east side. The northern half of the enclosure is encircled by further, much slighter walls which may have been connected with prehistoric agriculture. More round house sites are scattered all over the western flank of the hill.

Stowe's Pound must date from at least the Bronze Age, and the possibility of a neolithic origin cannot be ruled out.

20 **Taphouse Ridge, round barrow cemetery,** West Taphouse.

SX 143633.
N of the A390, ¾ mile W of West Taphouse, at junction with side road to Lanhydrock.

This linear cemetery of Bronze Age bowl barrows, aligned roughly west-east, consists of two groups of four. The western group, west of the present barn, are from 15m to 22m in diameter, and from 2.1m to 4.0m high. All have central mutilations. Of the eastern group only three barrows are at all prominent. These range from 17m to 28m across, and from 0.5m to 5.2m high. They also have central pits, indicative of past grave-robbing. The fourth barrow, just to the south of these, is almost ploughed out, but was about 30m across.

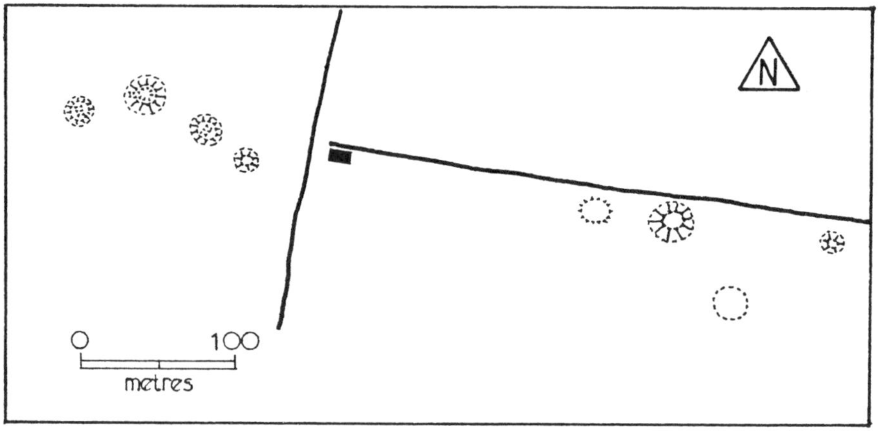

Right: above *Taphouse Ridge barrows (20)*
below *Taphouse Ridge (20)*

21 **Trethevy Quoit, Penwith chamber tomb,** St Cleer.

SX 259688. DE.

2½ miles N of Liskeard, reached from there by the B3254. Left fork after 1 mile to St Cleer and Darite. Site stands at angle of narrow lane between Tremar and Darite.

This massive neolithic tomb consists of a capstone 4.2m long balanced above a chamber 2.1m by 1.5m and more than 3.0m high at the eastern end. The chamber is formed by six stones, one of which is a dividing slab between it and a small forecourt originally defined by two uprights; one of these is missing. A lower corner of the dividing slab has a rectangular piece cut from it, affording restricted access into the chamber. The corner of the capstone which towers 4.3m above the forecourt has a small, unexplained hole through it. Although still in place, the capstone slants alarmingly due to the collapse of the western support stone into the chamber, where it remains. The tomb was formerly surrounded by a large mound, little of which survives.

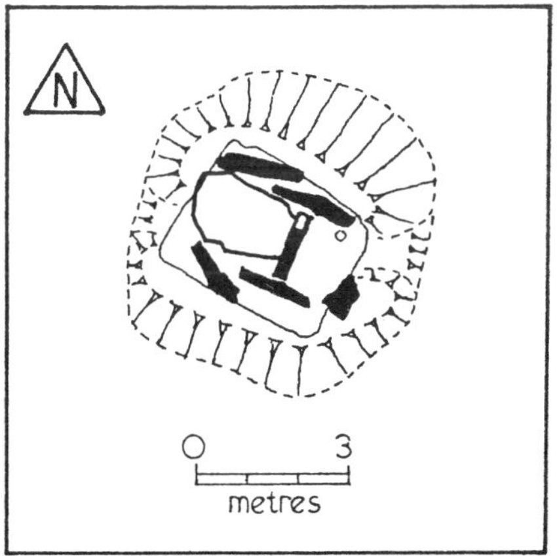

Trethevy Quoit (21)

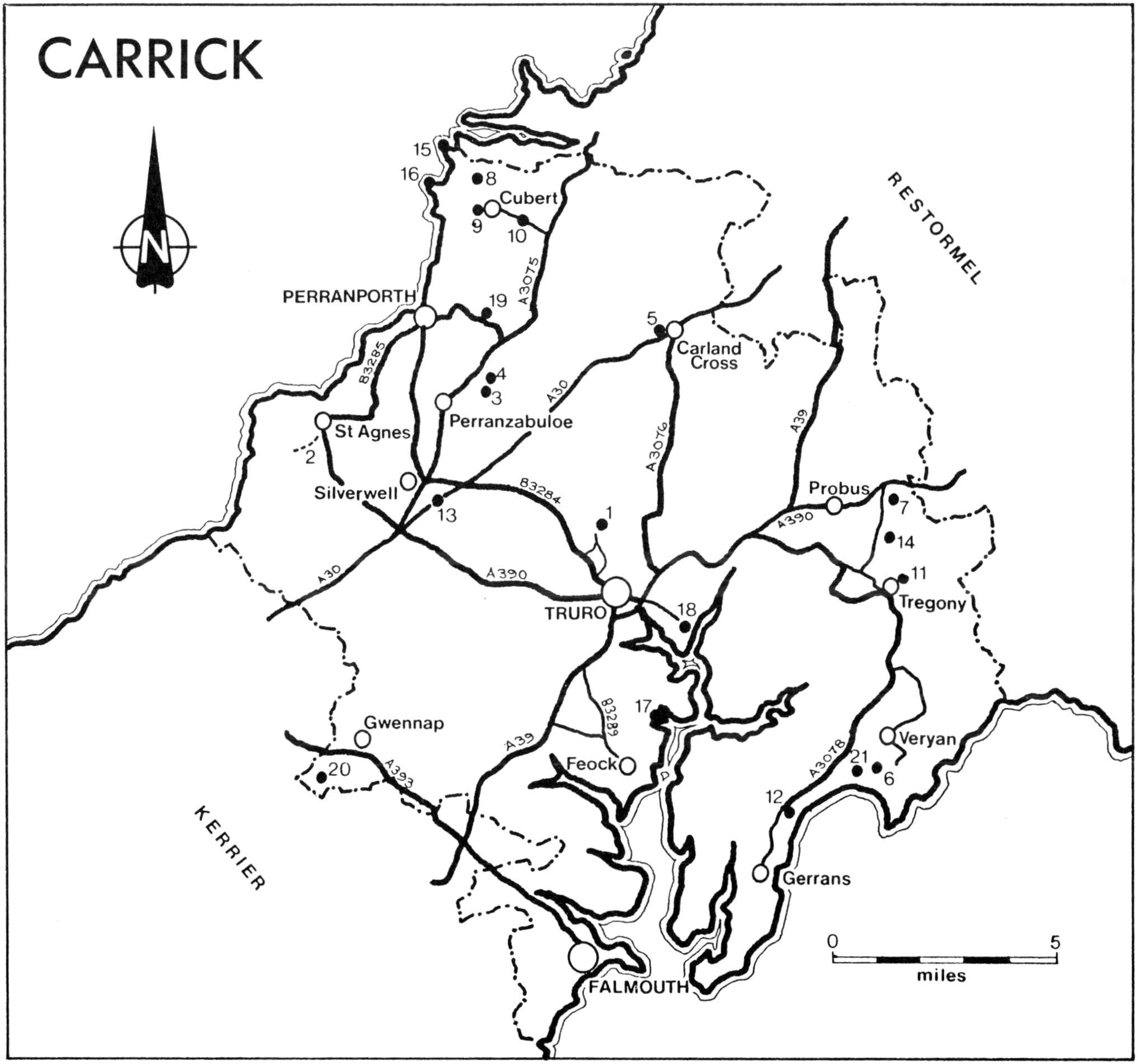
CARRICK
N
RESTORMEL
KERRIER
PERRANPORTH
Cubert
Carland Cross
Perranzabuloe
St Agnes
Silverwell
Probus
TRURO
Tregony
Gwennap
Feock
Veryan
Gerrans
FALMOUTH
A3075
B3285
A30
A3076
A39
B3284
A390
A393
B3289
A3078
0
5
miles
1
2
3
4
5
6
7
8
9
10
11
12
13
14
15
16
17
18
19
20
21

1 **Bishop's Wood, hill fort,** Truro.

SW 829487.
Minor road N from Truro to Idless, whence paths enter St Clement Forest (Lord's, Lady's and Bishop's Woods).

This Iron Age/Romano-British fort occupies a small hillside spur overlooking a deep valley to the east, rather than a hilltop position. Oval in plan, 167m by 150m, it has a single, well preserved earth rampart up to 3.7m high, surrounded by a ditch 1.5m deep. There are three entrances, facing west, north-east and south-east; it is not known whether all three are original. The site is forested, and no hut sites are known within the fort.

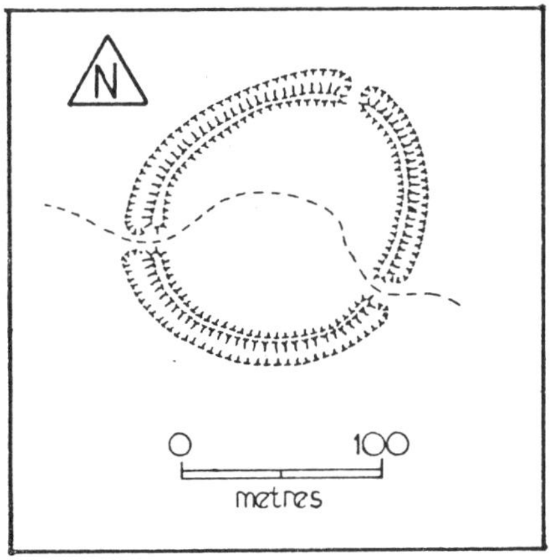

Bishop's Wood fort (1)

2 **The Bolster Bank, linear earthwork,** St Agnes.

SW 705494 to SW 716500.
Best seen where it abuts the S side of the St Agnes to Chapel Porth road, ¼ mile W of its junction with the B3277.

This earthwork originally ran for 2 miles, from approximately SW 703493 at Chapel Coombe, to SW 721508 above Trevaunance Coombe, cutting off nearly 500 ha of land including St Agnes Head and Beacon. Both extremities of the earthwork have been destroyed and the Bolster is now traceable only between SW 705494 and SW 716500. It is punctured by frequent breaches of recent origin; the best preserved section is immediately south of the St Agnes–Chapel Porth road. Here a length of bank rears 3.4m above its silted ditch, which is still 1.0m deep. The word 'Bolster' appears to derive from the Cornish *both-lester*, an upturned boat, and one short, isolated fragment close to Bolster Farm certainly resembles one. The name has been transferred to a famous Cornish giant, by whose hand the earthwork was supposed to have been raised. The reason for the Bolster's existence is not obvious. It could date from anytime between 500 BC and AD 1000, but opinion leans in favour of a post-Roman date, probably fifth or sixth century AD.

Bolster Bank (2)

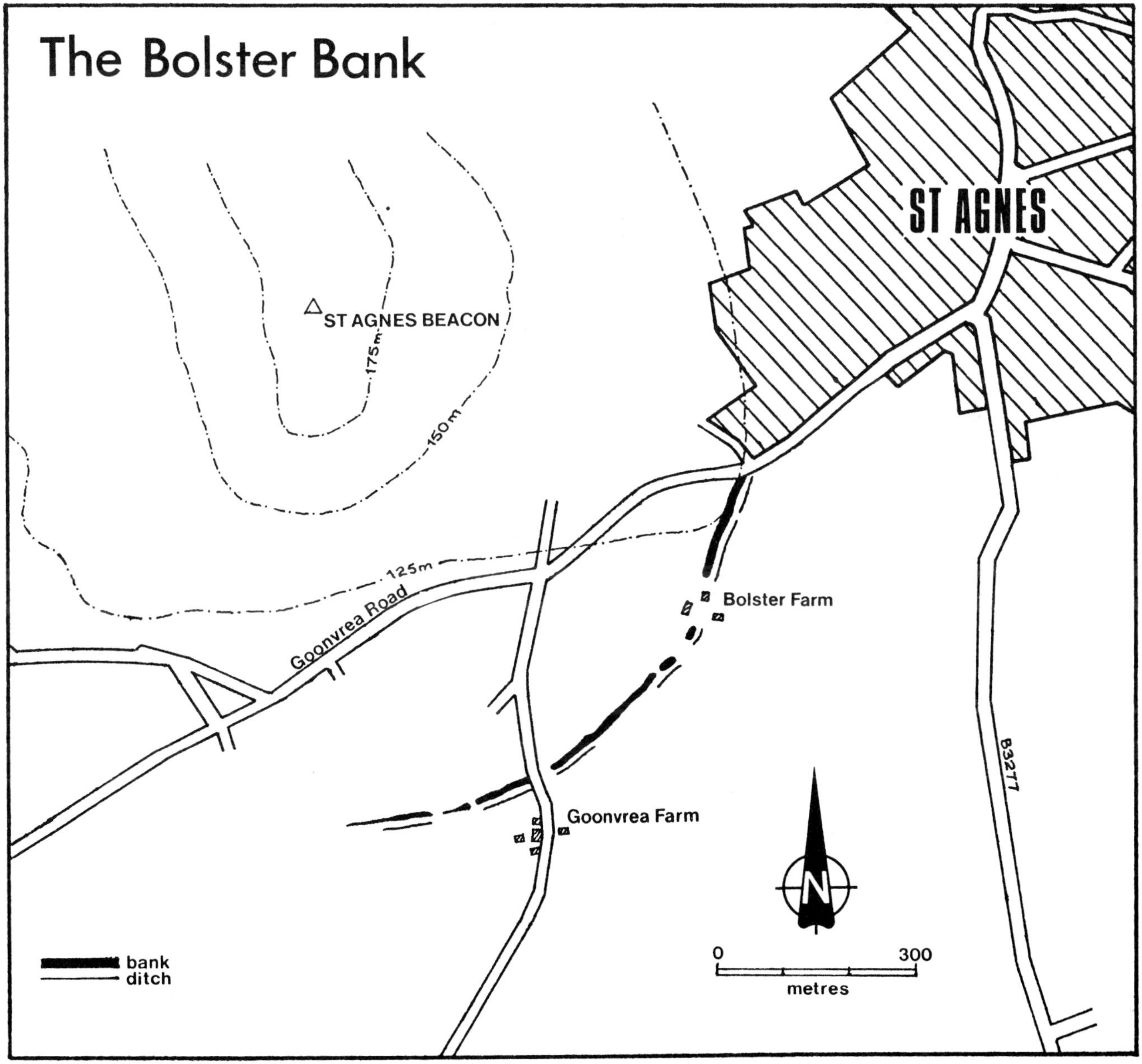
The Bolster Bank
ST AGNES
ST AGNES BEACON
175m
150m
125m
Goonvrea Road
Bolster Farm
Goonvrea Farm
B3277
N
0
300
metres
bank
ditch

3 **Caer Dane, hill fort,**
Perranzabuloe.

SW 778522.

Lane E from A3075 at Perranzabuloe towards Ventongimps. Track to site leaves N side of lane ¼ mile E of the A3075.

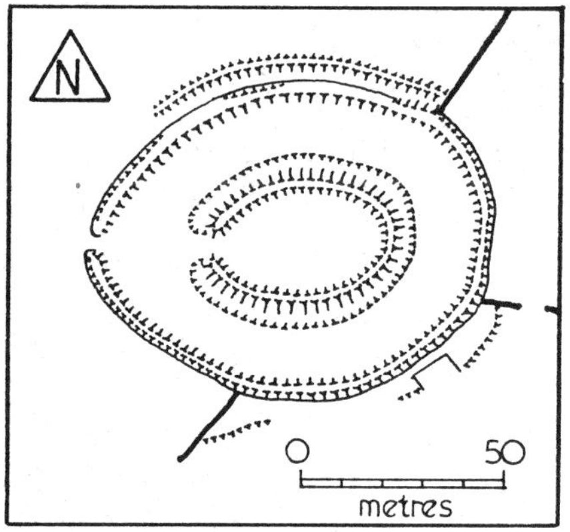

Caer Dane (3)

This small oval fort, 100m by 89m, is sited on a knoll overlooking a valley to the north. The outer bank, faced by modern walling, is 1.5m high. The ditch has been ploughed away, except for a low section of counterscarp bank on the north side of the fort, and the west entrance has been blocked. The central enclosure, 56m by 45m, is well-defined with a rampart 1.8m high, an outer ditch 0.5m deep and a fine, west-facing entrance. The site is heavily overgrown. Aerial photographs have revealed that the fort was virtually surrounded by a single outwork which becomes a double work in the north-west. The fort is Iron Age.

4 **Caer Kief, settlement enclosure,**
Perranzabuloe.

SW 783525.

On opposite side of valley from Caer Dane (Site 3) and reached by tracks running E from the A3075 at Perranwell. The site lies on the hillslope, in woodland.

A single bank 1.1m high, partly stone built, and a shallow outer ditch describe a trapezoid, the greater dimensions of which are 140m and 130m. Entrance gaps occur on the north and east; the former is probably modern. An isolated linear bank to the east, continuing the line of the north side of the enclosure, is the sole remnant of an adjoining enclosure 400m long, from west to east, by 200m. The site is not thought to have been a fortification, but is likely to be of Iron Age/Romano-British date.

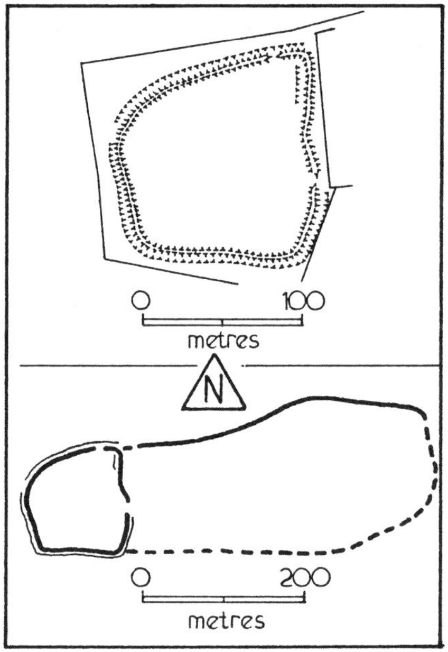

Caer Kief (4)

5 **Carland, round barrow cemetery,**
Carland Cross.

SW 845539.

On either side of the A30, just W of junction with the A3076 at Carland Cross.

Immediately north of the A30 is a prominent Bronze Age bell barrow 24m in diameter and 1.8m high. Known as 'Warren's Barrow', it has a deep excavation pit in its top. South of the A30, between it and the A3076, are six bowl barrows, some of which are much ploughed. These are the survivors of at least thirty barrows which spread across the land to the south-west of the road junction. A further five ploughed and mutilated barrows lie to the east of the junction.

Carland (5)

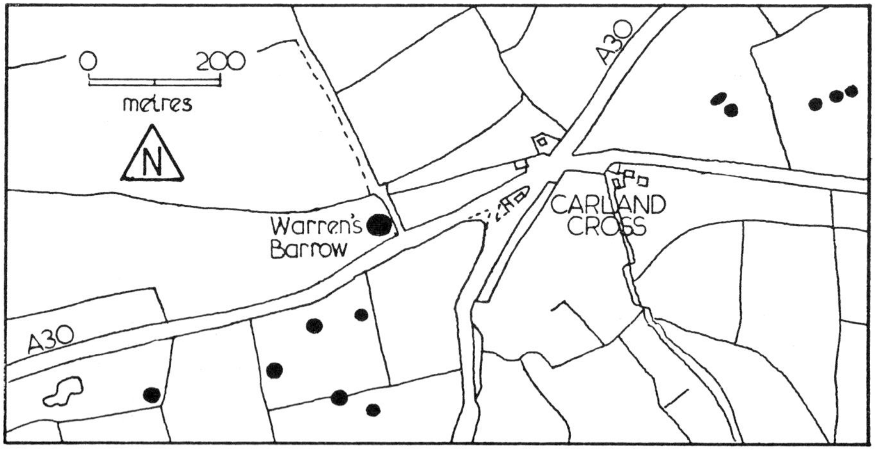

6 Carne Beacon, round barrow, Veryan.

SW 913387.
1¼ miles S of Veryan, at a sharp bend in the lane from Carne to Carne Beach.

This is one of the largest Bronze Age barrows in Britain, being 33m in diameter and 6.5m high. Local legend insists that King Gerent of Cornwall, whose supposed seat of Dingerein Castle (Site 12) is just across the bay, was buried here in a golden boat with silver oars. Unfortunately, excavation in 1855 failed to confirm this ancient belief. Instead a central stone cairn was found, covering a large cist 1.4m by 0.6m by 0.8m deep. This contained ashes and charcoal. Several secondary cremations were also found, but no pottery or other grave goods turned up. The flat top of the mound was mutilated by a former triangulation station, and ploughing has slightly cut back the base of this gigantic mound.

Carne Beacon (6)

7 Carvossa, settlement enclosure, Probus.

SW 919483.
Beside old turnpike road from Probus to Grampound, just S of the A390.

This rectilinear earthwork, measuring 190m by 165m, was formerly believed to have been a Roman camp. Excavation from 1968 to 1970 showed that the enclosure was of the pre-Roman Iron Age, but its most important period of use was between AD 60 and AD 130, when occupation outgrew the site and spilled into the outer ditch and surrounding area. Evidence was found of a road leading south-east to a mooring place on the then navigable River Fal; so was a great deal of pottery. This included amphorae and Samian ware, as well as Celtic Durotrigian ware originating from the region of Dorset. There was also evidence of iron-smelting.

Today only the northern rampart, 2.7m high, and its outer ditch are still impressive. Field walls overlie the west and south sides and the east rampart appears only as a low, irregular and spread bank within the field. An indistinct gap in this eastern bank represents the entrance which was found to have had a well-metalled roadway. Large postholes probably held the supports of an overhead gatehouse. Excavation also revealed a small rectangular enclosure within the north-west corner of the site. The entrance to this was equipped with gate-towers. Nothing of this smaller enclosure is now visible.

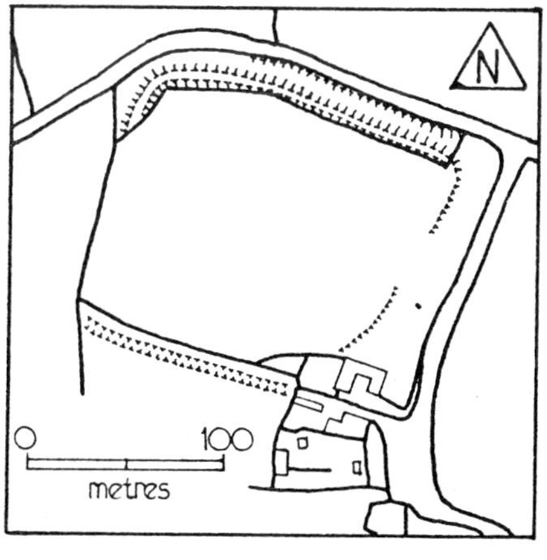

Carvossa (7)

8 **Cubert Common, round barrow,** Cubert.

SW 781594.
1 mile N of Cubert, on footpath from Cubert to Treago.

A fine Bronze Age bowl barrow 34m in diameter and 3.0m high. Its western side is slightly mutilated and wind-blown sand has gathered around its base. A local tradition warns that any attempt to dig the barrow will invoke violent thunderstorms.

Cubert Common (8)

9 **Cubert, inscribed stone,** Cubert.

SW 786577.
Built into W wall of church tower.

The inscription on this stone, CONETOCI FILI TEGERNOMALI (Conetocus, son of Tegernomalus), has been tentatively dated to the seventh century AD. The first name may contain the Brythonic word *cuno* (chieftain), and the second certainly contains *tigernos* (king). So the stone probably commemorates local royalty.

Cubert stone (9)

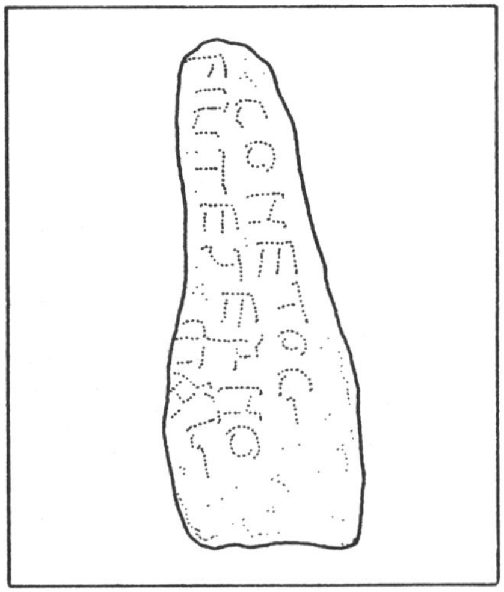

10 **Cubert Round, settlement enclosure,** Cubert.

SW 796574.
The road to Cubert from the A3075 passes through the site.

This circular, univallate earthwork is 70m in diameter; its rampart remains to a height of 1.7m. The entrance is no longer traceable and was probably obliterated by the road which bisects the site. The outer ditch is largely ploughed in and only parts, up to 0.4m deep, survive.

Cubert Round (10)

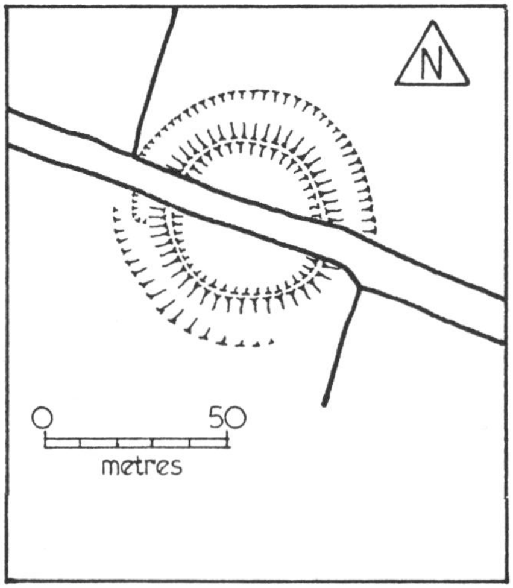

11 **Cuby, inscribed stone,** Tregony.

SW 927453.
The stone is built into the SW corner of Cuby church.

This inscribed stone, dating from the sixth or seventh century AD, carries the words NONNITA ERCILINI RIGATI . . . TRIS FILI ERCILINI (Nonnita, Ercilinus, Rigatus . . . the three children of Ercilinus).

Cuby stone (11)

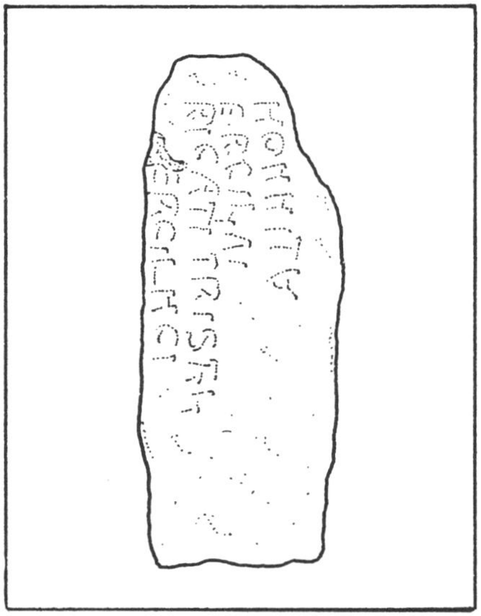

12 **Dingerein Castle, hill fort,** Gerrans.

SW 882376.

By E side of the A3078, ½ mile NE of turning to Gerrans and Portscatho.

106m in diameter, this Iron Age fort is circular with two concentric ramparts. Of these, the inner is traceable throughout its extent, reaching a height of 3.0m on the north-west side, but its southern half has been ploughed down. The outer rampart survives only around the north-west side of the fort, best preserved where it adjoins the road and reaches a height of 2.7m. No trace remains of either ditch, nor of the entrance to the fort which is believed by some to have been the home of the Dark Age King Gerent of Dumnonia. His name has been given to both the hill fort (Cornish: *Dyn Gerent* – Gerent's castle) and the neighbouring village of Gerrans.

Dingerein Castle (12)

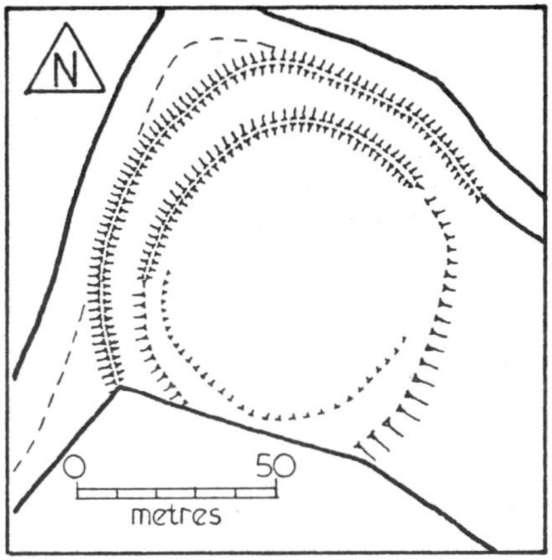

Dingerein Castle (12)

13 **Four Barrows, round barrow cemetery,** Silverwell.

SW 762248.

Beside the A30, ½ mile NE of Chiverton roundabout.

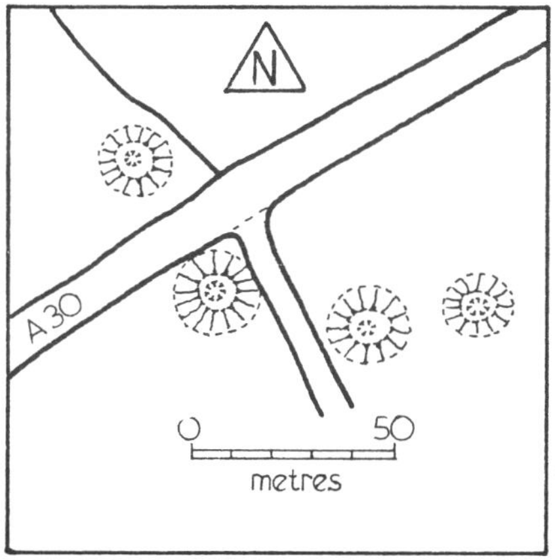

Like the Carland barrows (Site 5) these are sited beside the route of the main prehistoric trackway through Cornwall, which is closely followed by the A30. The prominent barrows lie in an arc on the highest ground in the neighbourhood. One, 3.0m high, is on the north of the road; the others, from 2.4m to 3.7m high, are on the south side. It is not known which of the mounds was 'Burrow Belles' which was opened during the reign of William III and found to contain a large burial chamber roofed by two capstones.

Four Barrows (13)

14 Golden, hill fort,
Probus.

SW 924469.

Reached by minor roads running S from the A390 1 mile E of Probus.

The impressive Iron Age fort of Golden, once thought to have been Roman, stands on a spur overlooking the valley of the Fal. It is of unusual plan, the north-western end being almost rectangular, but tapering to a point at the south-east end. It measures 330m by 200m and was defended by a single earth rampart which survives to a height of 3.2m, and a ditch up to 1.2m deep. The original entrance faces north-west; other breaches in the defences are of recent origin. There is speculation as to whether this fort is the trading settlement of Voliba listed and mapped by Ptolemy. Arguments for the case would apply equally to Carvossa (Site 7), but it is not clear whether or not Voliba lay on the Cenion River (probably the Fal).

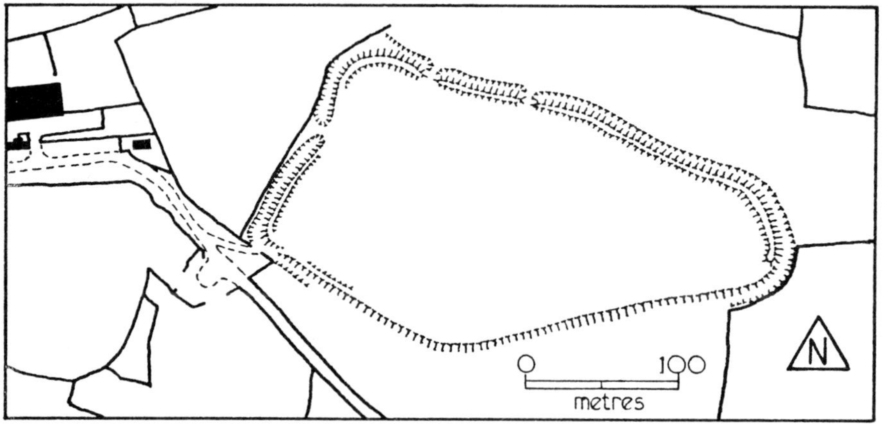

Golden hill fort (14)

15 Kelsey Head, cliff castle,
Cubert.

SW 765608. NT.

Minor road to Cubert and Holywell Bay leads W from the A3075 4 miles N of Goonhavern. Cliff path N from Holywell Bay leads to the site.

The headland is defended by a V-shaped Iron Age rampart and ditch 220m long, pierced by a single entrance 3.0m wide near the angle of the V. This entrance is somewhat indistinct and there is a scatter of loose masonry on its eastern side. The rampart, 1.5m high, incorporates natural rock outcrops and its ditch is 4.6m wide and 0.6m deep. The defended area totals 1.0 ha; traces of Iron Age dwelling sites have been found.

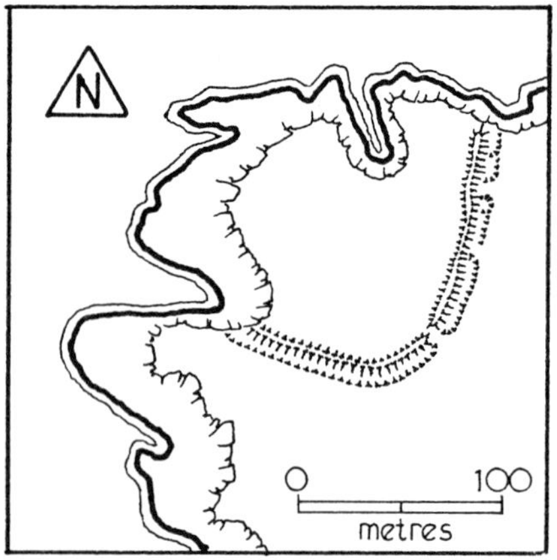

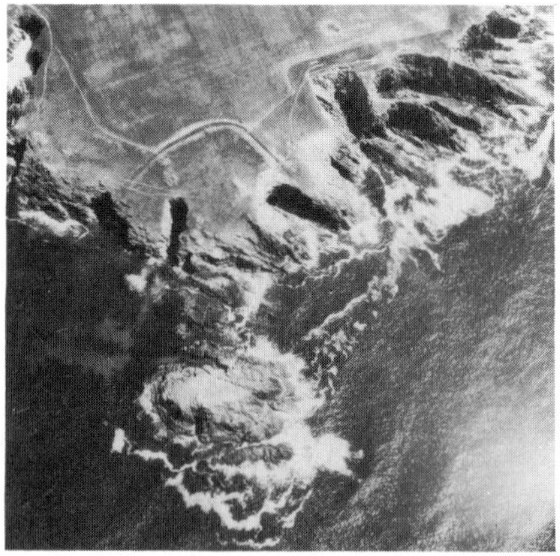

Kelsey Head (15)

16 **Penhale Point, cliff castle,** Cubert.

SW 758531.

Reached by cliff path leading S from Holywell Bay.

Past mining activity has damaged and buried the southern part of these Iron Age defences, but the headland still displays two impressive banks and ditches. Today these ramparts are 2.5m high and the outer ditch is 0.8m deep. A number of breaches occur in the defences, and it is not certain which was the original entrance. Recent surveys have discovered at least one hut site within the defences, and, at the time of writing, excavation of the site is projected.

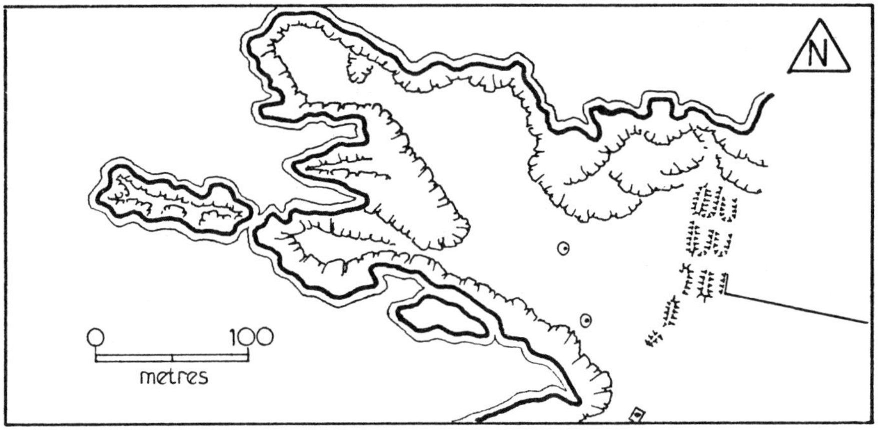

Penhale Point (16)

17 **Round Wood, cliff castle,** Feock.

SW 837404.

Minor road E from the A39 at Carnon Downs to Penelewey, whence a lane leads to the site.

This site is better described as a promontory fort. The Iron Age earthworks – two widely spaced banks and ditches, each with a central entrance – cross the neck of a thickly wooded promontory between Cowland and Lamouth Creeks. The inner rampart is the stronger of the two, reaching 3.0m in height and fronted by a ditch 1.5m deep. Within these defences, and on the highest part of the headland, is an oval bank up to 2.0m high, with parts of an external ditch. This enclosure is 115m from west to east, by 45m. The entrance faces west, directly in line with entrances through the outer banks. The fort is an unusual one and has not been excavated; however, this inner enclosure may be a secondary, perhaps post-Roman feature. The fort is cunningly sited in a semi-concealed position guarding the important confluence of the Fal and Truro Rivers.

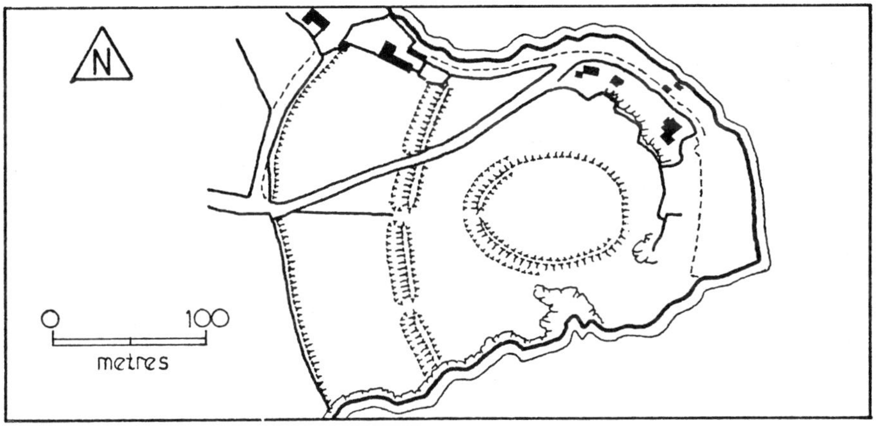

Round Wood (17)

18 St Clement, inscribed stone, St Clement.

SW 851439.
Inscription is on a cross shaft in St Clement churchyard.

The inscription on this tall, rough-hewn stone reads: IGNIOC . . . VITALI FILI TORRICI (Ignioc . . . Vitalus son of Torricus). The second part of the inscription was repeated in the Irish Ogam script, but this has now largely broken away. The name Ignioc is a later addition, as is the cutting of the cross at the top of the stone. The original inscription and the Ogam date from the first half of the sixth century AD; the cross, and possibly the first name, are seventh century at the earliest.

St Clement stone (18)

19 St Piran's Round, settlement enclosure, Goonhavern.

SW 779545.
By N side of the B3254, ¾ mile W of Goonhavern.

This remarkable earthwork encloses an area 45m in diameter. The surrounding earth bank rises 2.5m above the interior and is encircled by a ditch up to 1.5m deep. It is likely to have originated as an Iron Age/Romano-British settlement enclosure, but is better known for its medieval use as a *plen-an-gwary* (amphitheatre) for the production of miracle plays. The internal slope of the bank was cut into seating rows, no longer evident. There are entrances on the south-east and north-west; it is not known which was the original. Perran Round occasionally stages miracle plays today, and the Cornish Gorsedd has been held there three times.

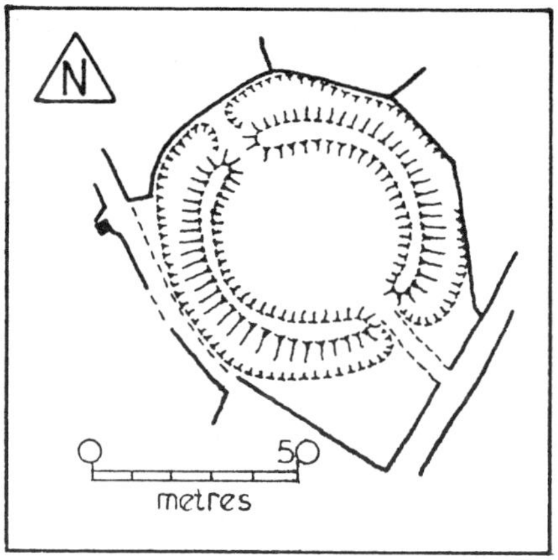

St Piran's Round (19)

St Piran's Round (19)

20 **Trebowland Round, settlement enclosure**, Gwennap.

SW 729387.

Lane to Trebowland Farm leads SW from the A393 ½ mile SE of Comford. Site lies at end of track beyond the farm.

An almost circular enclosure, 90m in diameter, defended by a single rampart and outer ditch, Trebowland Round stands on a gentle north-east facing slope. The western half of the enclosure is the better preserved, with a 1.5m deep ditch fronting a rampart 2.3m high. The eastern half has been ploughed so that the rampart appears as a spread bank 1.0m high, with only vague traces of the ditch remaining. There is no visible evidence of internal structures.

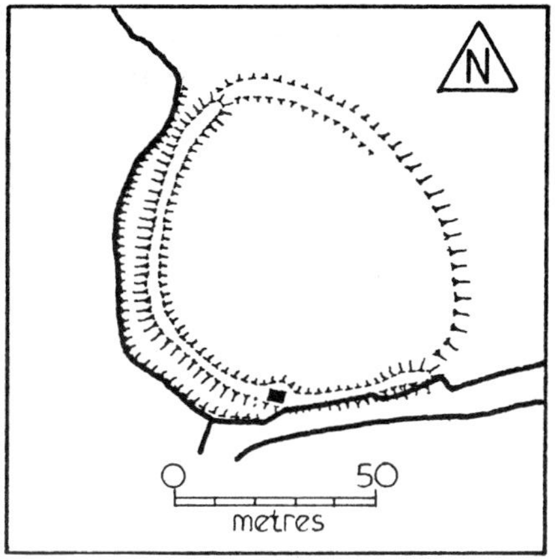

Trebowland Round (20)

21 **Veryan Castle, settlement enclosure**, Veryan.

SW 909388. NT.

To S of lane from Veryan to Carne Beach.

This impressive site is curiously positioned on the side of a steep valley which has been cut and filled artificially to accommodate it. The central enclosure measures 55m by 45m internally, and has a south-facing entrance. The uphill side of the enclosure is protected by a bank 2.0m high, with an outer ditch 2.5m deep. The ploughed remains of two outworks, one topped by a modern wall, lie beyond. The west side of the enclosure, formed by fill, falls away as a scarp at least 8m high. No occupation sites are visible.

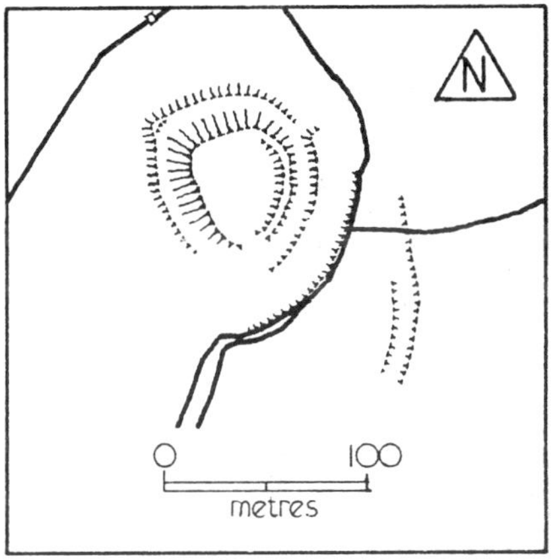

Veryan Castle (21)

Veryan Castle (21)

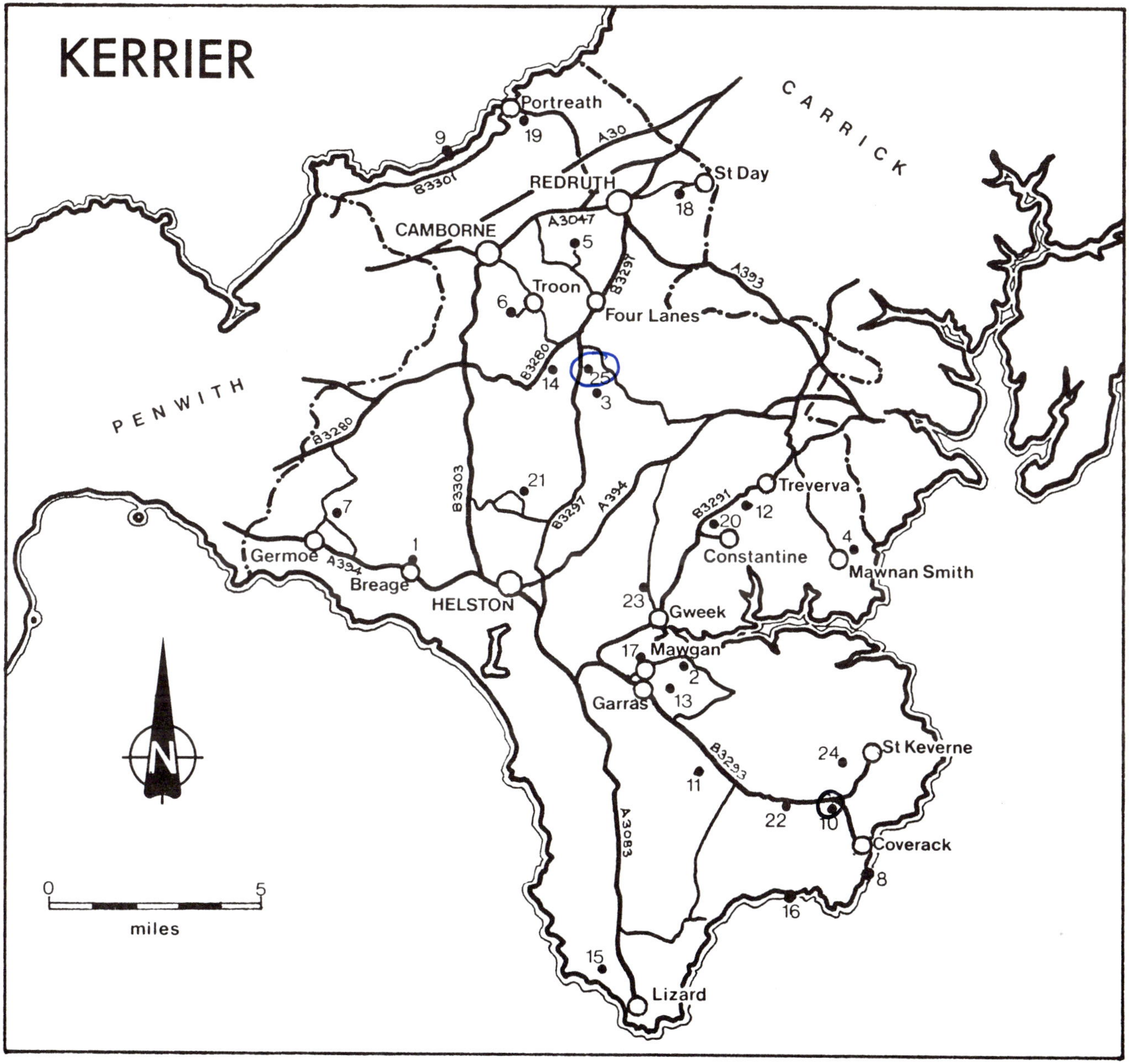
KERRIER
CARRICK
PENWITH
Portreath
St Day
REDRUTH
CAMBORNE
Troon
Four Lanes
Treverva
Constantine
Mawnan Smith
Germoe
Breage
HELSTON
Gweek
Mawgan
Garras
St Keverne
Coverack
Lizard
A30
B3301
A3047
B3297
A393
B3280
B3303
A394
B3291
B3293
A3083
N
0
5
miles

1 Breage, Roman milestone, Breage.

SW 618285.

The stone stands within Breage parish church.

Roman milestones are not milestones as such, but mark stones set beside an actual or intended road, inscribed to the glory of the Emperor. There is no Roman road in Cornwall, but native trackways may have been earmarked for conversion by the Romans. This example is inscribed in Latin to: 'the Emperor Caesar our Lord Marcus Cassianius Latinius Postumus, pious, fortunate, august'. It is the only stone dedicated to Postumus to survive in Britain, and dates from AD 258-268.

2 Caervallack, hill fort, Mawgan-in-Meneage.

SW 726246.

By SW side of minor road from Mawgan to St Martins, 1½ miles E of Mawgan.

This univallate earthwork, 100m in diameter, stands on a hillslope and consists of an outer ditch up to 2.5m deep surrounding an earth rampart 4.1m high. The ditch is heavily counterscarped on the south side of the fort. The entrance faces north-east; a breach in the south-west quadrant is probably recent. A large annexe extends eastward from the fort, but only its north and south arms survive. These consist of a substantial single bank and ditch. Just to the north-west is Gear Camp, a large enclosed settlement 6 ha in extent, with a single ditch and rampart which survives to a height of 4.6m.

3 Calvadnack, roundhouse settlement, Carnmenellis.

SW 690355.

Lane E from the B3297 at SW 681355 leads to Tolcarne Wartha, whence a footpath leading N passes close to W side of the site.

A small settlement on a west-facing slope, within easy reach of a stream. The fragmented remains of a rectangular field, covering about 0.8 ha, can be traced, in the north-west corner of which is an oval pound containing the remains of four round houses, one of which is badly mutilated. The walls of the field, pound and huts are no more than 0.5m high, but some of the huts still retain their upright doorjambs. Much of the surrounding area is heavily overgrown and it is possible that further huts and fields await discovery. The settlement probably dates from the Iron Age, although a Bronze Age celt was found close by.

Caervallack (2)

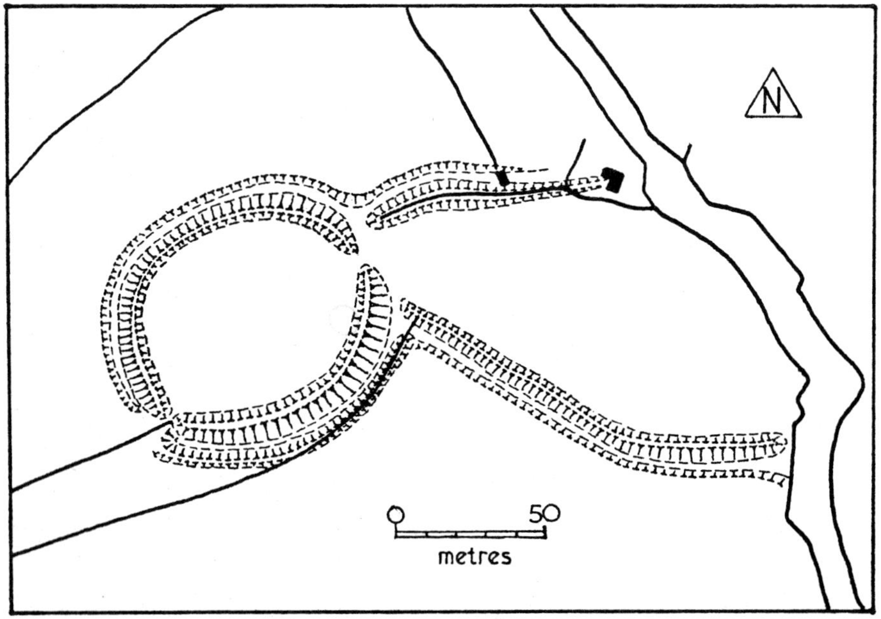

Calvadnack (3)

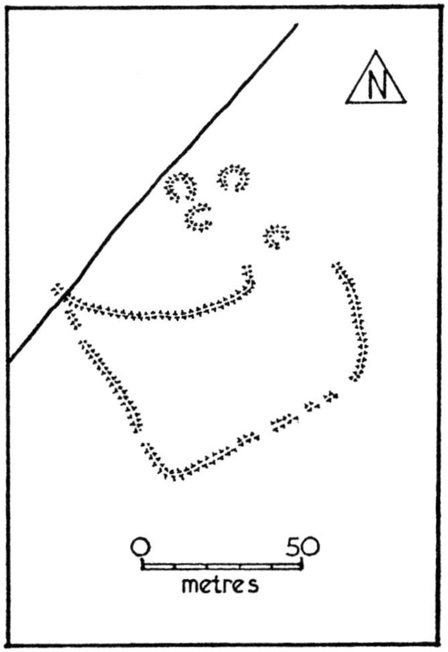

4 **Carlidnack, settlement enclosure,** Mawnan Smith.

SW 782293.
Lane to site from Carlidnack Road, Mawnan Smith. The site is private property, and permission to visit must be sought.

This splendid round commands the deep valley leading east to Maenporth Beach. It is oval, with diameters of 120m and 110m, and consists of a single rampart up to 4.0m high. The outer ditch is now incomplete, but stretches up to 0.7m deep survive. A modern house stands in the centre of the enclosure; trial excavation before it was built revealed that the site dates from the first century AD. The location of the original entrance is not clear.

5 **Carn Brea, tor enclosure,** Camborne-Redruth.

SW 686407.
Rough road to summit from Carnkie, reached by turning S off the A3047 at Pool.

This striking hill, 226m high, has three summits; one is surmounted by a giant nineteenth-century monument, another by Carn Brea Castle, which has medieval origins. Enclosing these two summits are massive prehistoric fortifications surrounding an area 520m long and 15 ha in extent. The fort is essentially bivallate, although the outer rampart is slighter on the steep northern slope than elsewhere. Both the southern ramparts show evidence of having been fronted by a deep ditch. A number of entrances pierce the defences, especially to the south where the hill slopes gently. The inner defence has far more gateways than the outer bank, and many retain massive gate jambs. The north entrance is halfway between the two peaks, and the ends of the inner rampart inturn on either side. The external height of these ramparts, which show much evidence of being either stone-faced or stone-built, varies from 1.0m to 3.7m. The summits carrying the monument and the castle are each surrounded by a single defence which utilizes the many large granite outcrops.

A concentration of neolithic objects pointed interest at the stone-walled enclosure which surrounds 0.7 ha of the castle summit, and the area was extensively excavated between 1970

Carlidnack (4)

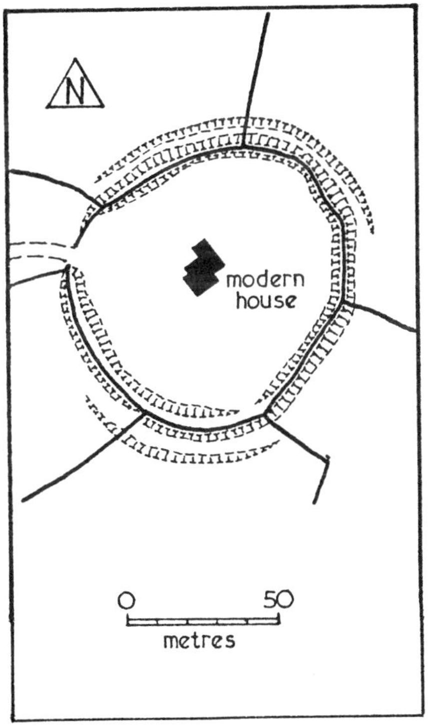

Carn Brea (5)

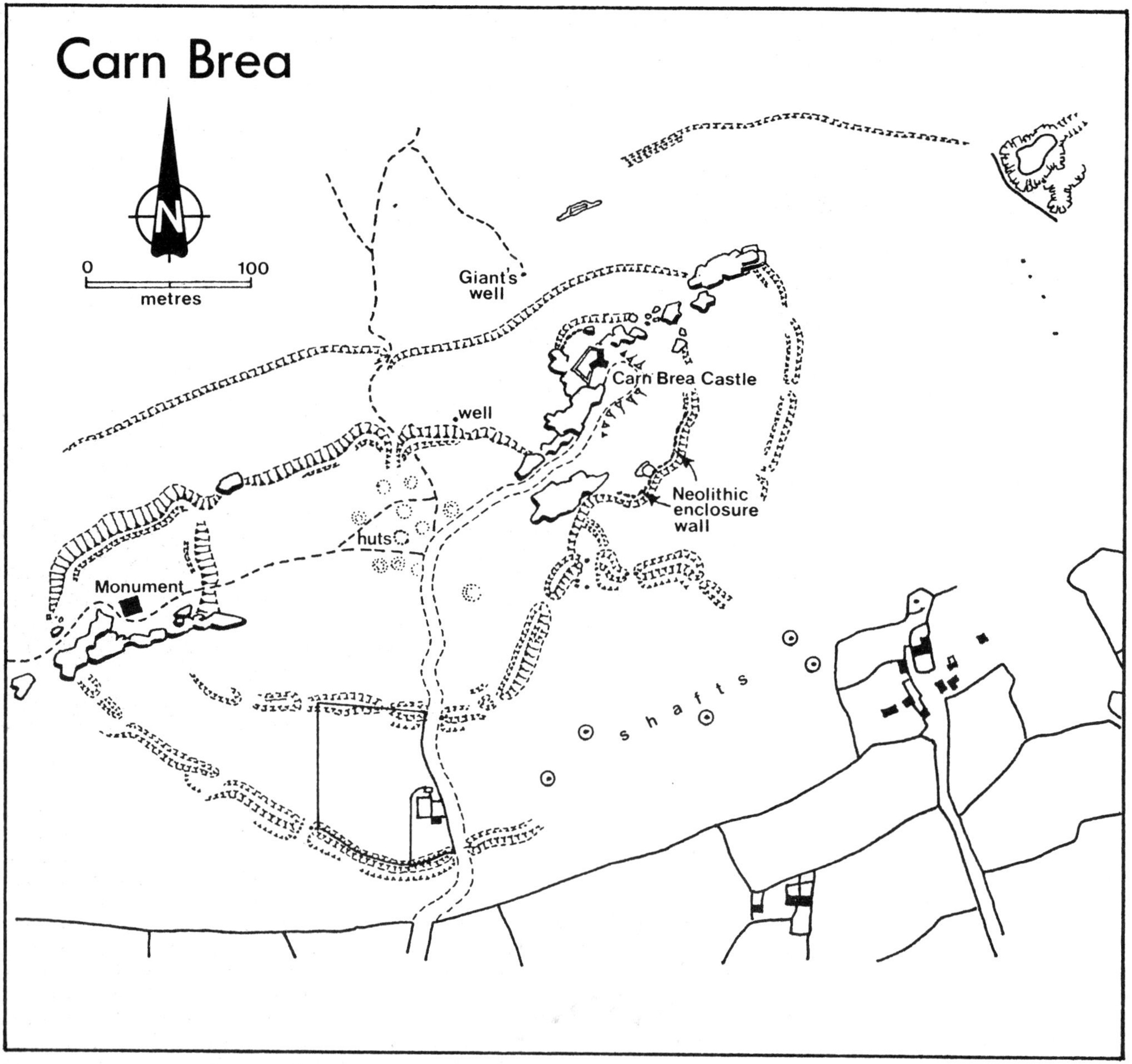
Carn Brea
N
0
100
metres
Giant's well
well
Carn Brea Castle
Neolithic enclosure wall
huts
Monument
shafts

Carn Brea (5)

and 1973. It turned out to be one of the most important archaeological sites in Britain, and one of the oldest known settlements. A village of perhaps 200 people may have been founded as early as *c.* 3180bc (3900 BC); evidence of their agricultural activities was found on the southern slopes of the hill. The village was defended by a substantial wall – the only part of the settlement still visible – yet enjoyed a peaceful existence for up to 300 years before being attacked and burned to the ground. More than 700 arrowheads bear witness to the ferocity of the attack, and the vain, desperate defence of the villagers.

The huge system of ramparts and ditches appears to be Iron Age, as are the eleven round houses in the interior of the fort, but excavation failed to verify this. It is even possible that the entire site, with the exception of the round houses, is neolithic. The importance of the site throughout the ages was illustrated by the discovery in 1749 of two hoards of Celtic coins, from south-east Britain and from Gaul, which dated from the Late Iron Age. Roman coins of the first century AD have also been found on the site.

6 **Carwynnen Quoit, Penwith chamber tomb**, Troon.

SW 650373.

Lane leads W from Troon to Carwynnen. Quoit lies in a field on N side of lane near foot of hill, and just E of Carwynnen.

Also known as the 'Giant's Quoit' and the 'Giant's Frying Pan', the capstone of this tomb formerly stood on three supports at a height of 1.5m. The quoit collapsed in 1834, was subsequently rebuilt, but fell again in 1967, since when it has remained in its collapsed state. The fallen capstone measures 3.3m by 2.5m by 0.3m thick. Two of the former support stones, both 2.7m long, lie on top of it, the third beneath it. Other stones are field clearance boulders. No trace remains of the former covering mound of this neolithic tomb.

Carwynnen Quoit (6)

7 **Castle Pencaire, hill fort.** Germoe.

SW 599300.

Minor road from Germoe on the A394 leads NE to Balwest, whence footpaths lead to the site on the summit of Tregonning Hill.

The two concentric stone ramparts of this Iron Age fort are tumbled and dilapidated, damaged by past quarrying, yet they are still imposing. The fort is oval, 125m from north to south, by 109m. It is best preserved on the west side where the outer rampart reaches a height of 2.7m. A war memorial stands atop the inner rampart on this side. Parts of the outer ditch can still be traced, and an inturned entrance on the south-west may be original. There were formerly as many as twenty round houses inside the fort and some may still survive, virtually indistinguishable from the many small circular quarry pits which pock the central enclosure. Castle Pencaire may be the *Loban Rath* to which fifth or sixth century Irish missionaries are said to have fled under threat from the pagan King Teudar. It may also be the *ker hyr* (long fort) after which Kerrier is named.

On the north slope of the hill are two well preserved rounds. Both are oval, with dia-

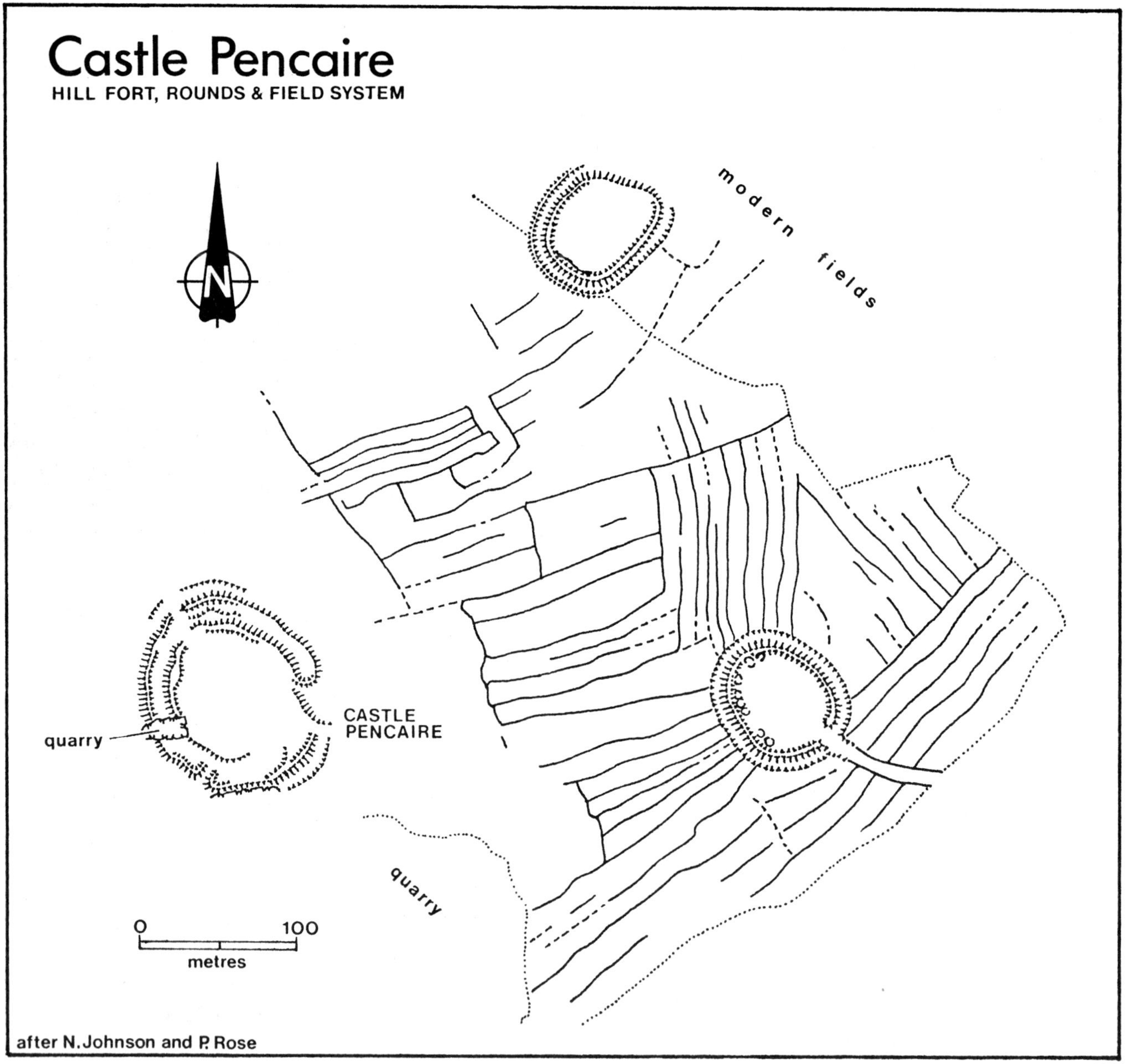
Castle Pencaire
HILL FORT, ROUNDS & FIELD SYSTEM
N
modern fields
CASTLE PENCAIRE
quarry
quarry
0
100
metres
after N.Johnson and P. Rose

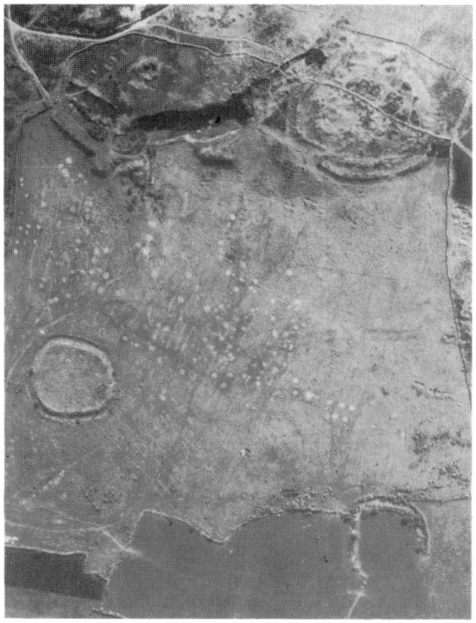

Castle Pencaire (7)

meters of about 90m and 80m, and are defined by single ramparts each of which reaches a height of 2.6m. The round at SW 602303, north-east of the hill fort, has an outer ditch 2.4m deep, but its north side has suffered from ploughing. The other round, east of the fort at SW 603300, is surrounded by a ditch up to 1.5m deep; two round houses are visible against the inside of the rampart in the north-west quadrant. Others have been traced, including a central hut recorded in 1932. A clearly traceable road, lined by low banks, runs from this round's south-east facing entrance through the remarkable field system which covers this flank of the hill right up to the hill fort itself.

Right: above and below *Chynhalls Point*

8 **Chynhalls Point, cliff castle,** Coverack.

SW 785174.
Reached by cliff path running S from Coverack.

The neck of this prominent headland displays two Iron Age ramparts with an intermediate ditch. The outer bank, best preserved on the northern side of the headlands, is 1.1m high. The inner is more massive, reaching a height of 2.7m, and is revetted with stone. A simple central entrance pierces both defences. No occupation sites have yet been noted.

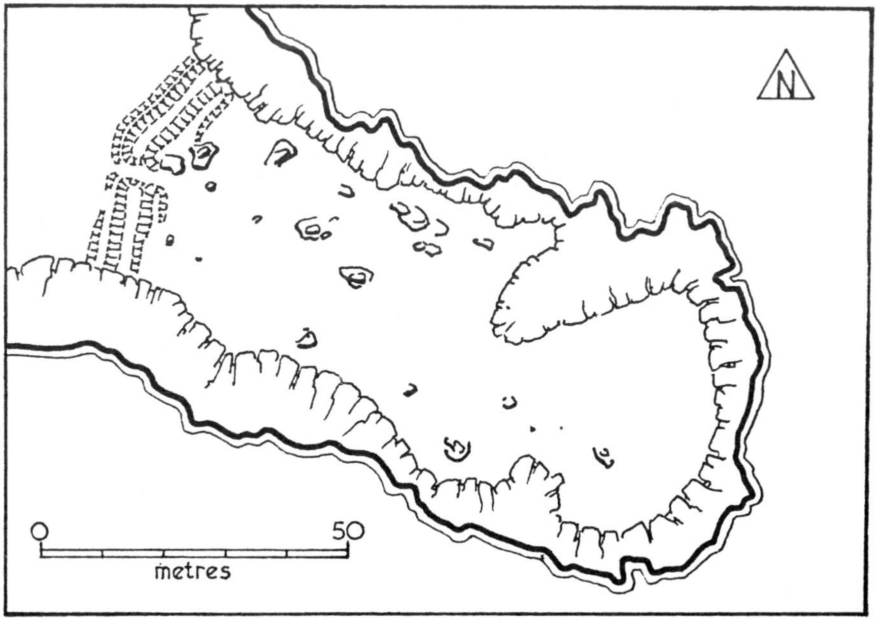

9 Crane Castle, cliff castle, Portreath.

SW 774196. NT.

On cliff path, 1½ miles SW of Portreath; best reached by footpath from the B3301 at SW 641439.

The interior of this Iron Age fort has been eroded away by the sea, so the inner of the two ramparts now sits on the very edge of the cliff. It is 2.2m high and its ditch, known as the 'Bowling Green', is 1.8m wide at its foot. The outer rampart which, like the inner one, is of earth and stone reaches a height of 2.7m and is 85m long. Beyond the 1.2m deep outer ditch is a rectangular annexe 103m by 68m, defined by a very slight bank with mere traces of an outer ditch. Early Iron Age pottery has been found on this site, whose name is derived from the Cornish ***ker hen*** (old fort). The castle will probably be totally destroyed by erosion within the next century or so.

Crane Castle (9)

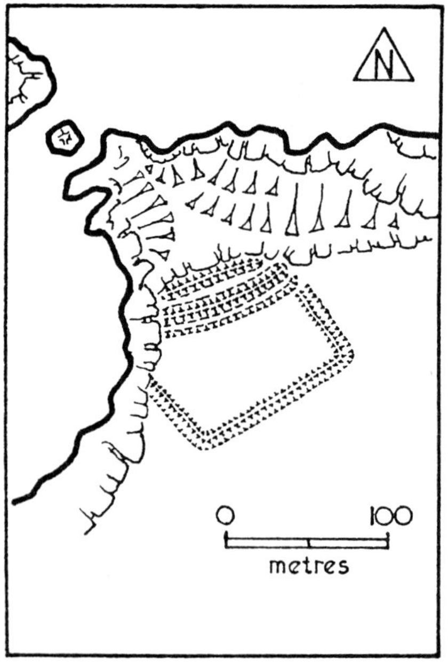

10 Crousa Common, round barrow. St Keverne.

SW 774196.

1½ miles SW of St Keverne, just S of the B3293 near track to Coverack.

Crousa Common – indeed the whole of Goonhilly Downs – is rich in Bronze Age round barrows. This is one of the finest and most easily accessible, 12m in diameter and 1.2m high. Originally it had a stone kerb. It contains traces of a burial cist. On the north side of the B3293, at SW 775201, are a pair of Bronze Age menhirs, one of which has fallen, the other standing 1.9m high.

11 Dry Tree, menhir, Goonhilly.

SW 726212.

Just outside SE perimeter fence of the Goonhilly Downs satellite tracking station which adjoins the B3293.

Here on Goonhilly downs is a fascinating juxtaposition of ancient and modern, for this fine stone stands in the shadow of the giant Space Age dish aerials. 3.2m high (the total length of the stone is 4.5m), it was re-erected in its original socket in 1927 after lying prostrate for many years. Its Bronze Age erectors must have transported it at least two miles, for it is of Crousa Downs gabbro. It is surrounded by three round barrows, and in the late eighteenth and early nineteenth centuries the site was notorious as the haunt of the Goonhilly highwaymen.

Dry Tree menhir (11)

12 **Eathorne, menhir,** Treverva.

SW 746313.

In a field on SE side of the B3291, ¾ mile SW of Treverva and opposite turning of lane leading to Longdowns.

A fine but little known Bronze Age menhir, 2.4m tall. Slim and regular in shape but with a curiously bent top, it is of local granite.

Eathorne menhir (12)

13 **Halligye, fogou,** Garras.

SW 877254.

Reached by minor road and path N from the B3293 at Garras. The site is in a private garden, and permission to visit must be sought. A torch is essential.

The largest of the mysterious Cornish fogous, this one is well preserved. It is Iron Age and was recently excavated. It was built beneath the inner rampart of a former defended settlement and opened into the ditch. The structure is T-shaped, the bar of the T being a large, wide gallery running north-west to south-east. The northern end is lower and narrower, with a heavy lintel in a place where there may have been a door. This was the entrance from the ditch which was recently reopened, having been blocked for centuries. The upright of the T, joined to the first passage by a low doorway, is a gently curving passage 20.7m long, lying south-west to north-east. The south-west end is cut into solid rock. An entrance cut in the nineteenth century enters the south side of this gallery; at its western end is a small side passage running south. In the main gallery, close to its tiny entrance, a natural block of granite protrudes from the floor; some hold that this was left as a deliberate stumbling block. The fogou has a known total of 39.0m of passages. There are large lintels and jambs for its small doorways, and it has corbelled walls and a roof of heavy slabs. The height of the two main passages averages 1.9m.

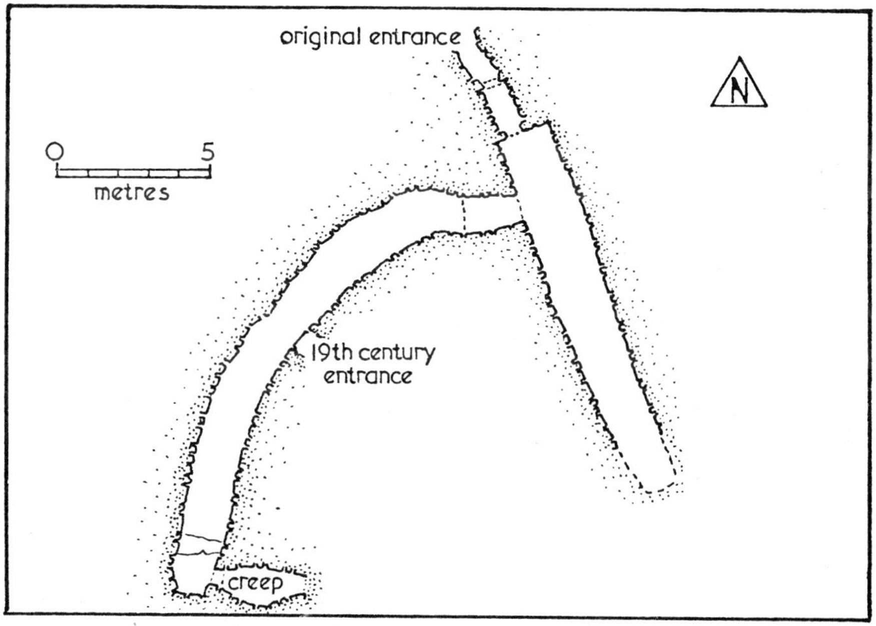

Halligye fogou (13)

14 Hangman's Barrow, round barrow, Troon.

SW 673367.
Close to SE side of the B3280, 200m SW of turning to Troon.

This massive cairn occupies a prominent ridge-top position. Built entirely of stone, it is 3.0m high and 20m in diameter. Its centre is mutilated and cratered due to past tomb-rifling and stone-robbing. Nothing is known of the cairn's contents.

15 Kynance Gate, round house settlement, Lizard.

SW 688139.
½ mile walk up valley from Kynance Cove. Site stands above NW side of valley.

The settlement is divided into two main groups of dwellings. The northern group has five

Kynance Gate (15)

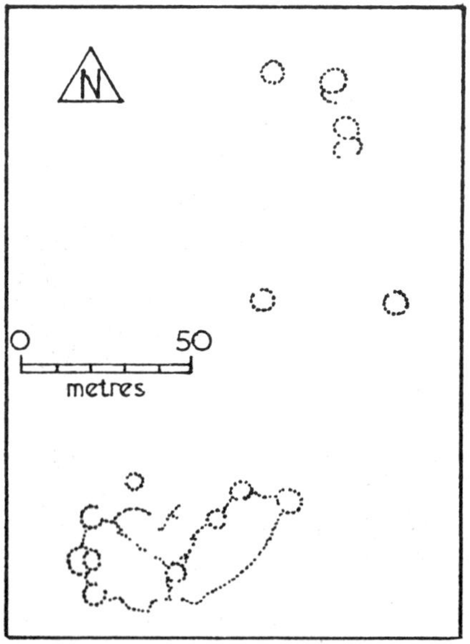

Hangman's Barrow (14)

Lankidden (16)

detached round houses averaging 9m in diameter and standing on artificial terraces. Other huts may lie beneath the dense scrub. The southern group, 60m away, is clustered around a natural rock outcrop and consists of eight huts connected by an irregular ring wall. Bronze Age hearths and pottery – over 2,000 sherds – were found here, indicating that the Early Iron Age settlement is on a Middle Bronze Age site which seems to have been abandoned *c.* 1000 bc (1250 BC), then resettled in the Iron Age. Hut walls exist to a height of 0.5m.

16 **Lankidden, cliff castle,** Coverack.

SW 755166.

On cliff path between Kennack Sands and Coverack, 1 mile E of Kennack Sands.

The Iron Age defensive work on this headland consists of a single massive rampart 4.0m high, with a simple entrance set east of centre. The outer ditch is somewhat silted up and now reaches a depth of only 0.6m.

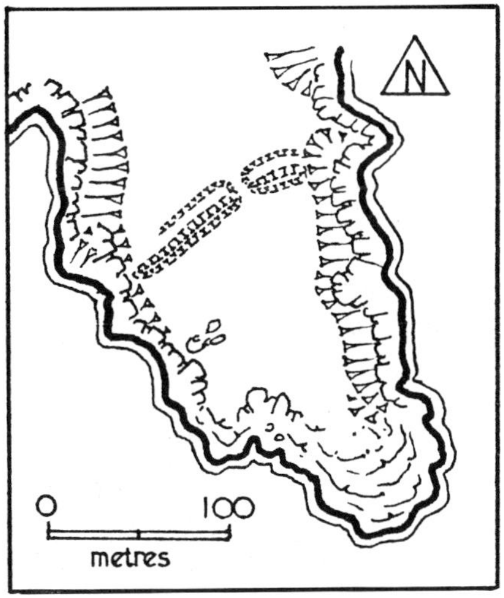

17 **Mawgan Cross, inscribed stone,** Mawgan-in-Meneage.

SW 707249.

In centre of village, at meeting of three roads.

A headless cross-shaft 1.9m high, inscribed with the words: CNEGUMI FILI GENAIVS (Cnegumus, son of Genaius). The lettering is of a late form, possibly tenth century AD.

18 **Menheer Farm, Roman milestone,** St Day.

SW 719421.

Left fork to Busveal and Gwennap Pit from St Day passes Menheer Farm, which lies on S side of road. The stone stands in the private garden of the farmhouse, and permission to view must be sought.

This stone was discovered during ploughing in 1942, and was subsequently set up in its present position. The inscription is a dedication to 'The Emperor, Caesar, Antonius Gordianus, pious, fortunate'. Dated to AD 238-244, it is the earliest of the Roman milestones so far found in Cornwall.

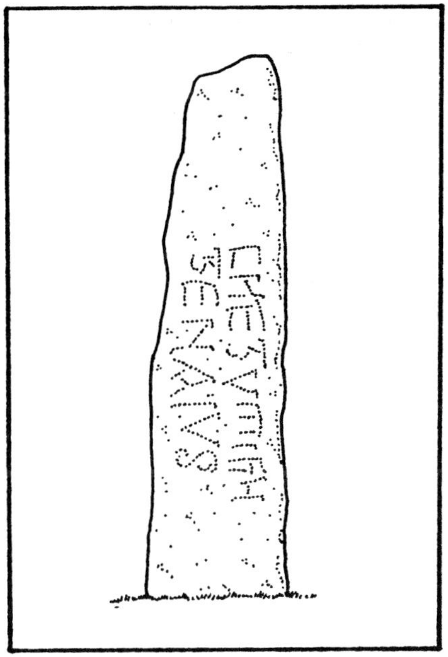

Above and below: *Mawgan Cross stone (17)*

19 Nance, hill fort,
Portreath.

SW 664450.

Reached by footpath from Portreath, or by track from Nance Farm, Illogan.

Standing on a spur overlooking the junction of two valleys and the cove of Portreath, this roughly oval fort has diameters of 116m and 104m. It is essentially univallate with an earth rampart up to 1.8m high, but an outer bank 2.0m high, with a ditch 0.7m deep, protects the south-west side. A further, isolated stretch of this outer defence occurs to the north. The position of the entrance is unclear; it may have corresponded to a cattle track through the rampart on the east. A roughly rectangular area of slightly raised ground outside this gap possibly represents the remains of an annexe.

Below: *Nance (9)*
Far right: *Piskey Hall (20)*
Bottom right: *Piskey Hall fogou (20)*

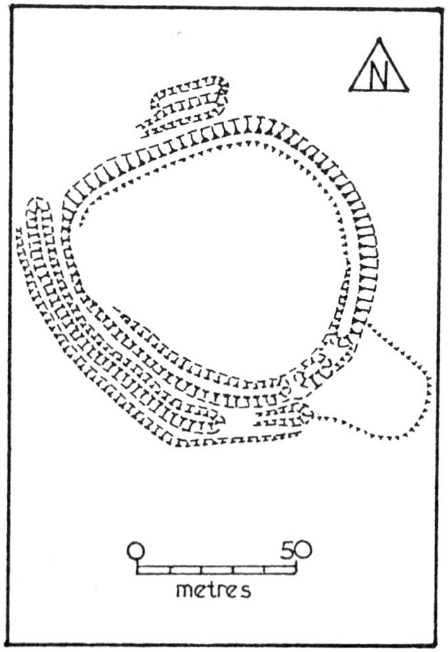

20 Piskey Hall, fogou,
Constantine.

SW 728300.

In a field directly opposite the gates to Trewardreva House, ½ mile N of Constantine on the B3291.

A semi-underground structure once associated with a now-destroyed Iron Age enclosed settlement. It is a slightly curved passage, the roofed part of which is 8.2m long. Piskey Hall is unusual among fogous in that its walls are vertical, not corbelled inward; as a result, the eight roof slabs are enormous. The fogou probably extended a little way further to the north-east where the present end wall is modern – as are the two jambstones at the present south-western entrance. It was once thought that a branch passage may have run southwards from the inner end of the fogou, but this is now considered unlikely. The structure was built against a low outcrop of granite, and its half-underground nature makes it a prominent object in the field.

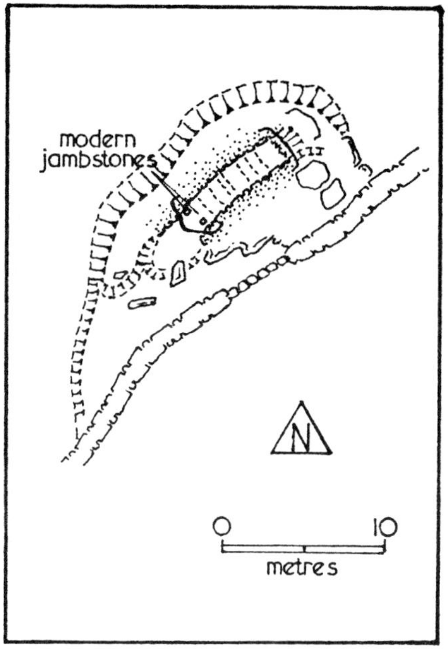

21 **Prospidnick, menhir,** Helston.

SW 659316.
Reached by lane leading E from the B3303 at Crowntown.

This fine stone is situated just below the summit of Prospidnick Hill, on the east side of the lane, and stands 3.0m high. Like so many other Bronze Age menhirs, it is known locally as 'The Longstone'.

22 **The Three Brothers of Grugwith, burial cist**, St Keverne.

SW 761198.
Behind Zoar Garage, on the B3293, 3 miles W of St Keverne.

A heavy capstone 2.4m by 1.5m is balanced on two stones which form the parallel sides of a chamber 2.4m long, 0.9m wide and 0.9m high. The other two sides are missing, and there is no trace of any barrow which may once have covered it. A number of shallow depressions in the capstone, once thought to have been artificial cup-marks, may be a product of natural weathering. This monument is probably Bronze Age.

23 **The Tolvan, holed stone,** Gweek.

SW 706283.
In back garden of Tolvan Cross Cottage, on minor road 1 mile due N of Gweek. Permission to view must be sought.

A large upright slab, triangular in shape, 2.3m tall and 2.2m wide at the base. The centre of the stone is pierced by a circular hole 44cms in diameter, the purpose of which is unknown. It is probably Bronze Age.

The Tolvan (23)

24 **Tremenheere Farm, menhir,** St Keverne.

SW 778210.
1 mile W of St Keverne, turning N off the B3293, and right after ½ mile to Tremenheere (farm track and footpath).

The farm is named after this fine, tapered Bronze Age standing stone which is 2.9m tall.

25 **Wendron, stone circles,** Four Lanes.

SW 681365.
In a field on E side of the B3267, ¾ mile S of its junction with the B3280.

There were formerly two circles here, standing about 18m apart. The south-eastern circle, 16.0m across, originally contained fourteen or fifteen stones, but only six survive. Four of these are free-standing, the others are built into the hedge – one still in its original position. The stones are from 0.8m to 1.2m high and represent only the south-eastern half of the circle. The north-western circle, once about 21m in diameter, has just two stones left, both *in situ* but built into the modern walls. The original number of stones is unknown; ten were noted by Dr Borlase *c.* 1760. The circles date from the Bronze Age.

Wendron (25)

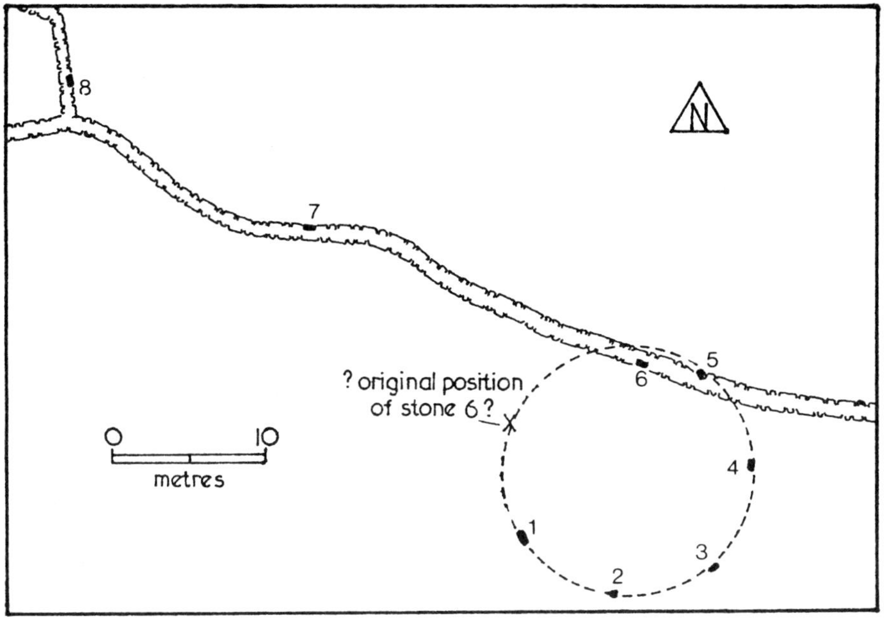

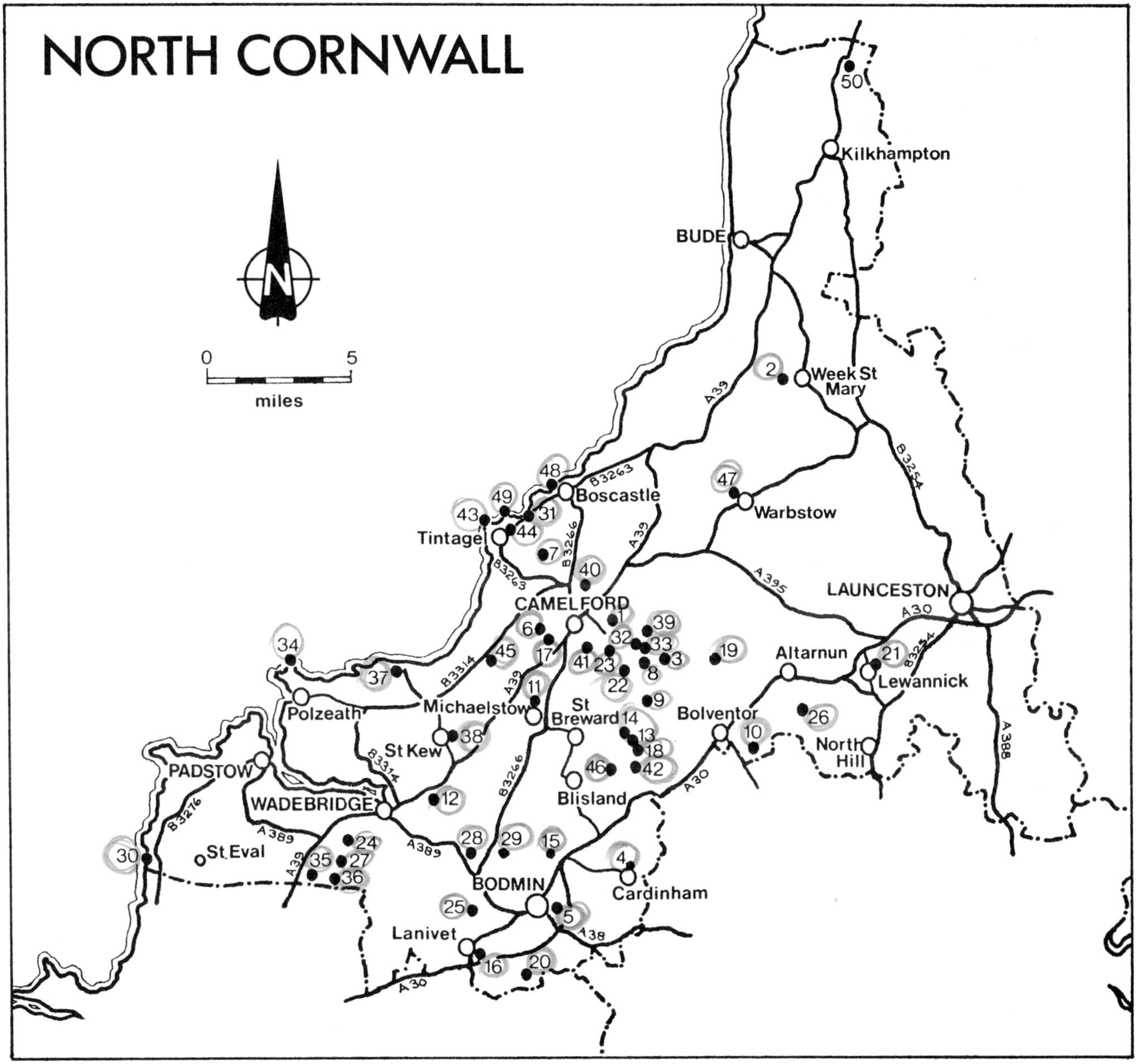
NORTH CORNWALL
N
0
5
miles
Kilkhampton
BUDE
Week St Mary
Warbstow
Boscastle
Tintagel
CAMELFORD
LAUNCESTON
Altarnun
Lewannick
Bolventor
North Hill
St Breward
Blisland
Michaelstow
St Kew
Polzeath
PADSTOW
WADEBRIDGE
St Eval
BODMIN
Cardinham
Lanivet
A39
A395
A30
A388
A38
A389
B3263
B3266
B3254
B3314
B3276

1 **Advent, triple barrow,** Camelford.

SX 137834.
2 miles E of Camelford, by N side of minor road running SW from Davidstow Woods.

Bronze Age triple round barrows are rare outside Wiltshire. This example has three mounds about 1.2m high and 24m in diameter, aligned roughly north-west to south-east, surrounded by a shallow, oval ditch with diameters of 67m and 37m. There are no records of any finds, even though all three mounds have hollowed centres.

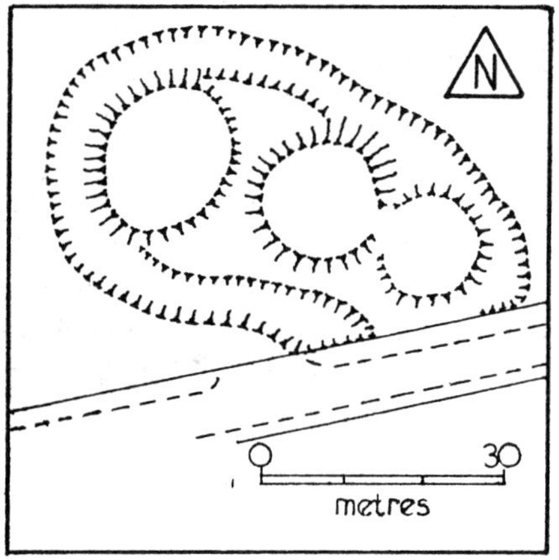

Advent (1)

2 **Ashbury, hill fort,** Week St Mary.

SX 228975.
Reached by lane running S from Week St Mary to Poundstock road, 1 mile NW of Week St Mary.

This Iron Age fort is univallate, forming an irregular oval with diameters of 210m and 150m. The earth rampart reaches a height of 3.2m above the foot of its outer ditch, this being 0.9m deep and edged on the north-west by a heavy counterscarp bank as much as 1.4m high. Entrance gaps face north-west and south-east; the latter has been damaged by quarrying activity. The south-eastern approach to the fort is crossed by two outlying linear earthworks, the outermost is 3.2m high, the inner one 1.4m. Both retain traces of their outer ditch.

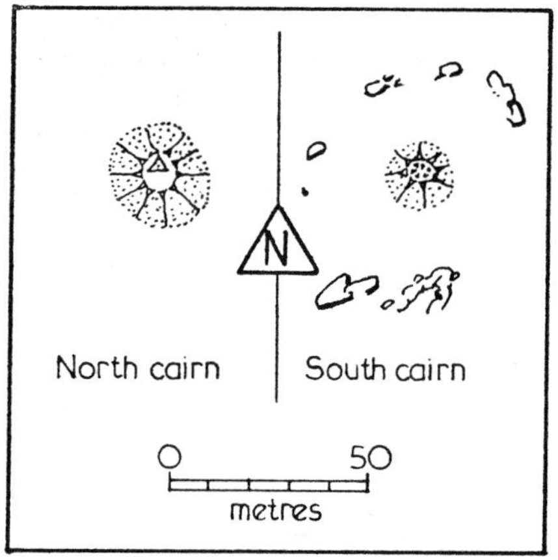

3 **Brown Willy, round barrows,** Bolventor.

SX 159798.
Brown Willy can only be reached on foot, from either Bolventor or the car park at the end of the Camelford to Rough Tor road.

At 420m the summit of Brown Willy (the northern peak) is the highest point in Cornwall – hence its name: Cornish *bron ughella* – highest hill. On this northern peak is a Bronze Age stone cairn 25m across and 3.2m high, topped by a recent cairn and the Ordnance Survey triangulation pillar. To the south, half-way along the hilltop ridge, is a second cairn 19m in diameter and 1.8m high.

Left: *Brown Willy barrows (3)*
Below: *Ashbury hill fort (2)*

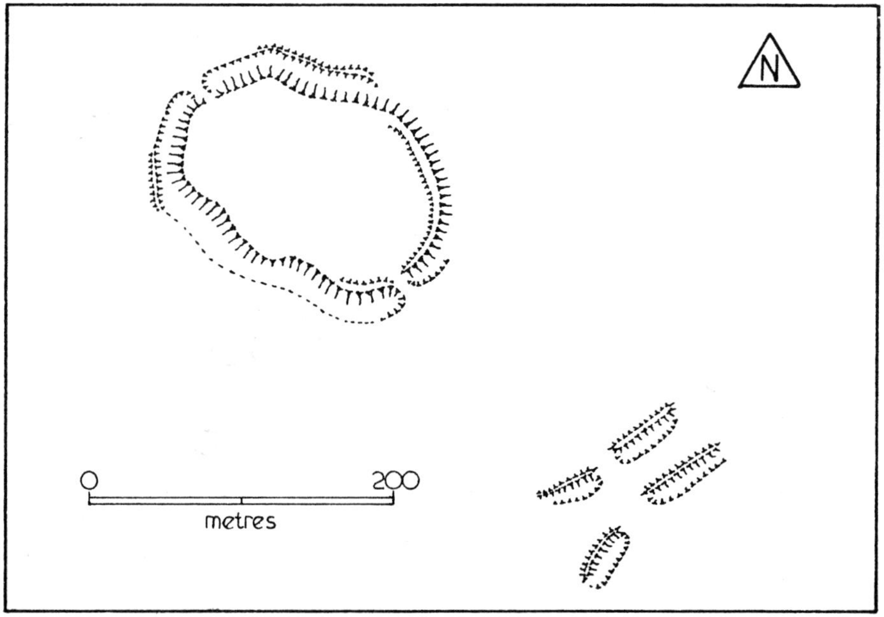

4 **Cardinham, inscribed stones,** Cardinham.

SX 123687 and SX 136677.

There are two Dark Age inscribed stones in the vicinity of Cardinham. One is on the east side of the churchyard and is inscribed: RANOCORI FILI MESGI (Ranocorus, son of Mesgus). The stone is 3.3m long, of which 1.9m is above ground.

The second stone is at Welltown, 1 mile to the south-east, and stands against the wall of a farm building. This is inscribed with the words: VAILATHI FILI VROCHANI (Vailathus, son of Urochanus). It is 1.5m high and was formerly used as a gatepost. Both stones have been ascribed to the sixth or seventh century AD.

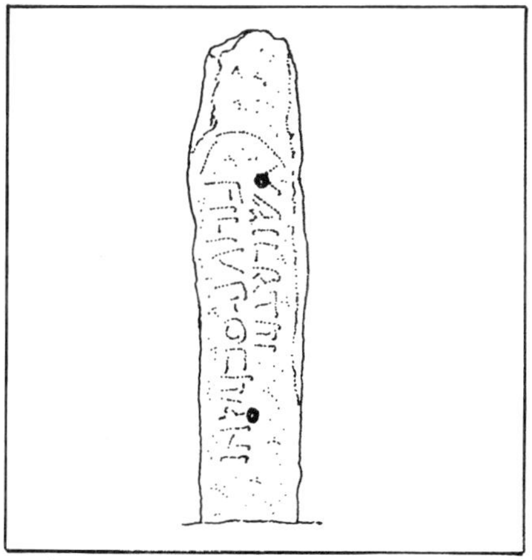

Welltown Stone (4)

5 **Castle Canyke, hill fort,** Bodmin.

SX 086658.

On SE outskirts of Bodmin. Leave new bypass at Carminow Cross, where minor road running NW passes the fort.

A large, bivallate Iron Age fort, now neatly quartered by modern field walls. The outer bank and ditch describe an oval with diameters of 348m and 308m. The best preserved section is on the south-west side, where the ditch, which is 1.0m deep, fronts an earth rampart 3.0m high. The inner rampart has long been destroyed, leaving only a scarp up to 0.4m high.

This fort is a candidate for the Arthurian location of Kelliwic; a place-name 'Callywith' occurs just over a mile to the north (see also Site 12).

Castle Canyke (5)

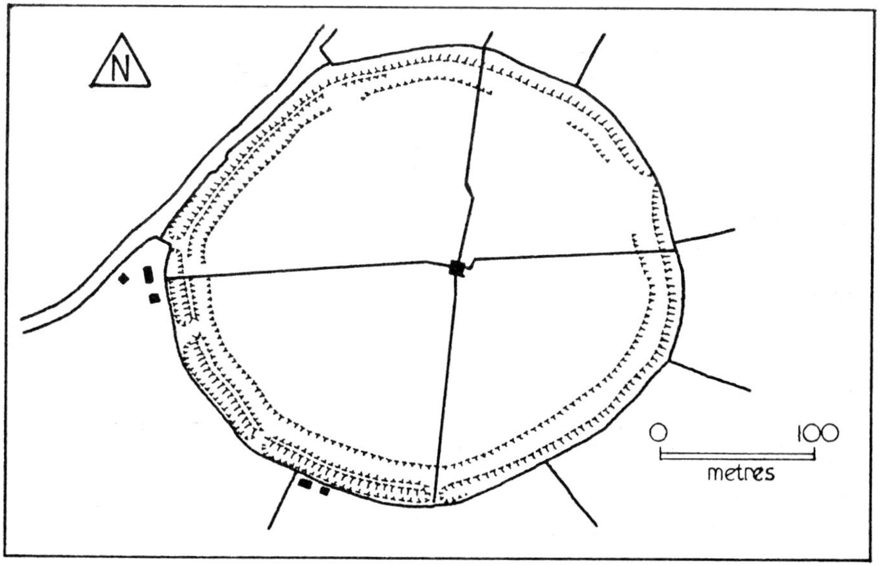

6 Castle Goff, hill fort, Camelford.

SX 083826.
Just to the NW of Lanteglos, reached by minor road leading SW from Camelford.

Castle Goff is a small univallate Iron Age fort 80m in diameter. Its impressive earth rampart is 3.5m high; the outer ditch averages 0.8m deep. A simple entrance faces west, blocked by a modern field wall which utilizes the defences. At a later stage in the fort's occupation an annexe was added on the west side. The bank which defines this reaches a height of 2.0m at one point, but ploughing has generally lowered it and filled the ditch.

To the north-west, at SX 081830 and bisected by a track, is a univallate earthwork 150m in diameter. Known as The Rounds, or Delinuth Camp, its rampart has been ploughed away until it is no more than 0.6m high. Correspondingly, the ditch is very poorly defined. This site is now surrounded by modern field walls.

Castle Goff (6)

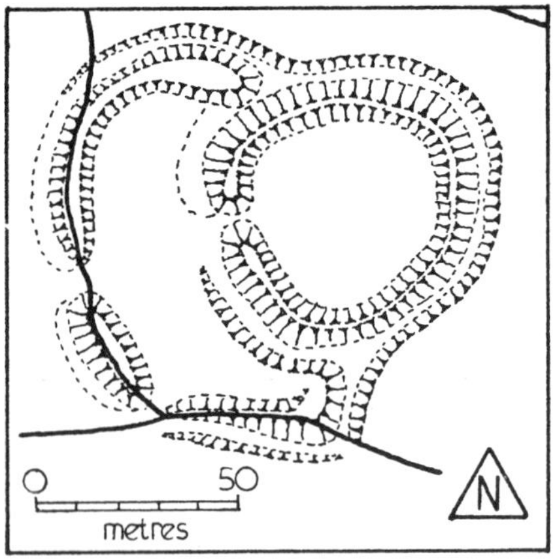

Castle Goff (6)

7 Condolden Barrow, round barrow, Tintagel.

SX 090872.
On hilltop, beside minor road leading N from the B 3263 at SX 093864.

An excellent Bronze Age bowl barrow stands on a hilltop 300m above sea level. 26m across and 2.8m high, it is surrounded by traces of a wide ditch which has suffered from ploughing. An Ordnance Survey triangulation pillar stands on top of the barrow. The name 'Condolden' is derived from the Cornish *godolghyn* (tump – a steep-sided mound); the alternative name, Cadon Barrow, is merely a contraction of Condolden.

Condolden Barrow (7)

8 **Fernacre, stone circle,** Camelford.

SX 144799.
½ mile due S of Rough Tor, reached by footpaths from car-park at SX 139819 at end of minor road from Camelford.

This large Bronze Age ring has thirty-five upright stones, and seventeen fallen ones. Many more are buried in the peaty soil. The stones describe an ellipse with diameters of 46m and 44m; they are irregular both in size and spacing. The tallest stone is 1.3m high. Large prehistoric settlements lie close by to the east, west and north.

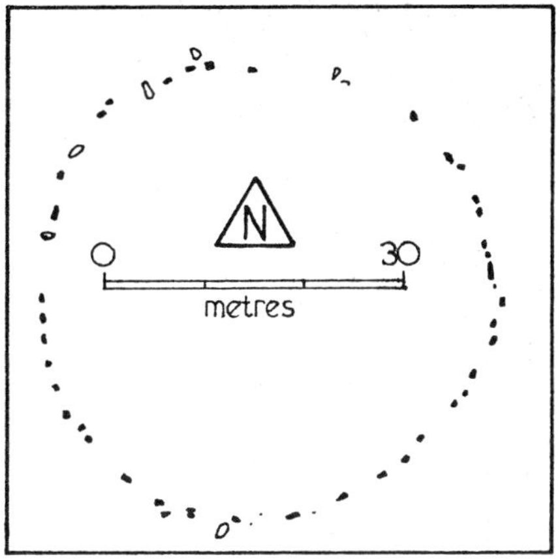

Above and below: *Fernacre (8)*

9 **Garrow Tor, round house settlements,** St Breward.

SX 145785.
Reached by footpaths across Emblance Downs from St Breward.

The slopes of Garrow Tor are strewn with the remains of settlements and fields which probably date from the Middle or Late Bronze Age. Most of the fields are of strip type, with their long axes at right angles to the contours. The main centres of settlement are at SX 147786, SX 144780 and SX 143781. The huts, of which well over a hundred are visible, are from 6.0m to 8.0m in diameter, with walls up to 1.5m thick and 0.9m high. At SX 145780 are the ruins of an extensive settlement of medieval longhouses. Excavated huts have produced pottery, beads, slate bangles and querns.

10 **Goodaver, stone circle,** Bolventor.

SX 210752.
Site lies on hilltop on E side of minor road from Bolventor to Redgate, 2 miles SE of Bolventor.

A dramatically sited Bronze Age ring with diameters of 32.7m and 31.5m. Twenty-four stones remain; only one has fallen, and a stone on the north side has broken (the sheared-off fragment has since been erected beside its parent stone). The site was badly restored in 1906 by the Revd. A.H. Malan; some stones were re-erected upside-down, some are not in their original sockets. The stones are between 0.8m and 1.3m high; the tallest, to the south-east, is opposite the smallest. From the present appearance of the site it seems that originally there may have been some thirty-two stones.

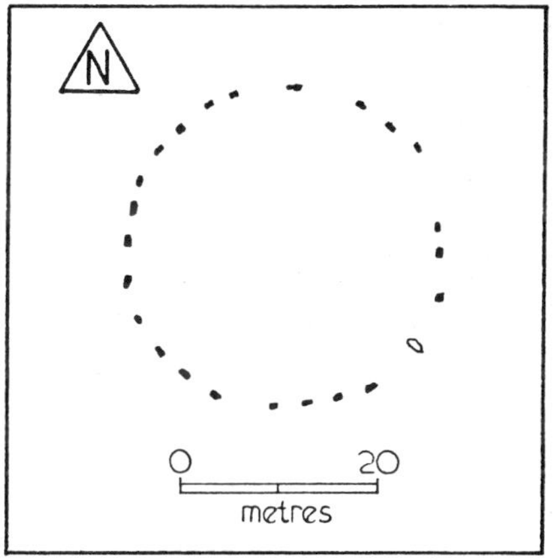

Goodaver (10)

11 **Helsbury Castle, hill fort,** Michaelstow.

SX 083796.
Due W of the B3266, 2½ miles S of Camelford, on minor road to Treveighan.

A fine oval Iron Age fort with diameters of 170m and 160m, although some damage has been inflicted by agriculture and quarrying. It has a single rampart and ditch with a mutilated sub-rectangular annexe on the east side. The fort and annexe entrance faces east and is approached by a sunken track which may be of the same date. The main rampart of the fort reaches a height of 4.0m; its ditch survives on the south-west side. A square enclosure in the centre of the fort contains the foundations of St Syth's chapel. Numerous chunks of masonry, presumably from the chapel, lie scattered around.

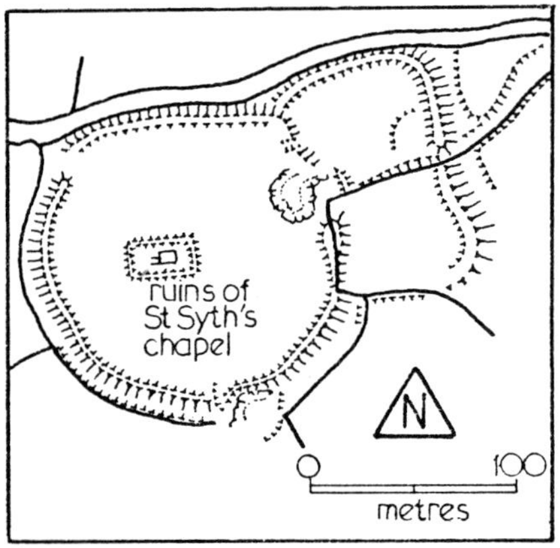

Helsbury Castle (11)

12 **Kelly Rounds, hill fort,** Wadebridge.

SX 019736.
Turn off the A39 1½ miles NE of Wadebridge, along lane heading due E. This lane cuts through the centre of the site; the SW side is overlaid by Sandylands Farm.

Kelly Rounds, or Castle Killibury, is a bivallate Iron Age hill fort 220m in diameter. The ramparts, each about 3.0m high externally, are widely spaced and fronted by ditches (often flooded) 1.8m deep. The north side of the fort is well preserved, but to the south of the lane the defences have been ploughed almost flat. The northern half of a rectangular annexe survives on the west side of the fort, the rest was obliterated by the building of the farm. On the opposite side of the fort cropmarks and traces of two contiguous annexes have been detected. Excavation found the inner ditch to have been cut 2.8m into the bedrock. It also showed that the earliest occupation of the site was during the eleventh or tenth century BC. It is not known if this was before the defences were built. The fort has long been a leading candidate as the location of Arthur's home fort of Kelliwic (see also Site 5), but only two post-Roman sherds have been unearthed.

Kelly Rounds (12)

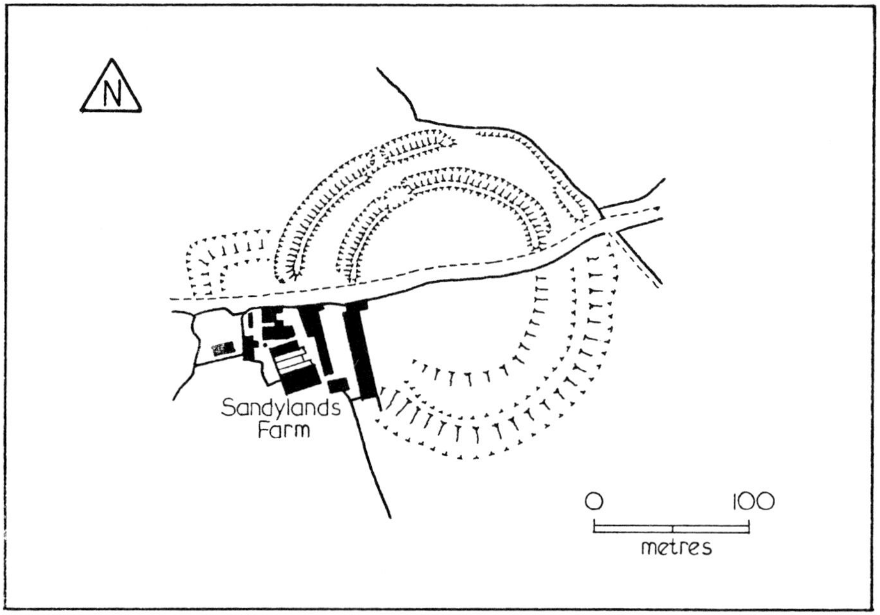

13 **King Arthur's Downs, stone circles,** St Breward.

SX 135775.

Reached by footpath E from St Breward. Site lies midway between Site 14 (King Arthur's Hall) and Site 18 (Leaze stone circle).

It seems there are the remains of two Bronze Age stone circles here, close together on a WNW-ESE line. The better preserved western ring is 23.0m across, with two upright stones, four stumps and two fallen stones. There are also two recumbent fragments near the centre. Of the eastern circle, only six stones remain, all belonging to its southern half. One is erect, two are stumps and three are fallen. The diameter of this circle appears to have been the same as that of its neighbour.

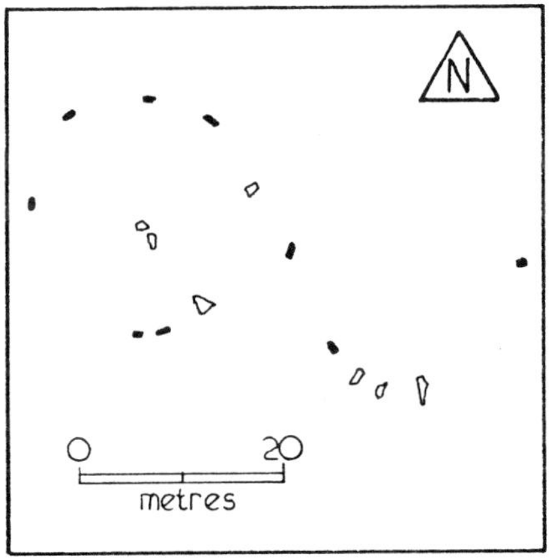

King Arthur's Downs (13)

14 **King Arthur's Hall, enclosure,** St Breward.

SX 130777.

On King Arthur's Downs, reached by footpaths E from St Breward.

This curious earthwork has been the subject of argument and discussion for centuries; its true date and purpose are still a mystery. At present fifty-six stones, from 0.3 to 1.8m tall, form an incomplete rectangle 48m by 21m. They appear to retain the inner side of a bank, 6.0m wide and up to 2.0m high, which is broken by a narrow entrance in the south-west corner. The interior is usually damp and boggy and devoid of any feature. The structure does not seem to have changed radically since its earliest known documentation in 1584. Guesses at its date have ranged from neolithic to medieval; similar enclosures in Ireland and south-west Wales are neolithic.

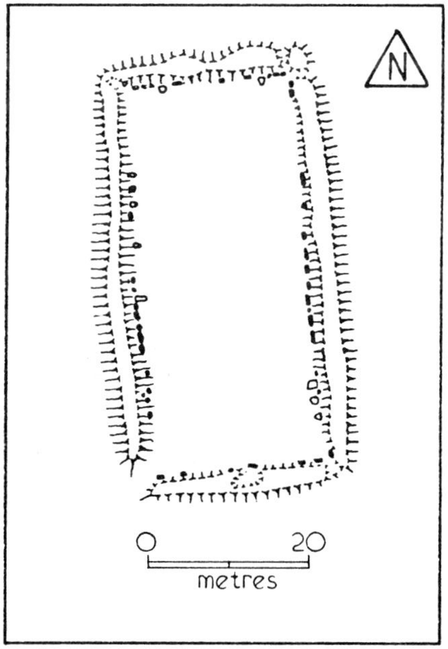

King Arthur's Hall (14)

15 **Lancarffe, inscribed stone,** Bodmin.

SX 082689.

Lancarffe lies 1 mile NE of Bodmin and may be reached by turning W off minor road which runs along the W side of the A30.

This stone is built into a farm building. It is inscribed: DVNOCATI HIC JACIT FILI MERCAGNI (Dunocatus lies here, the son of Mercagnus), and has been dated to between the fifth and seventh centuries AD.

16 **Lanivet, inscribed stone,** Lanivet.

SX 039642.

The stone stands inside Lanivet church.

This stone, 0.9m high, has a single name – ANNICUS – set within an incised border. It probably dates from the fifth or sixth century AD.

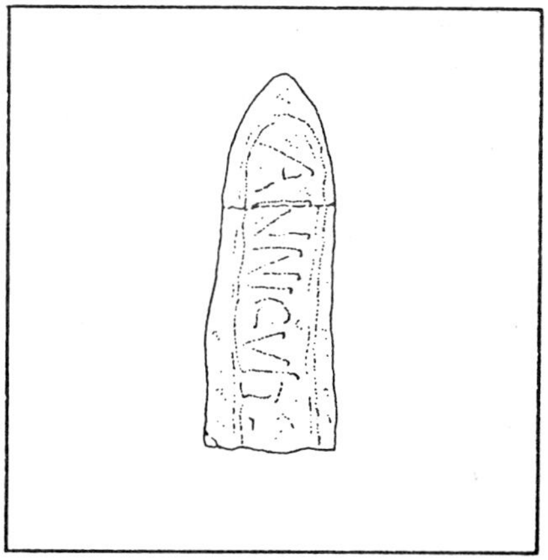

Lanivet stone (16)

17 **Lanteglos, inscribed stone,** Camelford.

SX 088824.

The stone stands in the churchyard on S side of church.

This stone was once used as a roof prop on a farm near Castle Goff. It is 2.4m high and has a rare Saxon inscription which reads: AELSELð 7 GENEREð WOHTE ðYSNE SYBSTEL FOR AELWINES SOUL 7 FOR HEYSEL (Aelseth and Genereth wrought this memorial for Aelwine's soul and for themselves). It probably dates from the tenth century AD.

Lanteglos stone (17)

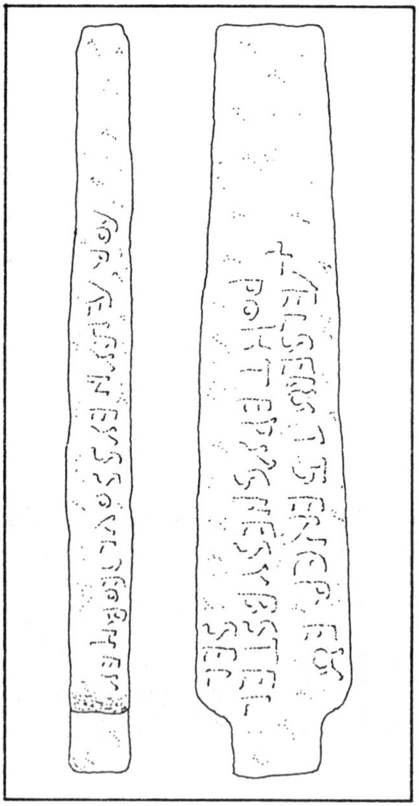

18 **Leaze, stone circle,** St Breward.

SX 137773.

Lanes E from St Breward to Leaze Farm. Site lies 500m NE of the farm.

Just 300m south-east of the King Arthur's Downs circles (Site 13) is this impressive single Bronze Age ring, a true circle 24.8m in diameter. There are fourteen stones, ten standing, surviving from a probable twenty-two. They are spaced 3.7m apart; the tallest is 1.1m high. One of the fallen stones lies beneath the hedge that bisects the site.

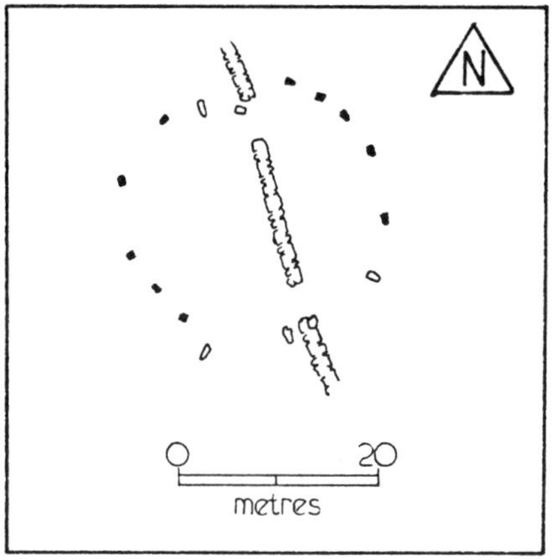

Leaze (18)

19 **Leskernick, stone circle,** Bolventor.

SX 188796.

Footpath from Codda, 1 mile N of Bolventor, to Trewint Downs, Altarnun passes just to S of site.

This circle was discovered as recently as 1973. Twenty-two stones have been traced, some buried, some fallen. There are no upright stones except for a stump on the east side. A true circle with a diameter of 30.6m is indicated. It dates from the Bronze Age and there is extensive prehistoric settlement on the southern slopes of Leskernick Hill just to the north-west.

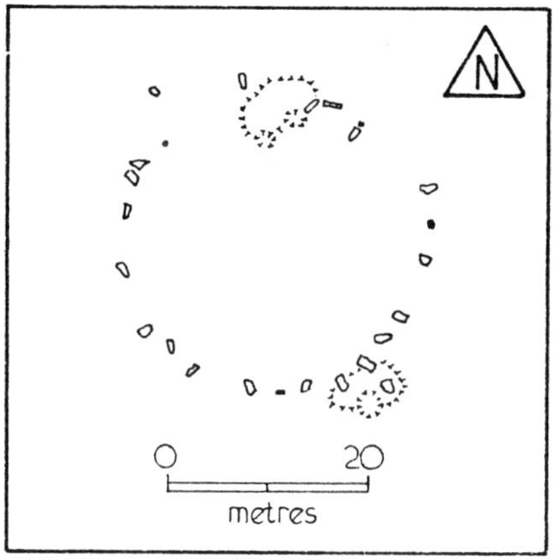

Leskernick (19)

20 **Lesquite Quoit, Penwith chamber tomb,** Lanivet.

SX 071628.

On N side of minor road leaving W side of the B3269 just S of Trebyan.

Also known as Lanivet or Trebyan Quoit, the ruined tomb consists of a fallen capstone 5.3m by 2.8m, leaning against an upright 1.9m tall. A second upright, at right angles to the first, is 1.7m high and 2.7m long. The capstone could not have been supported by both, which suggests that the original tomb was a fairly complex one. A pipe-laying trench cut just to the south of the remains in 1973 revealed several stone sockets and a post-hole which were possibly connected with the surrounding barrow of which nothing remains. The monument has been in its present condition since at least 1858.

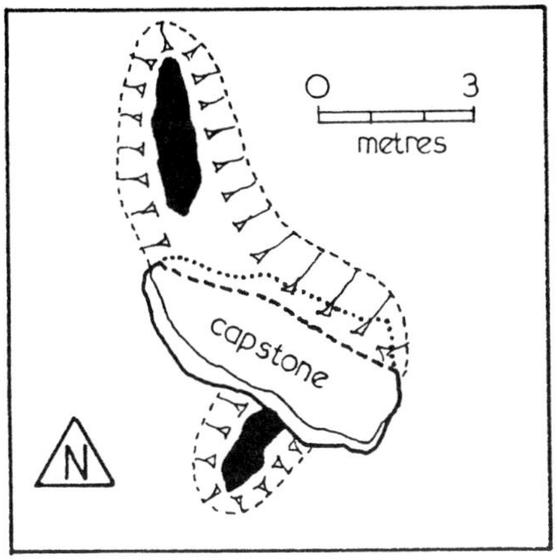

Lesquite Quoit (20)

21 Lewannick, inscribed stones,
Lewannick.

SX 276807.

Two Dark Age stones with inscriptions in both Latin and the Irish Ogam script. Within the church is a stone bearing the incomplete inscription: . . C IACIT VLCAGNI (Here lies Ulcagnus), and the name Ulcagni represented in Ogam on both front angles of the stone. On the south side of the oval churchyard, which preserves the shape of the original *lan* or monastic enclosure, is a second stone 1.6m high. This has an unusual form of inscription: INCEN. VI MEMORIA, the Ogam reading: IGENAVI MEMOR, which translates as: 'To the memory of Ingenavus'. Both stones date from the fifth to the seventh century AD.

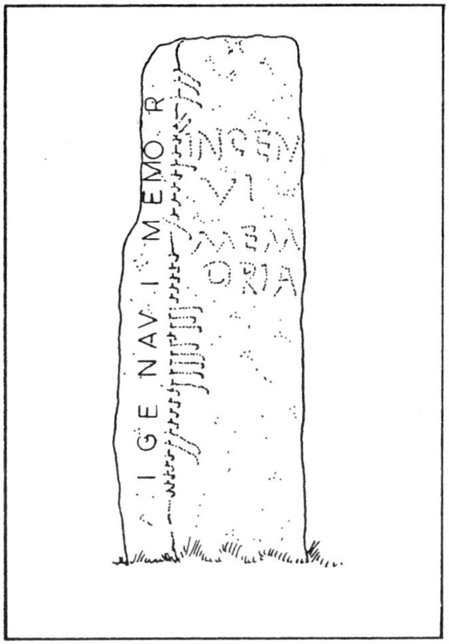

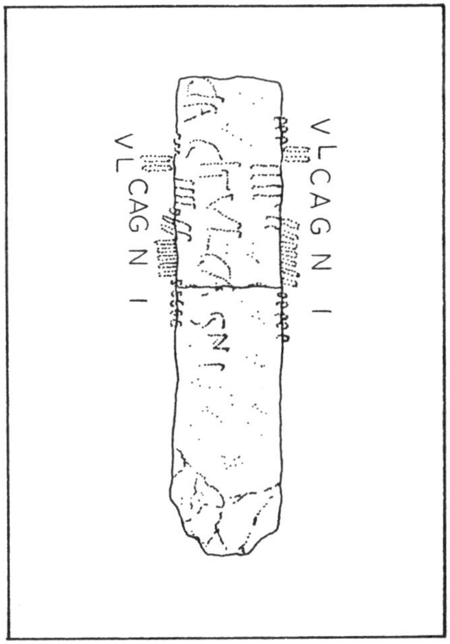

Right and above right: *Lewannick stones (21)*

22 Louden Hill, stone circle,
Camelford.

SX 132795.

Reached by footpaths from car-park at end of minor road leading SE from Camelford.

Discovered in 1973, this large Bronze Age ring retains only one erect stone, 1.4m high and leaning outward. Eleven or twelve fallen stones and four stumps also remain. It appears that the circle originally consisted of between thirty-three and thirty-nine stones, and that the slightly oval ring had diameters of 45.5m and 43m.

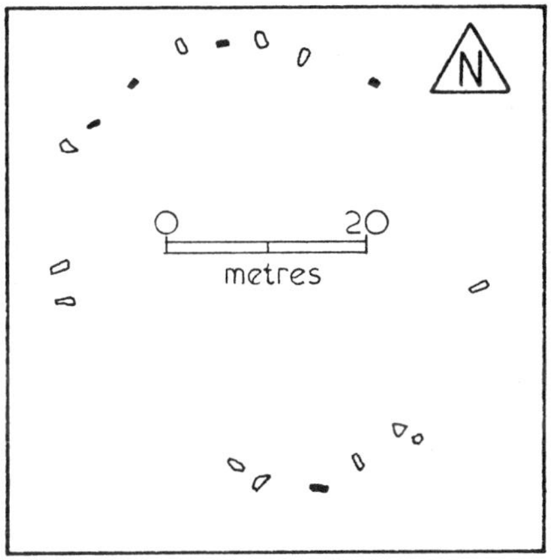

Louden Hill (22)

23 **Moorgate, menhir,** Camelford.

SX 113820.
Reached by footpath S from minor road which leaves E side of the A39 at Valley Truckle.

This fine pointed Bronze Age menhir, a thin slab of weathered granite, stands 3.0m high. It is the tallest of the few examples on Bodmin Moor.

24 **Nanscowe, inscribed stone,** Wadebridge.

SW 969708.
Minor road to Nanscowe Farm leaves S side of the A39 at Whitecross, 1½ miles W of Wadebridge.

This stone, 1.3m high, is in use as a gatepost. On the front of the stone is the inscription: VLCAGNI FILI and on the side is the name: SEVERI. The inscriptions probably date from the fifth or sixth century AD.

Nanscowe stone (24)

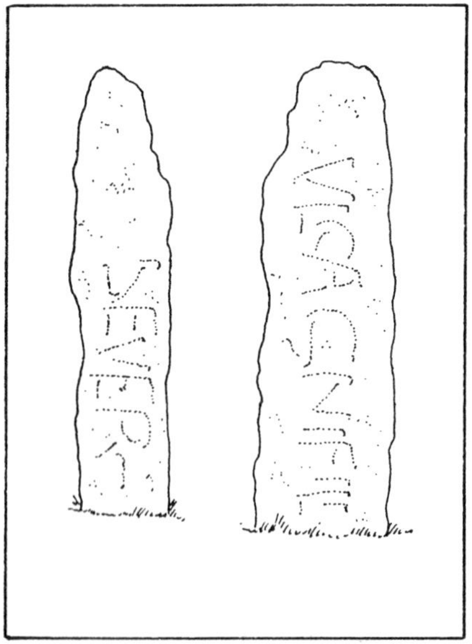

25 **Nanstallon, Roman fort,** Bodmin.

SX 034670.
At Tregear Farm, Nanstallon, reached by minor roads W from the A389 at St Lawrence's Hospital.

This is still the only known Roman fort in Cornwall. It was excavated between 1965 and 1969. Measuring 97m from north to south, by 87m, its eastern rampart was levelled in the nineteenth century. The three other ramparts are overlaid by modern field walls. The excavations were mostly confined to the eastern half of the fort where four barrack blocks, each measuring 32.3m by 8.2m, were found. In the centre of the fort was a building 14.6m by 12.2m which was the 'principia', or headquarters. At the mid-point of each of the four sides of the fort was an entrance 6.0m wide, equipped with double sets of gates. There were angle towers at each of the four rounded corners of the fort. The single earth rampart was originally 4.3m wide, fronted by a ditch 2.4m wide and 1.7m deep. Behind the rampart was a deep drainage gully and a well-metalled rampart road. The fort was quartered by roads leading from the four entrances. The finds indicate that the fort was occupied for only a short time, from AD 55/65 to AD 80.

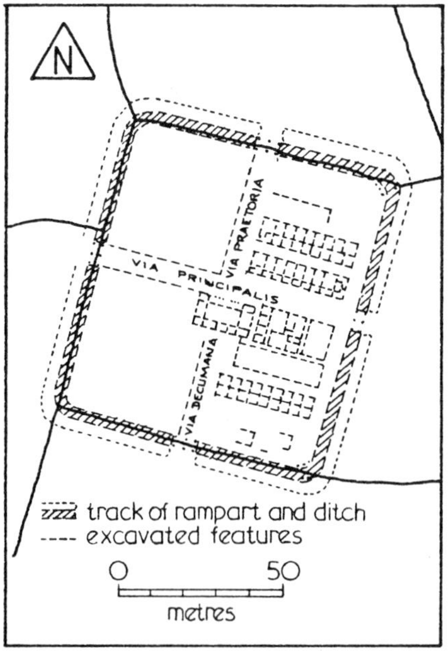

26 **Nine Stones, stone circle,** North Hill.

SX 236782.
Minor roads NW from North Hill to Clitters. Site lies ½ mile SE of Clitters on open moorland.

A small Bronze Age circle of eight stones, from 1.0m to 1.3m high, surrounds a central stone 1.1m high which may be a modern boundary marker. The circle has diameters of 15.2m and 13.7m. It was restored by the squire of Trebartha in 1889 when only two stones were standing. Today some of the stones are leaning, but only one has fallen. Originally there may have been ten or twelve stones.

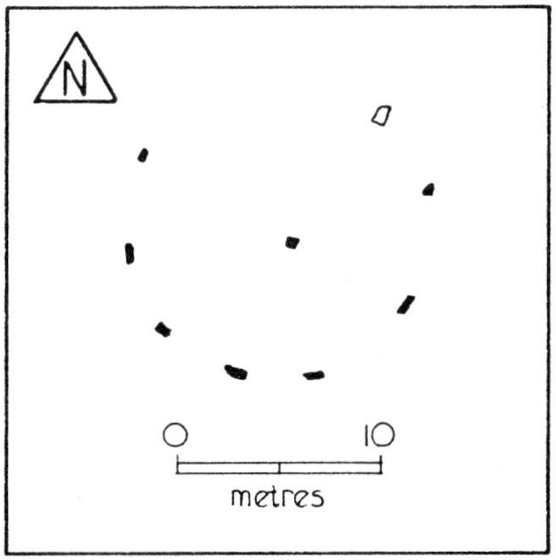

Nine Stones (26)

Left: *Nanstallon (25)*

27 Pawton Quoit, Penwith chamber tomb, Wadebridge.

SW 966696.

2 miles SE of Wadebridge, taking narrow lane to Haycrock Farm leading S from the A39 at Whitecross. Quoit lies in a field on W side of lane just before reaching the farm.

This neolithic tomb consists of nine short uprights forming a chamber 2.3m by 1.1m, and supporting a massive capstone 3.6m by 2.1m by 0.8m thick. This was originally 4.6m long, but a piece has broken off and lies in front of a façade formed by three of the support stones. There is no antechamber as at Trethevy (Caradon) and Zennor (Penwith). The tomb stands just south of centre of a ploughed down mound 21m by 15m, which still survives to a height of 1.2m. At an estimated weight of 14.4 tonnes, the capstone is the heaviest of all the Cornish quoits.

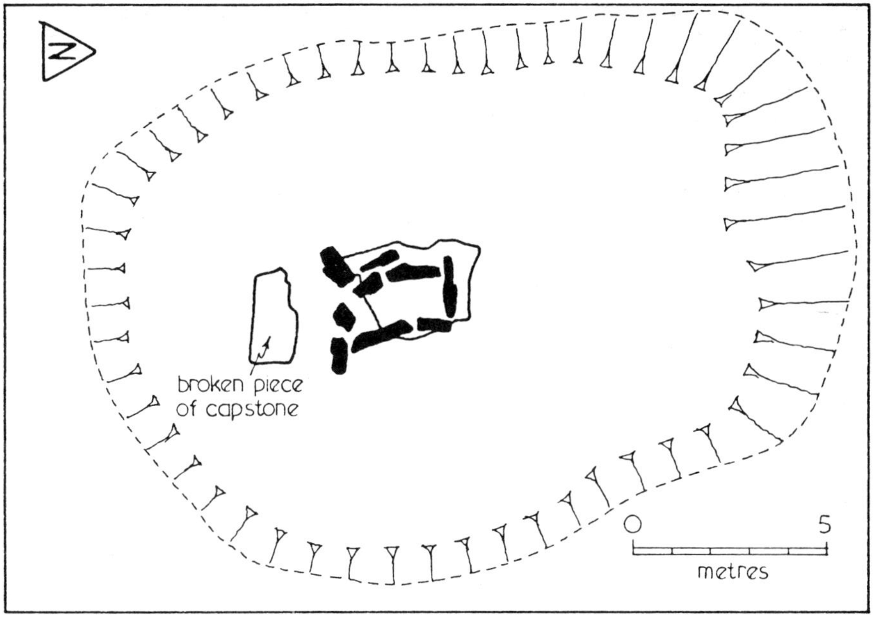

Pawton Quoit (27)

28 Pencarrow Rings, hill fort, Bodmin.

SX 040700.

The driveway to Pencarrow House from the B3266 near Washaway passes through the site.

A bivallate Iron Age fort with a small central enclosure 90m in overall diameter. It is closely surrounded on the south-east side by an ovoid outer work which bulges away on the north-west side so that the gap between them is as much as 24m. On the west side there is an incomplete annexe formed by a single bank and ditch. The inner rampart, up to 3.4m high, is encircled by a ditch 1.1m deep. The outer bank reaches a height of 3.0m and its ditch survives to a depth of 1.4m. The annexe is unusually strong, with an outer ditch 1.6m deep fronting a bank 3.1m high. The original entrance probably faced west, and is now utilized by the drive to Pencarrow House which penetrates to the centre of the fort and bends to pierce the southern defences. The fort has extensive outworks on all except the north-east side; these are set at a minimum distance of 200m from the outer rampart.

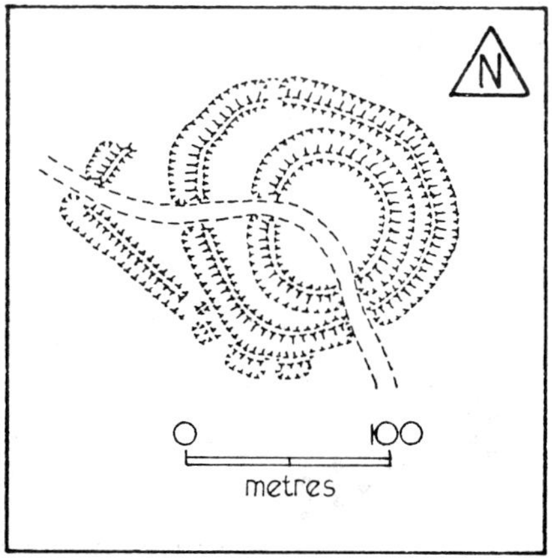

Pencarrow Rings (28)

29 **Penhargard Castle, hill fort,** Bodmin.

SX 058699.

Lane to Penhargard leaves W side of minor road from Bodmin to Helland, 2 miles N of Bodmin. Site lies in woodland just W of Penhargard.

This Iron Age fort, 89m in diameter, is essentially univallate, but an outer defence occurs on the south-west side. The fort perches on the brink of a steep slope above a valley to the west. The defences are fairly well preserved, especially the main rampart which is from 1.6m to 2.3m high. The lowest stretch is on the north side where there are no longer any remains of the outer ditch. The interior of the fort was artificially cut into two distinct terraces. The entrance faces south-west.

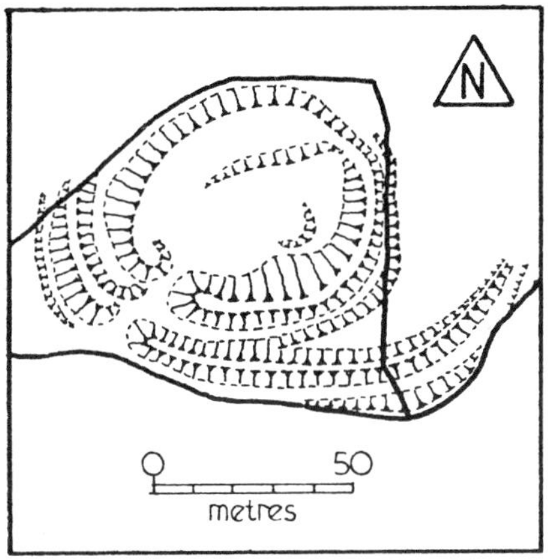

30 **Redcliff Castle, cliff castle,** St Eval.

SW 848696.

Overlooking Bedruthan Steps, approached off the B3276, ½ mile N of Trenance. Cliff path leads N from car park.

Two Iron Age ramparts and ditches cross this small headland, penetrated by a simple central entrance. The ditches are cut from solid rock and are from 0.7m to 2.1m deep, with the southern end of the outer ditch reaching a depth of 4.7m. The ramparts stand to a height of 2.0m. The fort's interior area has been much reduced by coastal erosion, and no dwelling sites have been found.

31 **Rocky Valley, carvings,** Tintagel.

SX 073893.

From car-park near foot of valley on the B3263, just N of Tintagel, a footpath leads seaward through the Rocky Valley. The carvings are on a rock face behind a ruined mill 400m from the road.

Two maze-like carvings, 23cm in diameter, are incised into the rock. They are similar to the Galician style designs attributed to the Bronze Age, and although these are fairly widespread throughout Britain and the Atlantic seaboard of Europe, no others are known in Cornwall. It is possible that they were carved by a miller in recent times.

Rocky Valley carvings (31)

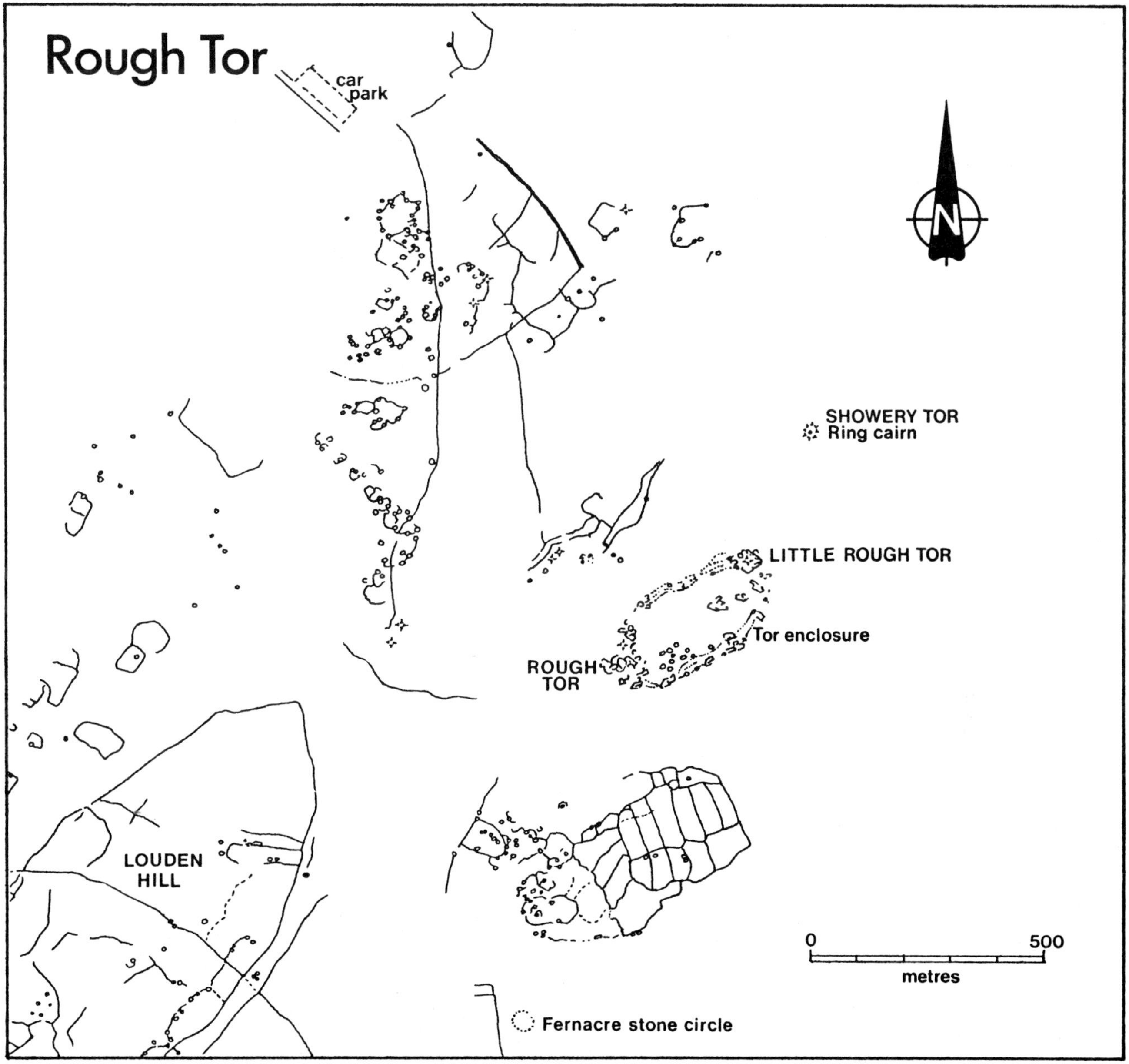
Rough Tor
car park
SHOWERY TOR
Ring cairn
LITTLE ROUGH TOR
Tor enclosure
ROUGH TOR
LOUDEN HILL
0
500
metres
Fernacre stone circle

32 Rough Tor, round house settlements, Camelford.

SX 142810. NT.

Minor road signposted 'Rough Tor' leads SE from the A39 at Camelford. Footpaths to Rough Tor lead from car park at end of road. (Rough Tor is pronounced 'Rowter', the first syllable rhyming with 'now', and is derived from the Cornish word Rowtor *– ruler, monarch.)*

At the western foot of Rough Tor is a large and extensive settlement of stone round houses, pounds and irregularly shaped fields edged with large blocks of granite. This extends for 900m in a southerly direction from a point 200m south of the car park. The round houses, many of which retain their upright door flankers, average 6.0m in diameter. A well preserved droveway approaches the settlement from the south, along the eastern foot of Louden Hill, leading from another large settlement at the south-western foot of Steping Hill. On the opposite side of the droveway, covering the lower south slopes of Rough Tor, is yet another extensive settlement site. To the north-east of the western Rough Tor settlement is a wide and massive boundary reave which leads up the hill. These fields and settlements are likely to date from the Late Bronze Age.

33 Rough Tor, tor enclosure, Camelford.

SX 142810. NT.

Directions as for Site 32.

The remains of a stone fort lie on the summit of Rough Tor, 400m above sea level. It utilizes the granite outcrops of Rough Tor and Little Rough Tor in its circuit. On the north-west side the ruins of three, and in places four, stone walls can be traced. Some are of piled stone, others of large slabs set upright. On the steeper eastern slope are traces of two walls and part of a third. The piled stone walls are now spread as much as 5.0m wide and none stands higher than 1.2m. The fort measures 305m from north-east to south-west, by 152m, and bears certain similarities to the neolithic enclosure on Carn Brea (Kerrier). However, without the benefit of excavation it is assumed to date from the Late Bronze Age. A dozen round houses can be traced in the south-west part of the interior, and several small kerbed cairns are incorporated into one of the entrances.

Rough Tor round house settlements (32)

Rough Tor, tor enclosure (33)

34 The Rumps, cliff castle, Polzeath.

SW 934811. NT.

Best reached by footpath from National Trust car-park at Pentireglaze at SW 943798.

This magnificent headland displays three lines of defence which were excavated from 1963 to 1967. There were probably two phases of construction, the earlier being represented by the outer rampart which is slightly out of alignment with, and, at 1.2m high, smaller than the other two. The stone walling along the back of the rampart is a recent addition. The second ditch, originally 4.6m, but now little more than 1m deep, fronts a massive bank 3.9m high, which was stone revetted on both sides. The inner rampart, 2.8m high, stands on a slight natural ridge. A simple central entrance penetrates all three defences, and all three originally had well-built stone and timber gateways. The area enclosed totals 2.4 ha, and a number of hut platforms were found. Other finds included sheep, cattle and pig bones, and wheel-turned pottery of the first century BC, some of which shows signs of influence from Brittany. An amphora of western Mediterranean type was also found. There is reason to believe that the Rumps may be the Dunocornavis, or Durocoronavis, named in Roman times.

Left and below left: *The Rumps (34)*

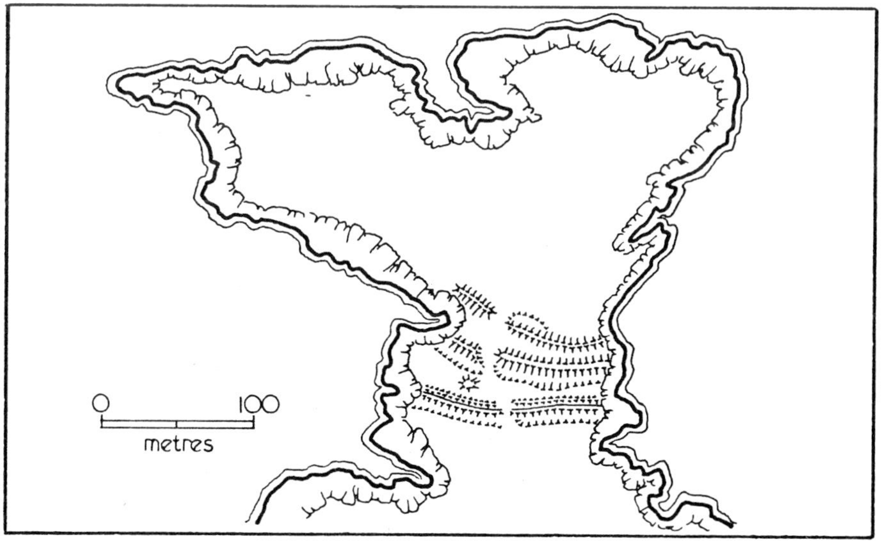

35 St Breock Downs, round barrows, Wadebridge.

Best reached by walking due E from the A39 at SW 937682.

More than sixty Bronze Age round barrows lie on the seven-mile ridge of St Breock Downs, the best preserved is at SW 941681. This measures 18m across and, despite some mutilation, is still 2.4m high. At SW 952682 is a fine barrow 29m in diameter and 2.0m high with an excavation hollow in its top. Two further barrows stand at SW 955681. These are 23m and 26m across, with their hollowed tops 2.0m above the surrounding ground. Also worthy of note is an unusual barrow at SW 974683. 1.0m high and 22m across, the mound is encircled by a ditch and outer bank, giving the monument an overall diameter of 34m.

36 **St Breock Downs, menhirs,** Wadebridge.

SW 969683 and SW 973683. DE.
Minor road S from Wadebridge to Burlawn, whence road leads SW to St Breock Downs.

The first of these Bronze Age menhirs stands on St Breock Beacon and is known as Mên Gurta. 3.0m high, it fell in 1945 and was re-erected eleven years later. Its overall length is 4.6m and, at 16.5 tonnes, it is the heaviest erected stone in Cornwall. Excavation revealed that a layer of white quartz stones had been laid around the menhir, perhaps forming a cairn 4.5m in diameter.

The second stone is 400m to the east. 2.4m tall, it stands in the centre of a low mound 6.0m in diameter.

St Breock Downs menhir (36)

Right: St Endellion stone (37)
Far right: St Kew stone (38)

37 **St Endellion, inscribed stone,** St Endellion.

SW 989797.
At crossroads on minor road half-way between St Endellion, on the B3314, and Portquin.

This cross-shaft, 1.5m high, is now back at its original site after standing for a while on Doyden Point. It is sometimes known as the Long Cross or Brocagnus Stone. The two-line inscription accompanies a Chi-Rho monogram and is worded: BROCAGNI HIC IACIT NADOTTI FILIVS (Brocagnus lies here, the son of Nadottus). This is repeated in the Irish Ogam script. Brocagnus is the Latin form of the name Brychan, and this stone may commemorate St Brychan, once king of a southern Welsh province – Brecon – and reputedly the father of a large number of Celtic missionaries to Cornwall. The back of the stone carries a cross carved in relief. The inscription has been dated to the sixth or seventh centuries AD.

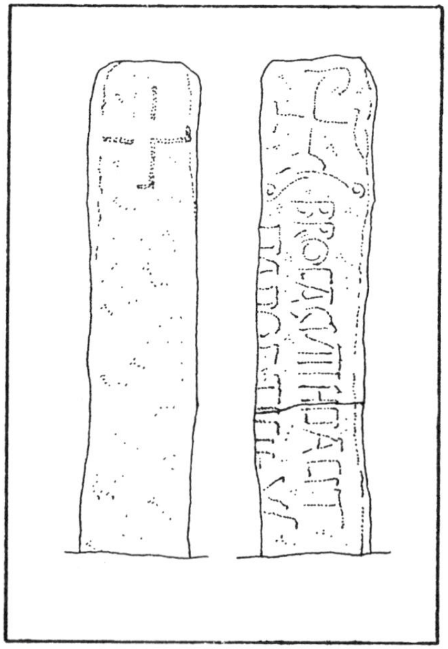

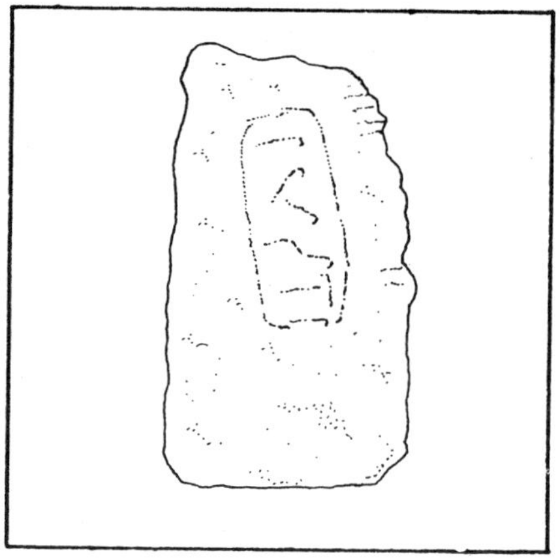

38 **St Kew, inscribed stone,** St Kew.

SX 021769.
The stone stands within St Kew church.

This stone is one of the few in Cornwall which carry inscriptions in both Latin and Ogam. The Latin inscription consists of a single name: IVSTI (Justus), which is repeated in Ogam. The stone is merely a fragment, and no further inscriptions remain. It is sixth or seventh century AD.

39 **Showery Tor, round barrow,** Camelford.

SX 149813.
Directions as for Rough Tor (Sites 32 and 33). The barrow stands 300m N of Little Rough Tor.

A natural formation of weathered granite, 5.0m high and reminiscent of the Cheesewring on Stowe's Hill, Caradon, is surrounded by a massive ring cairn of piled stone 30m in diameter and up to 1.2m high. The natural formation was evidently intended as a focal point. No excavations have been recorded at this site, so it is not known how many, if any, burials were associated with this presumably Bronze Age site.

40 Slaughter Bridge, inscribed stone, Camelford.

SX 109857.

Beside river 200m N of Slaughter Bridge, on minor road connecting the B3266 and the A39, 1 mile N of Camelford.

Once used as a footbridge, this massive stone, 3.0m long, now lies on the west bank of the Camel River. The sixth- or seventh-century inscription runs in two lines along the length of the stone and reads: LATINI IC IACIT FILIVS MAGARI (Latinus lies here, son of Magarus). The stone is known as King Arthur's Tomb, partly due to a misreading of the inscription, the last word being interpreted as MACATRY. It was suggested that the name Arthur had been contracted to Atry. A faint Ogam inscription repeats the Latin one.

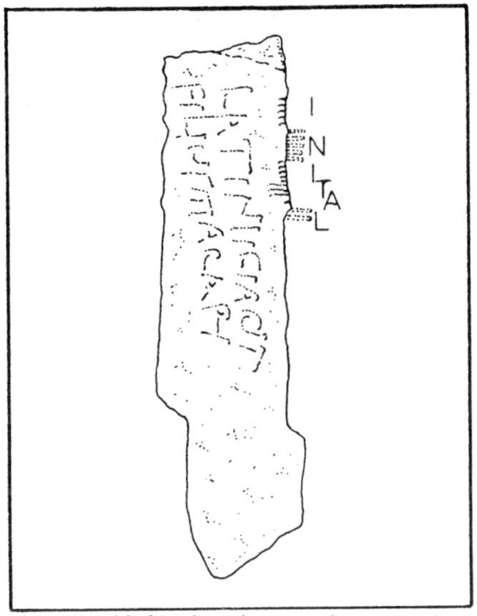

Above and left: *Slaughter Bridge stone (40)*

41 Stannon, stone circle, St Breward.

SX 125799.

Minor road from St Breward leads NE across Harpur's Downs to Stannon china clay works, where it becomes a track. Circle lies immediately S of china clay works.

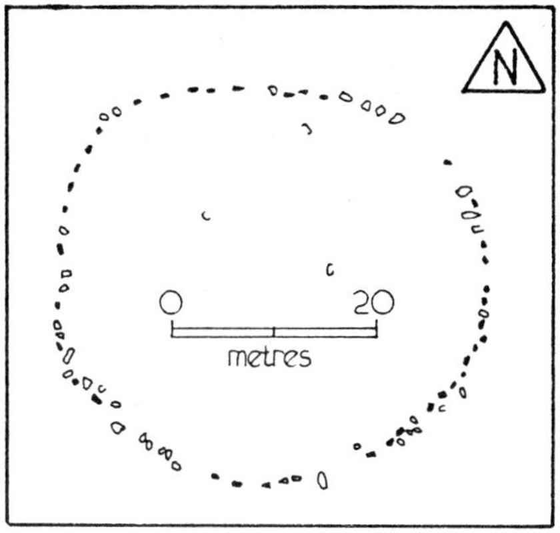

With diameters of 42.7m and 39.0m, this irregular ring has many similarities with the Fernacre circle (Site 8) 1¼ miles to the east. Of eighty-one visible stones, thirty-nine are standing. Their heights, from 0.3m to 1.2m, vary considerably as do the spaces between them. There is also a small central stump 15cm high.

80m to the north-west is a curious rough line of four low stones. These are diametrically opposite the Louden Hill circle (Site 22), but only from the Stannon ring can both the stone setting and the Louden circle be seen. Numerous barrows, settlements and field systems lie in the immediate vicinity of this Bronze Age ring.

Showery Tor (39)

Stannon (41)

42 The Stripple Stones, circle-henge, Blisland.

SX 144752.

Visible from the A30 near Temple, on slope of Hawk's Tor beyond china clay works. It is best reached from the Trippet Stones (Site 46).

Unfortunately this important neolithic site is rather battered and defaced. It is roughly circular, 68m in overall diameter, with a bank and shallow internal ditch which are poorly defined in places: nowhere is the bank higher than 0.6m. The bank was thought to have bulged into three deliberate apses, but these were probably the result of spread due to cart-tracks. Within the bank and ditch are the remains of a stone circle with diameters of 46.3m and 43.3m, originally of about twenty-eight stones. Fourteen of these remain, only four of which stand; a further stone, 3.7m long, lies near the centre. The four upright stones are between 1.2m and 2.0m tall. The site was excavated in 1905, when it was found that the ditch had averaged 2.7m in width and 1.2m in depth, but was irregularly cut. The entrance of the henge faces west, towards the Trippet Stones. The monument's south-east quadrant has been badly mutilated by the erection of field walls.

Stripple Stones (42)

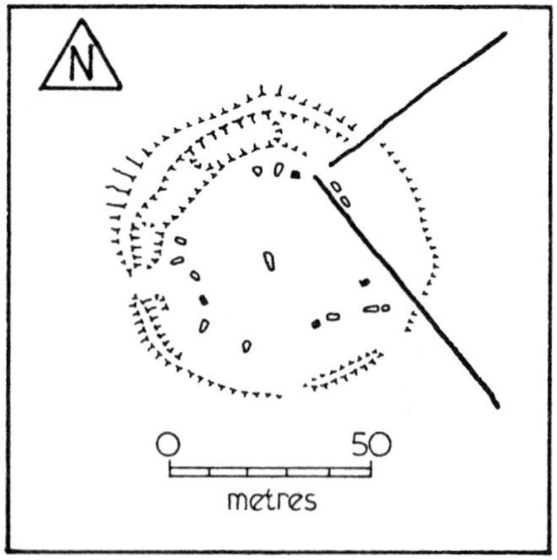

Left: *Stripple Stones (42)*

Tintagel, Site B (43)

43 Tintagel Island, settlement, Tintagel.

SX 050891. DE.

Footpath from Tintagel to 'King Arthur's Castle'. Site lies on headland beyond inner ward of the medieval castle and is indicated on notices as 'Monastery'.

The land bridge connecting the 'Island' to the mainland would almost certainly have carried the defences of an Iron Age cliff castle before its erosion and eventual collapse *c.*1300 AD. On the landward side, below the outer ward of the twelfth- and thirteenth-century castle, are a single bank and ditch which were certainly connected with the Dark Age settlement still surviving on the headland. The latter was excavated in 1933-4.

The settlement consists of rectangular dry-stone buildings. The most interesting part is Site A, on the flat top of the headland. Here a number of buildings cluster around the remains of a later, twelfth-century chapel built on the site of a much earlier chapel. Just to the south of this is the base of a *leacht*, or tomb-shrine, 1.5m square, of a type common in Ireland. Sites B, C and F were built on terraces cut into the cliff. At Site B one of the buildings was of two-storey height, and a stairway cut into the cliff led up to the top of the headland which also contains Sites D, E and G. Site D consisted of six buildings, one of which contained a corn-drying kiln. Little remains of Site G, perched on the cliff-edge; Site E mostly lies beneath the walled garden enclosure that belonged to the castle.

The Dark Age sites, occupied from the fifth to the eighth centuries AD, were formerly interpreted as a monastic settlement. Opinion now favours their having been a secular trading settlement, possibly a chieftain's stronghold. There is no evidence to support the notion that the settlement was a Celtic monastery.

Excavation revealed imported Mediterranean pottery of the fifth century. This was of two types: red bowls known as Tintagel A ware, and amphorae known as Tintagel B ware, both of which were found later on other important Dark Age sites such as South Cadbury Castle, Somerset. The settlement was fed by a pair of wells. A curious feature is a sinuous rock-cut tunnel of unknown purpose.

The name Tintagel is of Norman-French origin (*Tente d'Agel* – Stronghold of the Devil – a Cornish equivalent would be *Dynjawl*). The settlement's original name is not known.

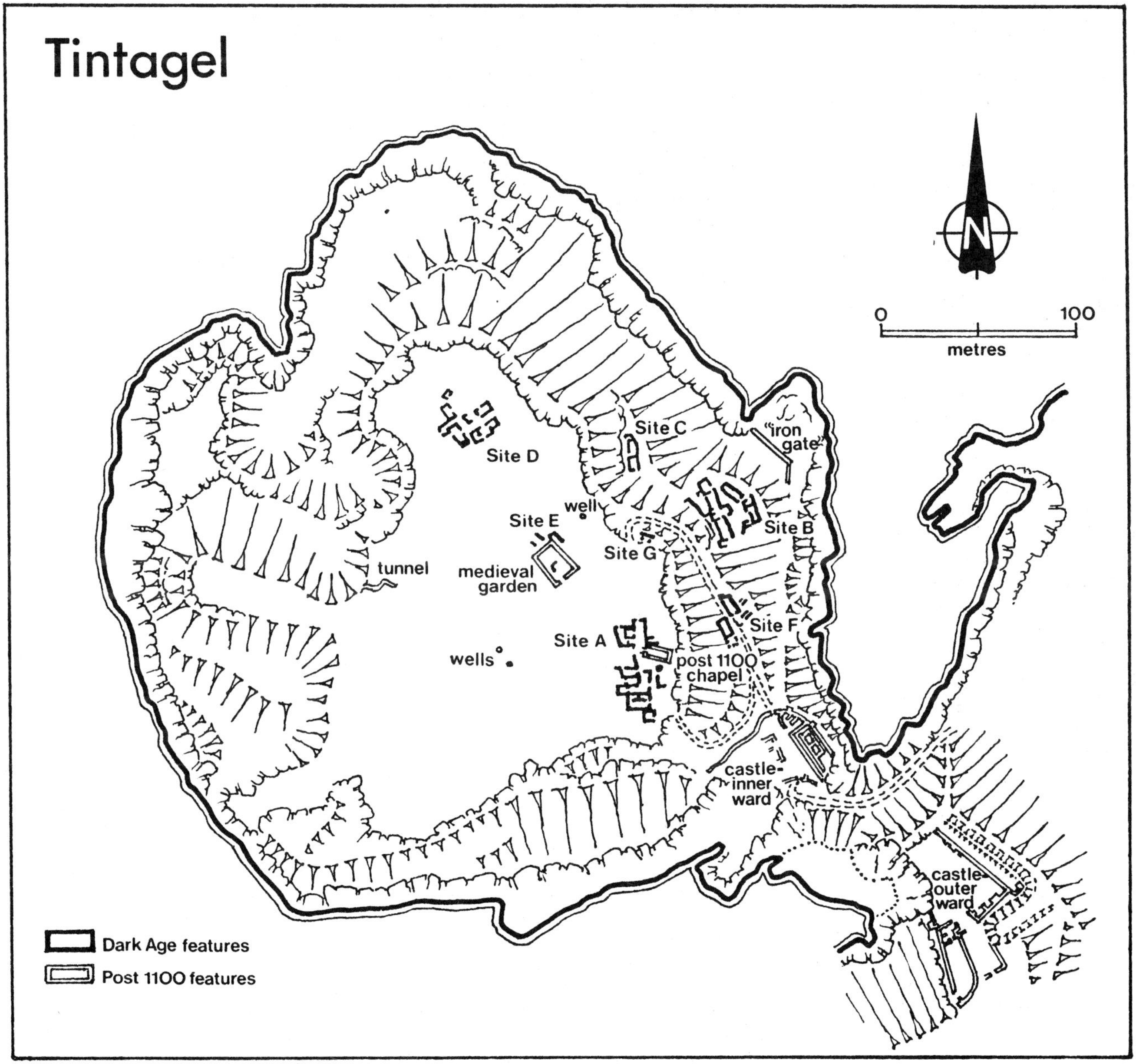

Tintagel
0
100
metres
N
Site D
Site C
"iron gate"
well
Site E
Site B
Site G
tunnel
medieval garden
Site F
Site A
wells
post 1100 chapel
castle-inner ward
castle-outer ward
Dark Age features
Post 1100 features

44 **Tintagel, Roman milestones,** Tintagel.

SX 051885 and 076892.

The first of these, in the south transept of the parish church, is a stone 1.5m tall inscribed: (I)MP C G VAL LICIN (To the Emperor Caesar Gaius Valerius Licinius), which dates from shortly after AD 250. It was found in 1889 serving as a lych stone at the south-east entrance to the churchyard.

The second stone is at Trethevey, 1½ miles north-east of Tintagel, in a private garden. Permission to view is required. Dated to AD 251, its inscription reads: C DOMIN GALLO ET VOLVS (To the Emperor Caesar our Lords Gallus and Volusianus). It is a squared granite stone 1.3m high.

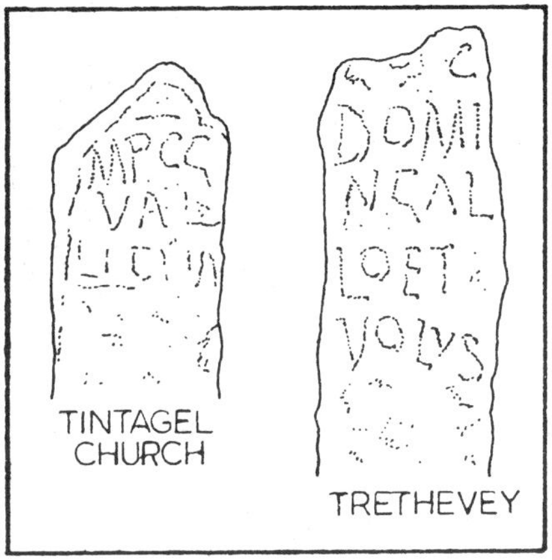

Tintagel Roman milestones (44)

45 **Tregeare Rounds, hill fort,** Pendoggett.

SX 033800.

On S side of the B3314, 1 mile NE of Pendoggett.

This Iron Age fort is not on a hilltop, but on a north-east facing slope. Two widely spaced ramparts and ditches surround a central enclosure 90m in diameter. The outer rampart averages 2.5m high internally; its steep-sided outer ditch reaches a depth of 2.4m. The inner ditch, up to 1.7m deep, is traceable in its entirety, but the inner rampart has been beaten flat except on the north where its internal height is 1.2m. In 1902 traces of first and second century BC occupation were found between the ramparts, but not in the central area which may have been used to corral livestock. A scarp 1.5m high forms a gently curving outwork on the eastern side of the fort. This is the remains of an annexed enclosure through which a partly sunken track leads to the fort's south-east facing entrance. A curious feature of the site is a post-medieval 'hull' which burrows under the south-west side of the outer rampart. It is 1.7m high and 15m long.

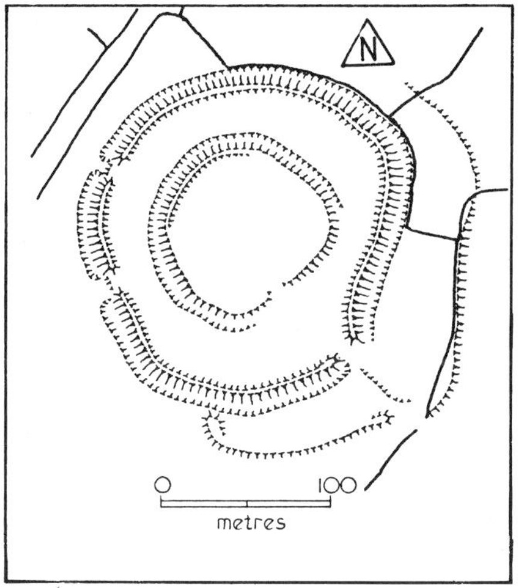

Tregeare Rounds (45)

Tregeare Rounds (45)

46 The Trippet Stones, stone circle, Blisland.

SX 131750.

On Manor Common, Blisland, best reached by minor road leading NW from the A30 near Temple, at SX 136736.

This Bronze Age ring is a true circle 33.0m in diameter. Twelve stones survive, from a probable original of twenty-six. Eight still stand (some lean considerably) and these are between 1.2m and 1.4m in height. A modern boundary stone lies prone near the centre of the ring. The Stripple Stones henge (Site 42) is just visible on the slopes of Hawk's Tor, ¾ mile to the east.

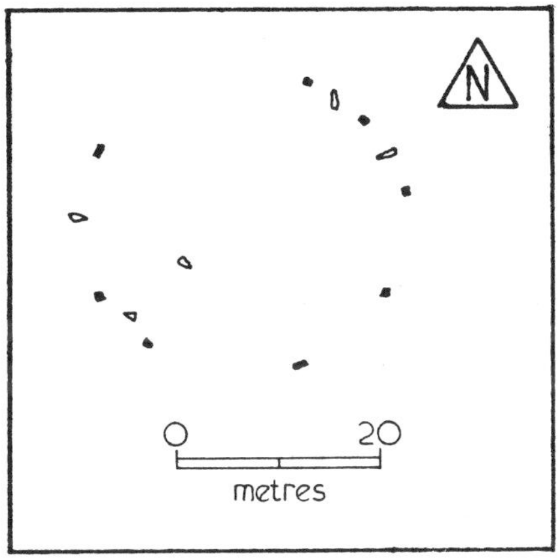

Warbstow Bury (47)

47 Warbstow Bury, hill fort, Warbstow.

SX 202908.

Minor road off the A395 at Hallworthy to Warbstow. Site lies ½ mile to NW.

Like Tregeare Rounds (Site 45) this Iron Age fort stands on the slope of the hill. It is oval in plan with diameters of 340m and 270m, and is one of Cornwall's most imposing hill forts. It comprises two massive and widely spaced ramparts up to 5.8m high, fronted by ditches as much as 2.7m deep. A third, slighter defence exists between these two on the higher, south-western side, where the outer ditch is also wider and bears a counterscarp 1.0m high. Three entrances can be seen, on the east, north-west and south-west sides. In the centre of the fort is a large mound, 22m long by 10m wide by 0.6m high, flanked by indistinct side ditches in the manner of a neolithic long barrow. This is known locally as 'The Giant's Grave' and as 'King Arthur's Tomb'.

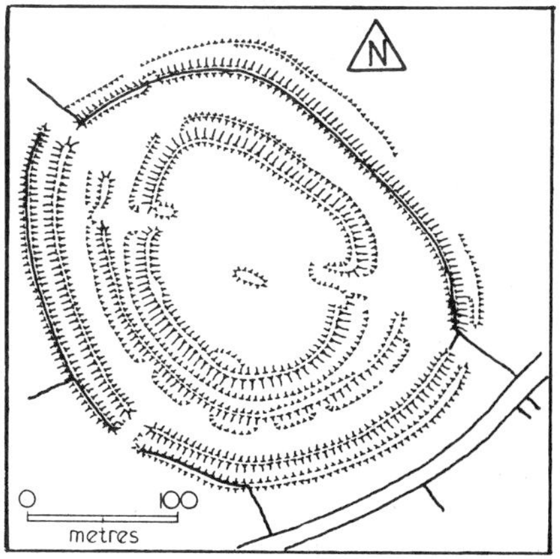

Warbstow Bury (47)

48 **Willapark, cliff castle,** Boscastle.

SX 091912. NT.
Reached by cliff path from S side of Boscastle harbour.

The Iron Age cliff castle on this headland consists of a single defence. The rampart, 110m long, survives to a height of 1.8m and is fronted by a ditch 0.8m deep. The position of the entrance is uncertain; it is probably where the footpath cuts through the bank. The rampart is comparatively weak at the higher south-western end, and is at its strongest at the opposite end, at the foot of a steep slope.

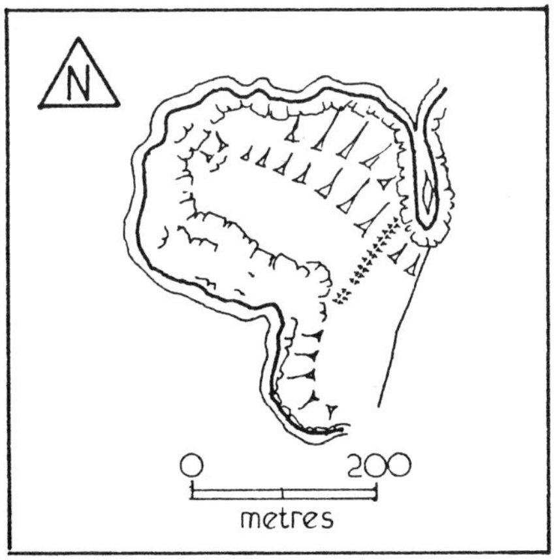

Willapark (Boscastle) (48)

49 **Willapark, cliff castle,** Tintagel.

SX 063896. NT.
Reached by footpath from the B3263 at Bossiney.

Like its namesake (Site 48), this Iron Age cliff castle relied on a single line of defence. This takes the form of an ill-defined bank and ditch 48m long. A modern wall stands on top of the mutilated rampart, the entrance through which is now unidentifiable.

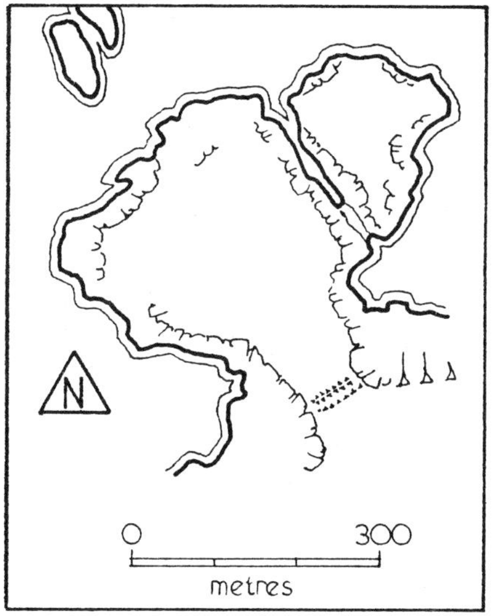

Willapark (Tintagel) (49)

50 **Woolley Barrow, long barrow,** Kilkhampton.

SS 263166.
By E side of the A39, 3 miles N of Kilkhampton.

Neolithic long barrows are rare in Cornwall; this is the finest of the few. It is 62m long, 21m wide and 2.5m high, with mutilations on the north-west and south-west sides. No evidence has yet been found of any internal structures, but one may well exist. A small excavation did locate a single side trench on the northern side of the barrow. This was 72m long and 1.6m deep.

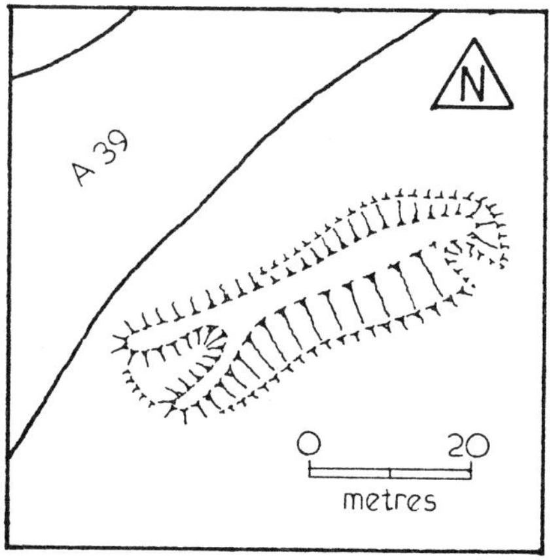

Woolley Barrow (50)

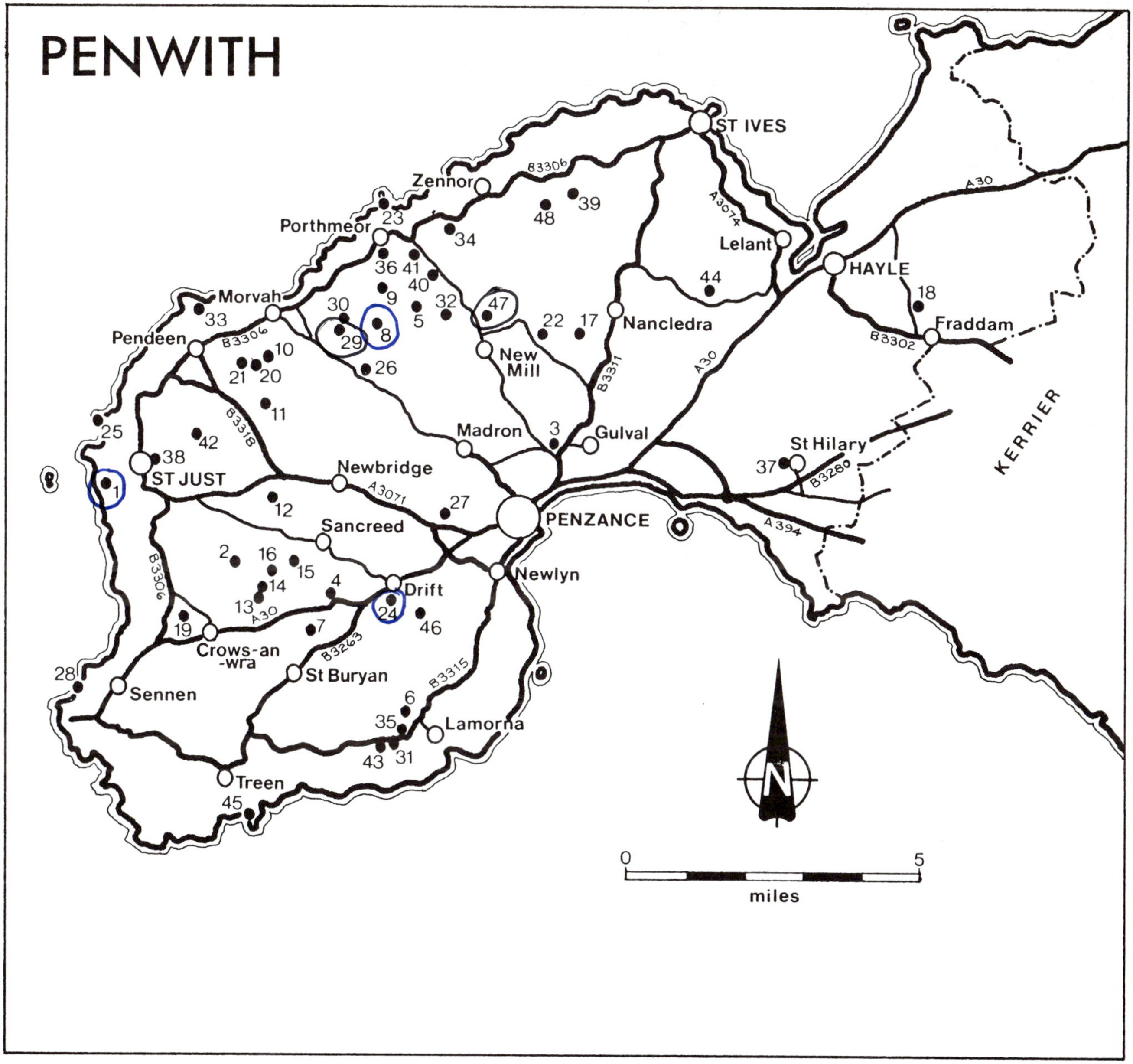
PENWITH
ST IVES
B3306
Zennor
39
48
23
Porthmeor
34
A3074
Lelant
HAYLE
A30
36
41
40
44
18
Morvah
9
30
47
33
5
32
22
17
Nancledra
Fraddam
B3302
Pendeen
B3306
29
8
New Mill
10
26
21
20
B3331
A30
11
B3318
25
42
Madron
3
Gulval
St Hilary
KERRIER
38
ST JUST
Newbridge
37
B3280
1
A3071
12
27
PENZANCE
A394
Sancreed
2
16
15
B3306
14
4
Drift
Newlyn
13
A30
24
46
19
7
Crows-an-wra
B3283
St Buryan
28
B3315
Sennen
6
35
Lamorna
43
31
Treen
45
0
5
miles

1 Ballowall Barrow, Scillonian chamber tomb, St Just.

SW 356312. DE.
1 mile W of St Just, take lane signposted 'Carn Gloose'. The site lies by roadside on clifftop.

This large, complex, multi-phase monument is unique. It consists of a large closed chamber within a central cone-shaped cairn, the latter being surrounded by a later collar or cairn-ring. The central chamber contained a number of stone cists and a T-shaped ritual pit; this alone remains. Two further cists can still be seen in the narrow space between the central cairn and the collar which contains a smaller chamber, again with a pit cut into its floor. Set into the outside of the collar, on the south-west side, is an entrance grave with two capstones in place. It is probable that a conventional Scillonian chamber tomb of neolithic type was the first structure here, followed in the Middle Bronze Age by the central cairn and its cists, and finally by the collar which incorporated the original mound and chamber of the entrance grave. The top of the central cairn is now missing, but the cairn survives to a height of 2.7m. The entire monument has diameters of 21.4m and 20.4m.

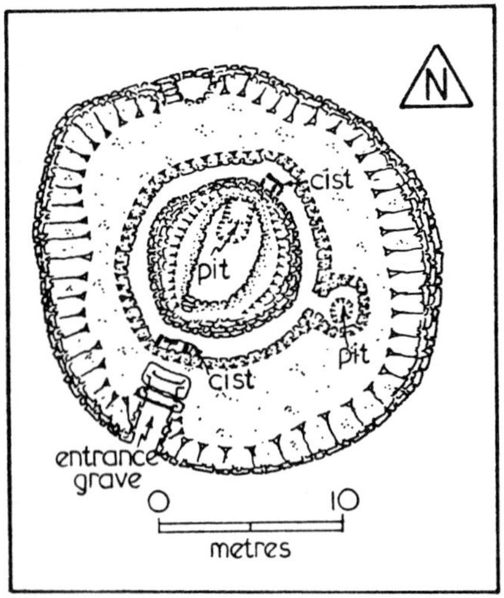

Ballowall Barrow (1)

2 Bartinnê Castle, enclosure, Crows-an-wra.

SW 395293.
On summit of Bartinney Hill, best reached by footpath from Carn Euny (Site 16), or from National Trust car-park at foot of Chapel Carn Brea (Site 19).

A circular structure consisting of a low, weak bank of earth and scattered stones 75m across, with little or no sign of any external ditch. In the centre of the enclosure are three small circular banks arranged in a tight triangular pattern: these may be either round house remains or ring-cairns. Although it lies at the heart of an extensive Iron Age field system (best seen from the air), this site may represent a ritual structure rather than an unfinished hill fort or settlement enclosure.

Left: *Ballowall Barrow (1)*

Right: *Bleu Bridge stone (3)*

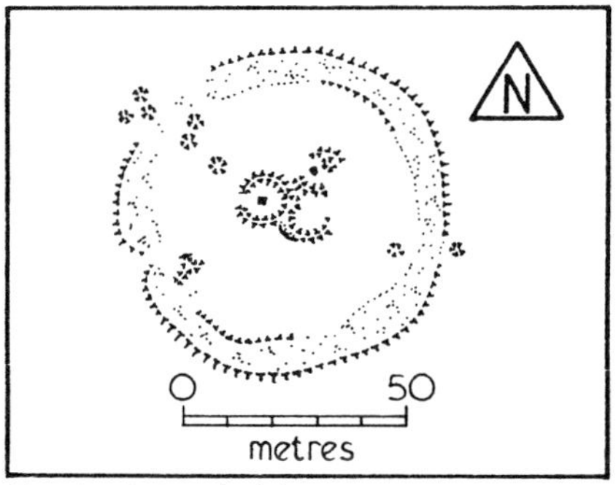

Bartinnê Castle (2)

3 Bleu Bridge, inscribed stone, Gulval.

SW 477318.
Track leads E from Penzance-Zennor road 200m NW of its junction with the B3311. The stone stands at the foot of the track near a footbridge.

1.7m tall, this stone is inscribed QVENATAVCI IC DINVI FILIVS: Quenataucus (lies) here, the son of Dinuus. Although the first of the two names is Irish, there is no accompanying Ogam inscription. The Latin inscription has been dated to the sixth century AD.

4 **The Blind Fiddler, menhir,** Sancreed.

SW 425282.
By N side of the A30, ½ mile W of Catchall.

Also known as the Trenuggo or Tregonebris Stone, this great Bronze Age slab stands 3.3m high. Fragments of bone were found at its foot during the nineteenth century.

5 **Bodrifty, round house settlement,** Newmill.

SW 445354.
Lane from Newmill to Bodrifty Farm. Site lies just to N, on edge of moorland.

Seven round houses of Iron Age date, some built on earlier foundations, lie within a low, oval earth and stone wall enclosing an area of 1.2ha. There are traces of at least three more huts and some fragmented field walls within the enclosure. The huts average 7.5m in diameter, and walls survive to a height of 1.2m. Many upright jambstones remain. The 1951-5 excavations revealed drains, hearths, more than 3,000 sherds of pottery, and spindlewhorls and slingstones. The original settlement, built in the fourth or fifth century BC, was an open one within a large field system, much of which can be traced. The existing huts and the pound wall date from the second century BC.

6 **Boleigh, fogou,** Lamorna.

SW 437252.
Track leads N from the B3315 half-way up S side of Lamorna valley. The site lies in the private garden of Rosemerrin House, and permission to view is required.

A fine Iron Age fogou, 11.0m long and 1.8m high, which once lay beneath the rampart of a small enclosed settlement, only traces of which remain. An L-shaped creep passage, ending in a false portal, leads from the west side of the main passage, just inside the entrance. The west jamb of the fogou entrance bears the relief carving of a human torso and head, perhaps representing a Celtic deity. This is the only Iron Age stone carving known in Cornwall and may indicate a ritual function for the fogou.

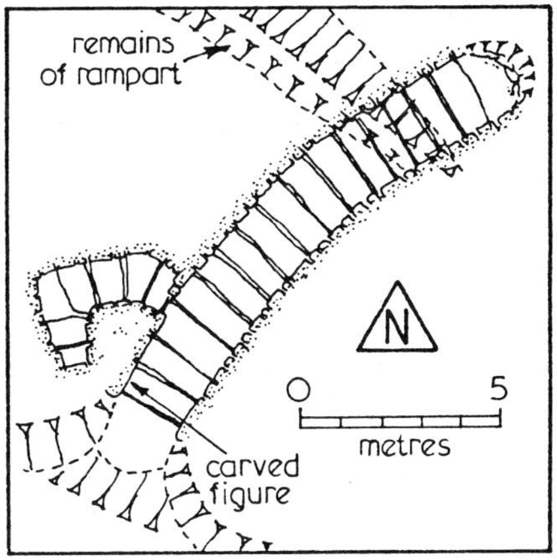

Boleigh fogou (6)

Left: *The Blind Fiddler (4)*

Bodrifty (5)

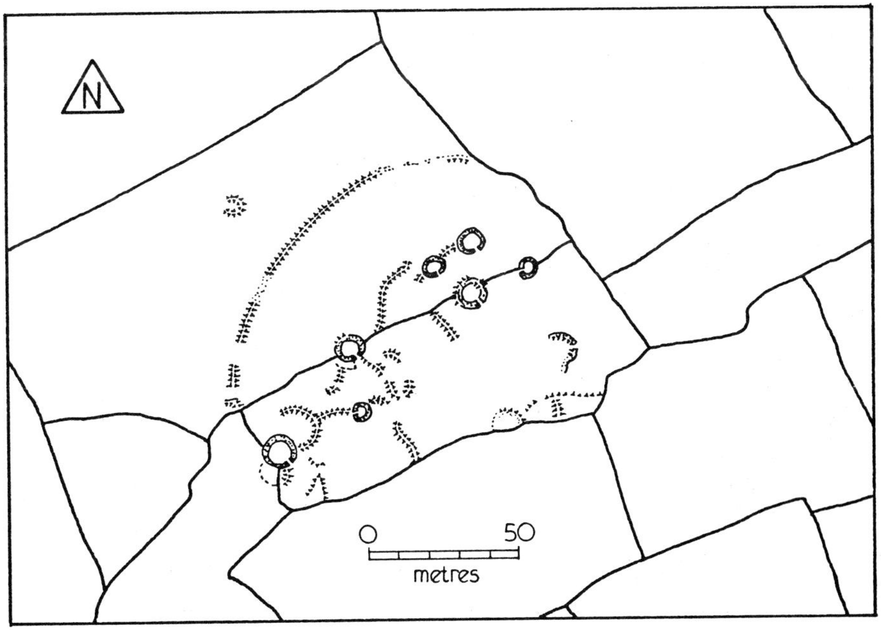

7 Boscawen-Ûn, stone circle,
St Buryan.

SW 412274.

Reached along farm track through Boscawen-noon Farm, leading S from the A30, 1 mile W of Catchall.

This Bronze Age ring, an ellipse with diameters of 24.9m and 21.9m, consists of nineteen upright stones from 0.9m to 1.3m high. Another stone, leaning sharply to the north-east, stands just south of centre: if erect, it would be 2.4m tall. The circle was restored in 1862: three fallen stones were re-erected and a hedge bisecting the circle was removed. The present hedge encircling the site was built at this time. An experimental trench cut through the site revealed nothing. A west-facing gap may have been an entrance. A notable feature of the site is a stone on the south-west perimeter which is of white quartz.

This monument is probably the *Beisgawen yn Dumnonia* named in the old Welsh Triads as one of the 'Three Principal Gorsedds' of the Island of Britain. The modern Cornish Gorsedd was inaugurated here in 1928.

To the north-east there are two outlying menhirs. The nearest, at SW 415276, is 2.6m tall – a longstone built into the foot of the nearby hedge may have stood beside it. The other, conical in shape and 2.3m high, is built into the hedge bordering the farm lane at SW 417277. Smaller outlying stones across the valley to the west of the circle have been removed in recent years.

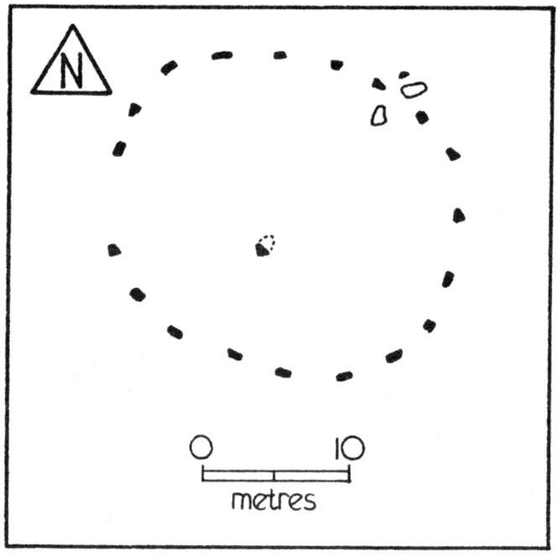

Boscawen-Ûn (7)

8 Boskednan, stone circle,
Madron.

SW 434351.

Lane to Ding Dong Mine leads N from Penzance-Morvah road 1½ miles NW of Madron. 200m N of the disused engine house a footpath leads NW to the site.

This ruinous Bronze Age circle, one of many known as the 'Nine Maidens', stands on a lonely, windswept moorland ridge. 21.9m across, it is apparently a true circle with eleven stones remaining out of a possible twenty-two. When seen by Dr Borlase in the mid eighteenth century, nineteen stones remained, thirteen erect; now only seven stones are standing, and some lean alarmingly. The tallest stone is 2.0m high; the rest are between 1.0m and 1.3m tall.

A round barrow touches the south side of the circle which revealed a central cist when it was opened in 1872. A fragment of Trevisker pottery had been found during another dig twenty-four years earlier.

55m north-north-west of the circle, beside the footpath, is the stump of an outlying menhir, the tapering sides of which suggest a former height of about 1.7m. Further to the north is a line of three round barrows, all denuded although the most northerly of the three displays a ring of unusually tall retaining stones.

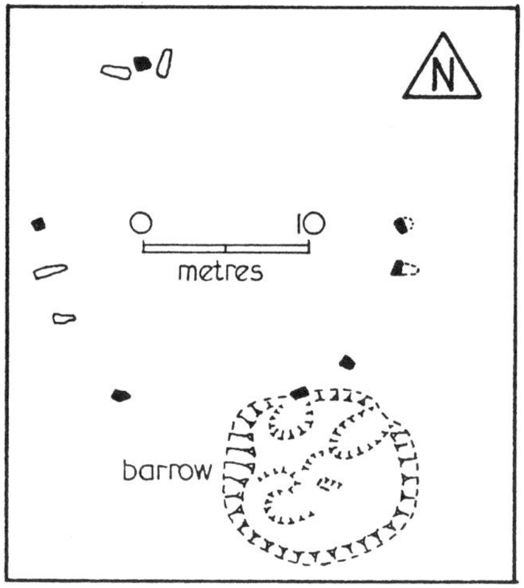

Above and below: *Boskednan (8)*

Bosporthennis 'beehive hut' fogou (9)

Bosporthennis (9)

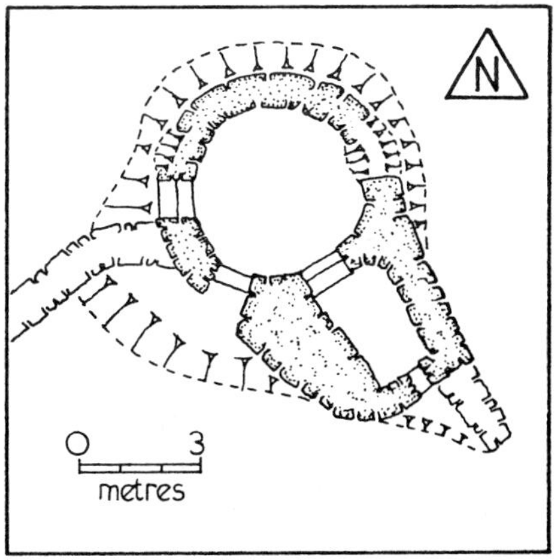

9 Bosporthennis, courtyard house settlement and fogou. Porthmeor.

SW 436360.

Reached through Bosporthennis Farm, off W side of Penzance-Gurnard's Head road, ½ mile SE of its junction with the B3306.

A scattered settlement of at least three Iron Age/Romano-British courtyard houses and several round houses in a sheltered spot at the eastern base of Hannibal's Carn. In a central position within the settlement is the intriguing 'beehive hut', now regarded as an above-ground fogou from its strong resemblance to the Phase I structure at Carn Euny (Site 16). It has a round, corbelled chamber 4.0m across (the lintelled entrance from the south-west is modern), connected by way of a low, heavily built portal to a small, oblong chamber 3.3m by 2.1m, which was its original entrance passage (the wall blocking the south-east end is also modern). Both chambers are now roofless. The best preserved of the courtyard houses, with an adjoining paddock and walls up to 1.5m high, lies 180m to the west of the fogou; another, 60m south of the fogou, has a medieval cow-house built inside its courtyard.

10 **Bosullow Trehyllys, courtyard house settlement**, Morvah.

SW 409342.

At base of hill 500m NE of Chûn Castle (see Site 20 for directions).

This superb, unexcavated Iron Age/Romano-British village consists of three detached courtyard houses, a number of detached round houses and an interlocking complex of round houses incorporating a fourth courtyard house and possibly the remains of a small above-ground fogou. Walls still reach a height of 1.8m in places and the buildings are surrounded by a bewildering array of tiny contemporary fields and garden plots. The settlement is situated immediately beside a preserved stretch of the main prehistoric trackway of the peninsula, and is known to have extended to the northern side of the track. The only remains there are a stone-lined well and a stone hump which preserves part of a fifth courtyard house.

Above and below: *Bosullow Trehyllys (10)*

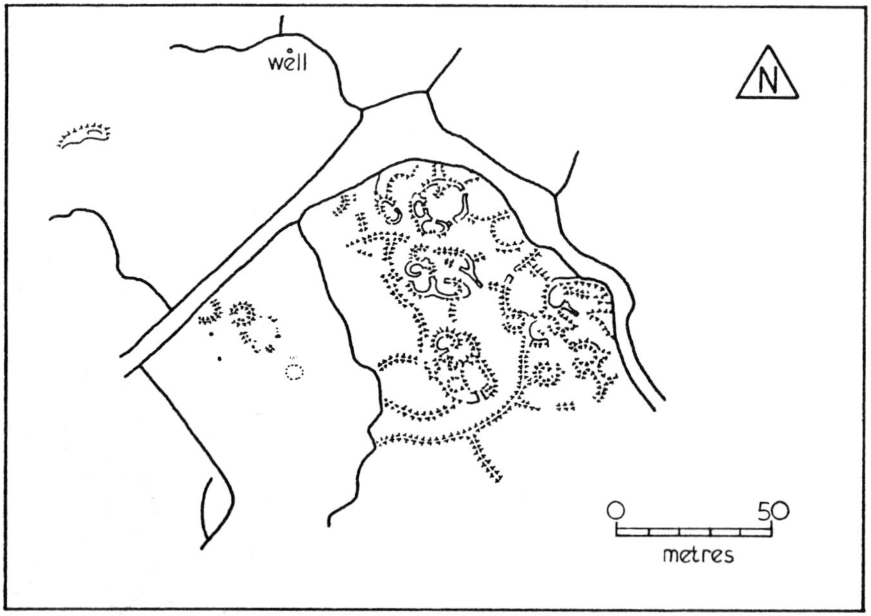

11 **Boswens, menhir,** Pendeen.

SW 400329.

On open moorland and visible from E side of the B3318, 1 mile S of Pendeen.

A fine Bronze Age menhir, 2.6m tall, which stands in the centre of a cairn 12m in diameter. The cairn is still traceable despite being denuded almost to ground level.

12 **Botrea, round barrow cemetery,** Newbridge.

SW 403312.

On hilltop immediately S of junction of the A3071 and the B3318.

On the top of Botrea hill are four unusual platform barrows, the largest of which is 38m in diameter. All are low, flat-topped mounds, none more than 1.2m high, with remains of raised rims. A couple of small bowl barrows lie just to the west; to the south are two large kerbed barrows, with a third, almost ploughed out, close by. Three of the platform barrows were explored in the nineteenth century, finds including ashes, a Bronze Age urn, and two superb barbed arrowheads.

Botrea (12)

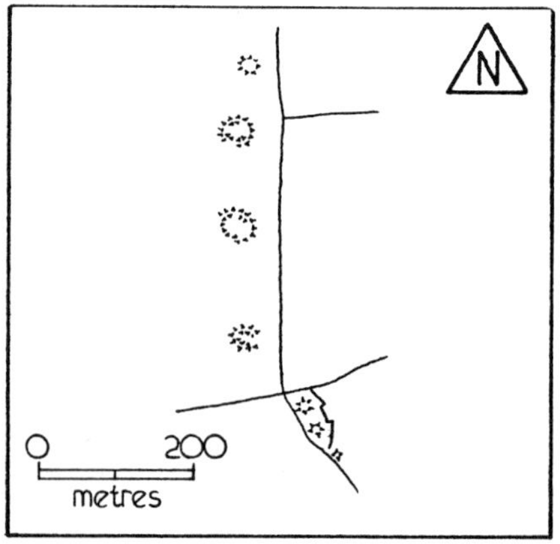

13 Brane, long barrow, Sancreed.

SW 402280.
200m S of Brane Scillonian chamber tomb (see Site 14 for directions).

A large mound, 40m long, 10m wide and up to 2.2m high, with sides spread by ploughing. Its antiquity has yet to be proven, but it does not appear to be a tinstreaming refuse mound, as some suspect. The south-western end of the mound has been truncated by a stream and a field wall.

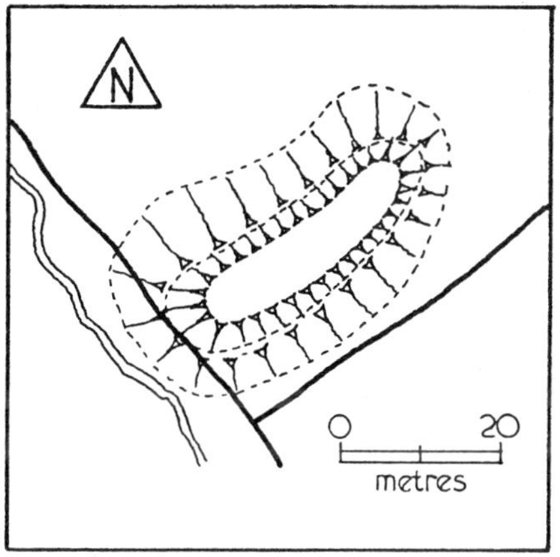

Brane long barrow (13)

14 Brane, Scillonian chamber tomb, Sancreed.

SW 401282.
In corner of a field 250m SW of Brane Farm, on lane from Sancreed to Carn Euny (see Site 16).

One of the best preserved of the mainland entrance graves, this neolithic tomb is small, just 6.1m in diameter and 2.0m high. The chamber faces south-south-east, and measures 2.3m by 1.2m by 0.9m high. Two large capstones remain in place; there may once have been a third. Although small, the mound is retained by a remarkably heavy kerb of granite blocks.

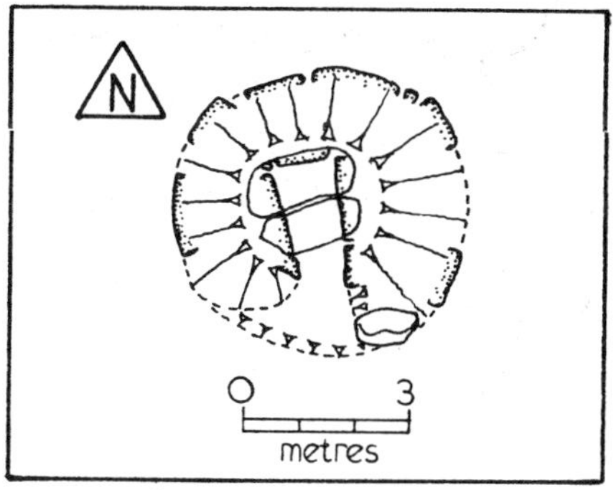

Brane Scillonian chamber tomb (14)

15 Caer Brân, hill fort, Sancreed.

SW 408290.
Reached by footpath and track N from Carn Euny (Site 16), or S from Grumbla on the Sancreed – St Just road.

A fine Iron Age fort 130m in diameter, with a deep outer ditch fronting an earth rampart up to 4.6m high. Just four low sections remain of the inner defence, which was of earth revetted with stone. There are a number of breaches in the defences; the original entrance was probably the one facing north-west. In the centre of the fort is a large round house cut through by a recent, but disused track. The fort is best preserved on the north side; the low, discontinuous state of the southern defences suggests that it may have been unfinished.

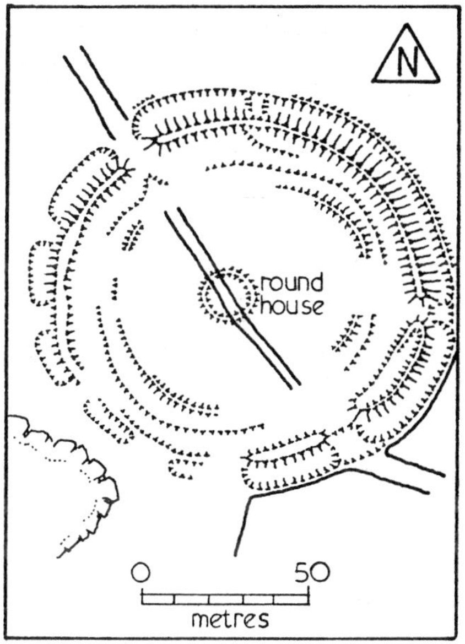

Right and below: *Caer Brân (15)*

16 Carn Euny, courtyard house settlement and fogou, Sancreed.

SW 403288. DE.

Signposted by Department of the Environment signs from the A30 at Lower Drift. Car-park just beyond Brane Farm.

The four interlocking courtyard houses of unusual design, plus a number of round houses, were built in the first century BC, replacing a timber-built settlement that was four hundred years older. Excavation showed evidence of settlement since the Bronze Age. Leading from the most northerly courtyard house is the magnificent fogou whose main gallery is 20m in length, 12.8m of which is still roofed. It is up to 2.0m high and is gently curved. At the southern end of the fogou is a low, angled creep passage leading to the surface. At the northern end is a low passage entering a remarkable circular corbelled room, 4.6m across and 2.4m high. The fogou, which had underfloor drainage, was found to have been built in successive phases. The corbelled chamber and its entrance passage was the first phase, *c.* 500 BC, followed within the next century or two by the long passage which originally was closed at both ends. During this phase the only way in and out of the fogou was the tiny creep passage. The north end of the fogou was opened at about the time the surviving settlement was built; it seems that the south end has been open only in recent centuries. The inhabitants of Carn Euny were farmers and stockbreeders, with a minor involvement in tin. It appears that they abandoned the village peacefully after about AD 400.

Carn Euny fogou (16)

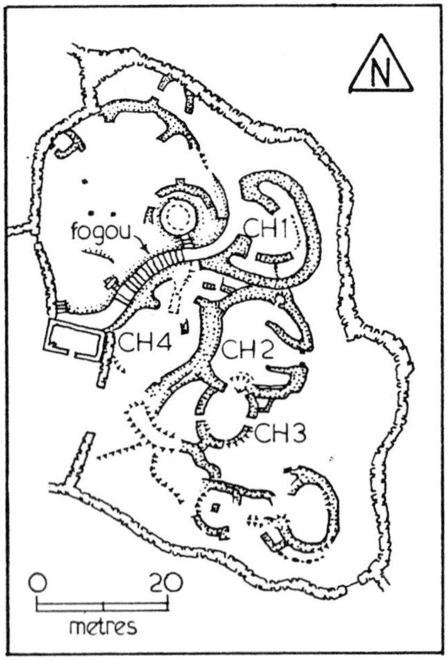

Carn Euny settlement and fogou (16)

17 **Castle-an-Dinas, hill fort,** Nancledra.

SW 485350.

Reached from the B3311 at Castle Gate, along track skirting quarry workings to top of hill.

133m in diameter, this Iron Age fort consisted of four concentric lines of defence. The innermost, a stone wall, has almost vanished, leaving little more than foundations. The next is another thick wall, tumbled but still 1.8m high in places. It is interrupted on the south-east side by a late eighteenth-century folly, Roger's Tower, built of stone from the castle walls. The third defence is a strong earth and stone bank; the outermost, another strong rampart of earth, reaches 2.3m in height, but exists only around the north-western half of the fort. Traces of an outer ditch can be seen, but the position of the original entrance is not known. A probable round house, the sole survivor of many, lies near the centre of the fort. It may be that the innermost wall represents the frontage of buildings constructed against the back of the main rampart, similar to those within Chûn Castle (Site 20).

Castle-an-Dinas (17)

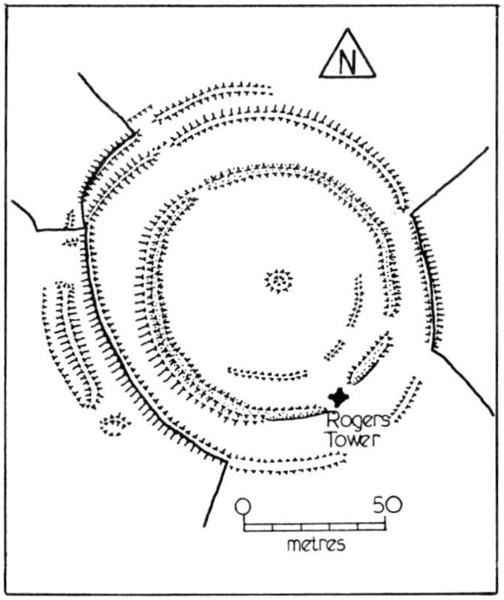

18 **Castle Kayle, settlement enclosure**, Fraddam.

SW 584357.

On E side of minor road running N from the B3302 just W of Fraddam.

A univallate 'round', probably of the Late Iron Age/Romano-British period, 100m in diameter. On the west its rampart is well preserved, if somewhat adapted to modern use, reaching a height of 3.0m. The rest of the rampart has been totally destroyed, but the outer ditch, partly used as a farm track and as much as 1.5m deep, extends around the southern half of the enclosure. A short length of ploughed-down scarp to the east, 0.7m high, may represent the remains of an attached annexe.

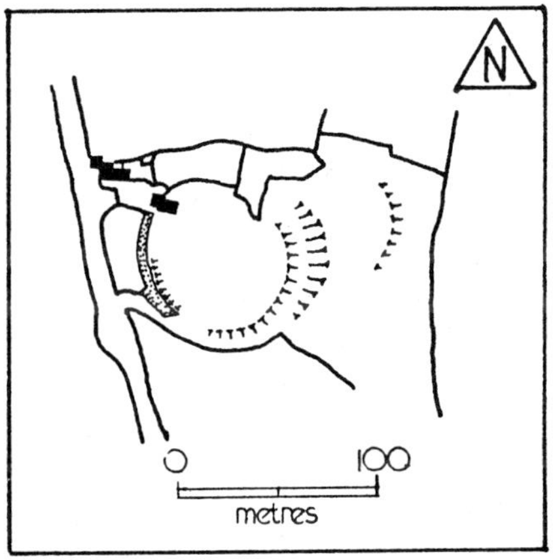

Castle Kayle (18)

19 **Chapel Carn Brea, Scillonian chamber tomb**, Crows-an-wra.

SW 386280. NT.

Minor road leads NW from Crows-an-wra on the A30. From small car-park on left, ½ mile from the junction, leads to hilltop.

The first barrow on the hilltop was of neolithic entrance grave type, 9.0m in diameter and containing a south-facing chamber 2.7m long by 1.2m wide. It was curiously tapered at its inner end and carried two capstones. It was subsequently covered by a gigantic cairn, 19m across and 4.6m high, containing three concentric retaining walls and the secondary cist which is now exposed on the south side. In the thirteenth century the tiny hermitage chapel of St Michael of Brea was built on top of the cairn, but this was dismantled in 1816 after falling into dangerous decay. The present dilapidated state of the cairn is due to the erection of a radar station on it during World War II, which reduced its height to the present 2.7m and exposed the cist which has a heavy capstone 1.5m square. Just west of the cist is a corner of stonework which betrays the entrance to the buried Scillonian chamber. The hill is the site of eight barrows which include at least one further entrance grave.

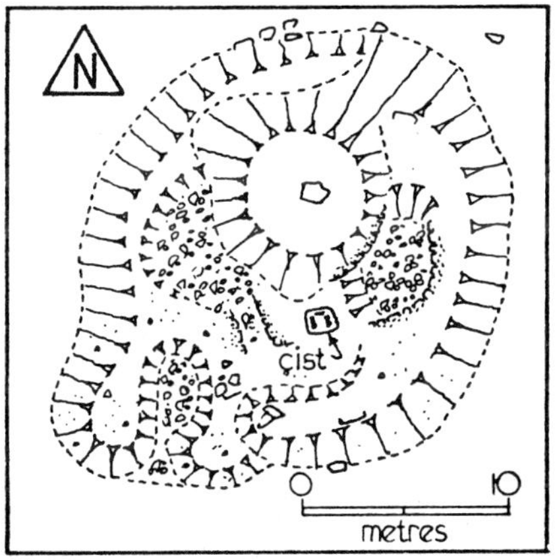

Chapel Carn Brea (19)

20 **Chûn Castle, hill fort,** Morvah.

SW 405340.

Lane signposted 'Chûn Castle' leaves the Penzance-Morvah road at Bosullow Common, 3 miles NW of Madron. Parking at Trehyllys Farm at the end of the lane.

This superb Iron Age fort is entirely stone-built. 85m in diameter, it has two massive concentric walls, the inner of which is, for the most part, 4.6m thick. This widens to nearer 7.0m on either side of the tapered entrance which retains its massive gateposts. The original outer gate can be seen more or less in line with the inner one. At some point this was blocked and another was built about 15m to the south, creating a twisting, staggering entry that would force intruders to expose their unshielded right sides to the defenders on the inner wall. This wall probably stood to a height of about 6.0m; now, after centuries of stone robbing, it has been reduced to a maximum height of 2.4m. The outer wall, 2.0m thick, and once about 3.0m high, stills stands to 2.1m in places. The outer ditch, choked and indistinct, was 6.0m wide, and beyond the later outer gate are traces of a short bank and ditch forming a protective hornwork.

Within the fort is a stone-lined well and the foundations of Dark Age buildings constructed against the back of the inner wall during the sixth century AD. These overlay the sites of at least a dozen Iron Age round houses, each about 5.0m in diameter, associated with finds of pottery bearing curvilinear decoration,and duck-stamped ware of the third and second centuries BC. The Dark Age reoccupation was probably responsible for the reconstruction of the entrance. Just south of the well, excavation revealed an elaborate smelting furnace and a lump of tin slag weighing about 5.5 kg, showing that the fort, built astride the prehistoric trackway, was closely connected with the tin trade.

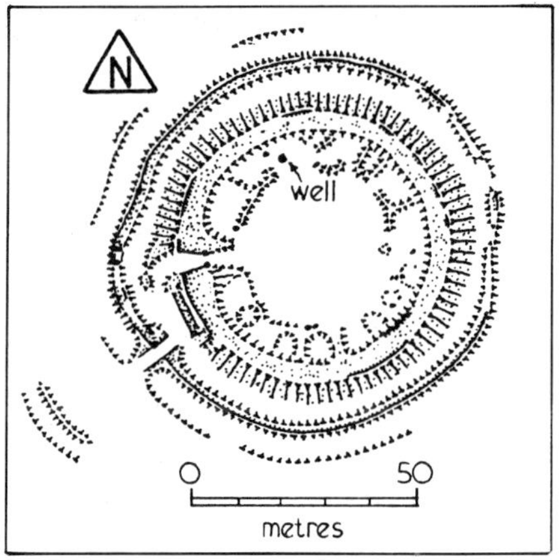

Chûn Castle (20)

Chûn Castle (20)

21 **Chûn Quoit, Penwith chamber tomb**, Morvah.

SW 402339.
Just W of, and visible from, Chûn Castle (Site 20).

Resembling a giant mushroom, this neolithic tomb has the most perfectly preserved chamber of its type in Cornwall. It is a closed chamber formed by four large slabs supporting a convex capstone 3.4m by 3.1m and up to 0.8m thick. The chamber is 1.8m high internally, and considerable remains of its circular mound can be seen. This was of stone, 13.5m across; it survives to a height of 0.8m. A few small kerbstones also survive. A pair of slabs, one still set on edge, the other fallen, can be seen on the mound south of the chamber. These may be the remains of a secondary cist, or of an entrance passage through the mound to the chamber.

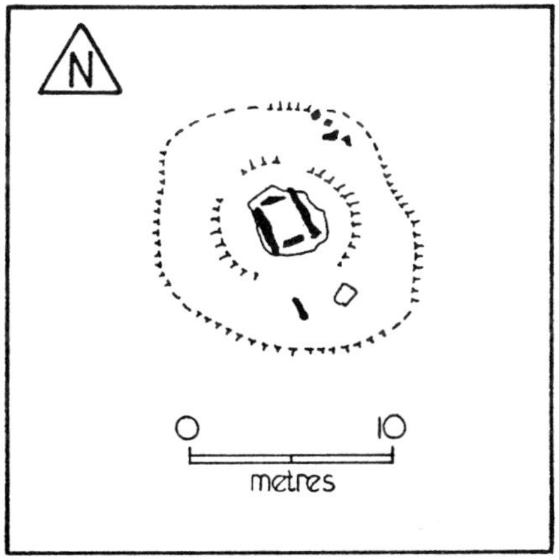

Chûn Quoit (21)

Chûn Quoit (21)

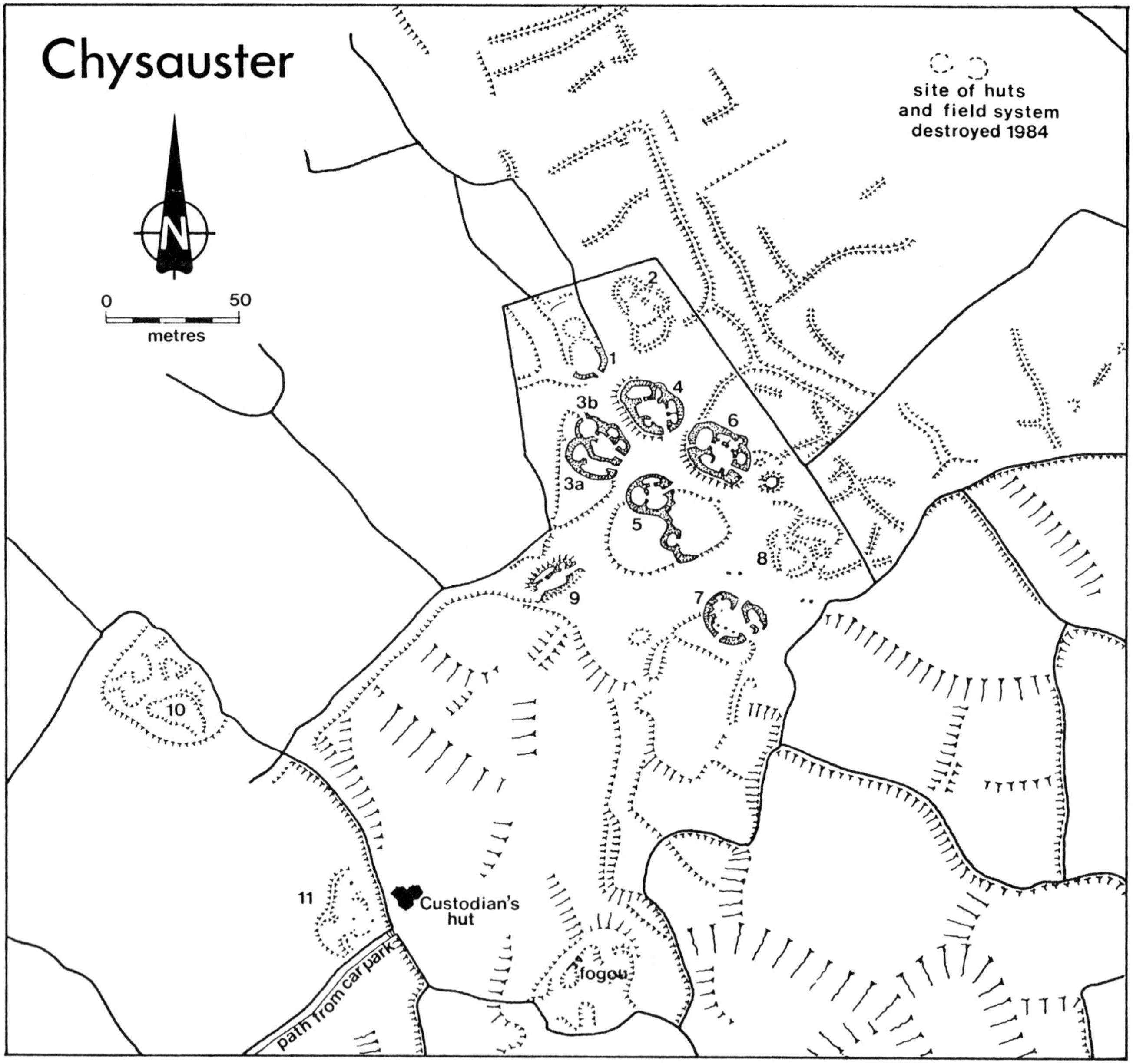

Chysauster
N
0
50
metres
site of huts
and field system
destroyed 1984
1
2
3b
3a
4
5
6
7
8
9
10
11
Custodian's
hut
fogou
path from car park

22 **Chysauster, courtyard house settlement**, Newmill.

SW 473350. DE.
Well signposted from the B3311 at Badger's Cross, and from the Penzance–Gurnard's Head road at Newmill. A car-park is provided.

The classic and largest example of its type, this Late Iron Age/Romano-British village consists of nine courtyard houses in a group, eight of which are arranged in pairs on either side of a winding village street, with a further pair a little way down the hillside. Five of the houses, one of which is a semi-detached unit, have been fully excavated and walls stand from 0.6m to 2.1m high. Houses 4 and 6 are the best preserved, lacking only roofs, doors and a lived-in atmosphere. Drains, hearths, stone paving and the socketed stone which held the base of the main roof post all remain. Most of the houses have a terraced garden plot attached.

To the north-east was a vast and well-preserved field system which had been farmed by the occupants. Sadly, much of this was destroyed early in 1984. To the south of the main body of the village is the inner end of a ruined fogou, originally about 15m long, now reduced to just 4.5m. Two of its roofing stones remain in place. Chysauster was founded during the first century BC and peacefully abandoned four centuries later. A fine, detailed guide may be purchased from the Department of the Environment's custodian on site.

Chysauster: House 6 (22)

Chysauster: the fogou (22)

23 Gurnard's Head, cliff castle,
Treen.

SW 433385.
Reached by footpath from Treen on the B3306.

Two dilapidated stone ramparts 60m long, with outer ditches, cross the high, narrow neck of this rugged headland, defending an area of 3 ha. The inner bank, 3.0m thick, reaches a height of 1.8m; the outer rampart is now no more than 1.2m high. The two halves of each rampart are slightly out of alignment, forming staggered entries that are now difficult to see. 10m south of these defences is a short length of ditch above the eastern cliff, apparently an unfinished outer defence. Excavation in 1939 showed that the back of the inner rampart had been fashioned into three steps, providing a stance for slingers, as in some Breton cliff castles. Within the ramparts, on the lower eastern side of the headland, are sixteen round houses averaging 6.0m in diameter. They and the ramparts are second century BC.

Gurnard's Head (23)

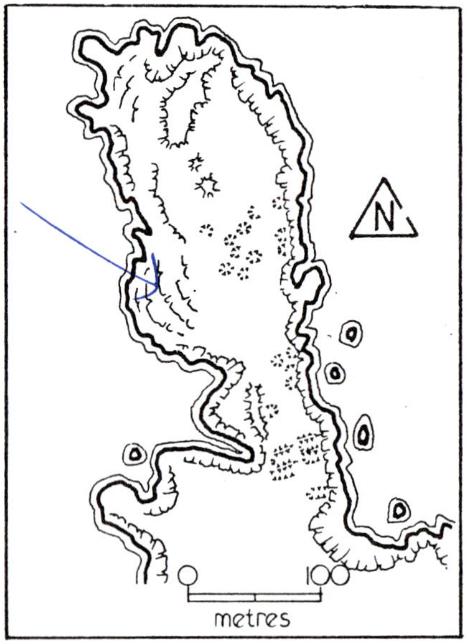

Higher Drift menhirs (24)

24 Higher Drift, menhirs,
Drift.

SW 437283.
In a field on S side of the A30, ¼ mile W of Lower Drift.

Also known as the 'Sisters', or Triganeeris Stones, these two Bronze Age menhirs stand 5.5m apart. They are 2.7m and 2.3m high. In 1871 it was found that a rectangular pit 1.8m long had been cut just north of a line between the two stones. This apparently contained nothing.

Kenidjack Castle (25)

25 Kenidjack Castle, cliff castle,
St Just.

SW 355326.
Reached by lane and track leading W from the B3306 at bottom of Nancherrow valley ½ mile N of St Just.

The high central spine of this headland is protected by natural outcrops, but there are faint signs of a wall here. North of this is a well preserved triple Iron Age defence. The outer ditch is 1.2m deep and the stone ramparts behind it are 2.4m, 3.3m and 2.1m high. An entrance roadway, its north side revetted with stone, hugs the foot of the central rocky spine; two round houses lie beyond. The southern defences are behind a natural rocky ridge, and consist of two battered stone banks 1.2m high with traces of outer ditches. There are two hut platforms immediately behind the inner bank.

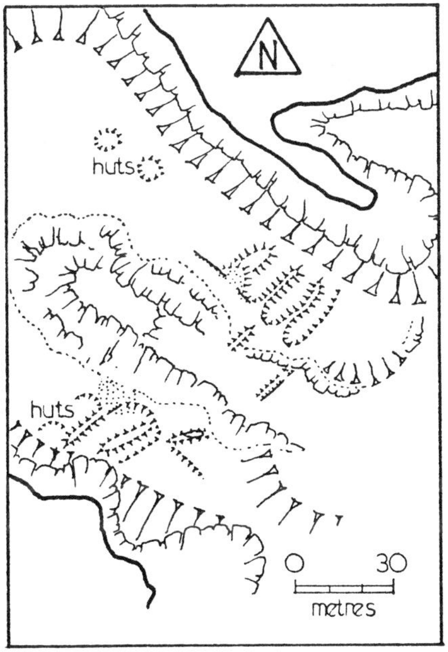

Kenidjack Castle (25)

26 **Lanyon Quoit, Penwith chamber tomb,** Madron.

SW 430337. NT.
Beside Penzance–Morvah road, 2½ miles N of Madron.

The present appearance of Lanyon Quoit bears little resemblance to its original form. It fell during a storm in 1815 and some stones were broken, making true reconstruction impossible when it was re-erected in 1824. The capstone stood about a metre higher than its

Lanyon Quoit (26)

present elevation of 1.5m, and there were four uprights, one of which was too short to reach the capstone. Now the capstone (5.3m by 2.7m by 0.3m thick) stands on three supports; a fourth is on edge at the north end of the tomb. Another broken slab lies at the foot of the southern support.

It was thought that this neolithic tomb stood at the north end of a long barrow measuring 27m by 12m, but it now looks as if this is, in fact, the spread remnants of two round mounds in juxtaposition. The southern barrow contains a jumble of stones which are the remains of two or more cists. The chamber of Lanyon Quoit was excavated in 1754 when a pit was dug in previously disturbed soil: it is said that a rectangular pit 1.8m deep had been dug there a few years previously.

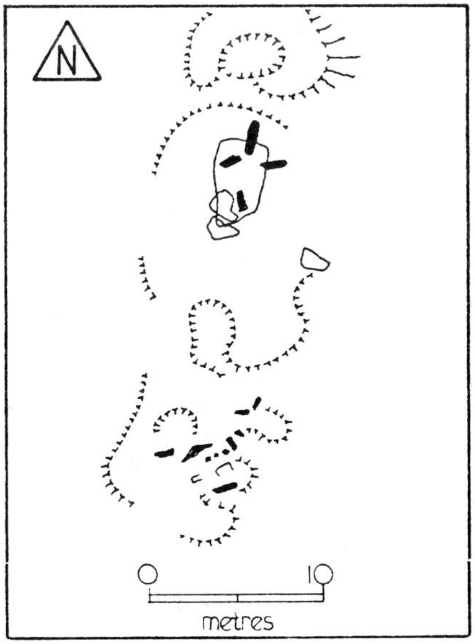

Lanyon Quoit (26)

27 **Lesingey Round, hill fort,** Penzance.

SW 453304.

The site lies beneath a prominent clump of trees visible from N side of the A3071, ½ mile NW of its junction with the A30 on the edge of Penzance.

79m in diameter, this Iron Age fort is surrounded by a modern stone hedge. It has a single massive earth rampart 3.7m high fronted by the remains of an outer ditch. The ill-defined west-facing entrance leads into the tree-grown interior which was raised artificially above the level of the surrounding landscape.

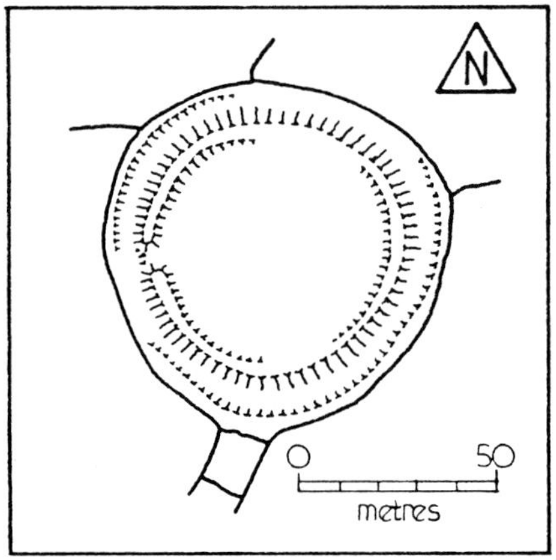

Lesingey Round (27)

28 **Maen Castle, cliff castle,** Sennen.

SW 348258. NT.

Beside the cliff path, half-way between Sennen Cove and Land's End.

The oldest known of the cliff castles, built during the fourth century BC. A rock-cut ditch of up to 2.4m deep has a pronounced stone-revetted counterscarp on its outer lip: this reaches a height of 2.0m. Set back from the ditch is the main rampart, a massive stone wall 3.7m thick, 60m long, and surviving to a height of 1.5m. The gateway is well preserved and a former gate-jamb lies within it. A pair of postholes, still visible at the inner end of the entrance passage, indicates the former position of the timber gates. This entrance may have been additionally protected by a pair of curtain walls curving out from the main rampart on either side. The south side of the headland has no fortification; steep slopes and rocky outcrops provide a natural defence. Pre-war excavations detected no permanent dwelling sites within the fort, which enclosed an area of less than 1 ha, but many stone-walled Iron Age fields can be seen terracing the coastal slope which overlooks the site.

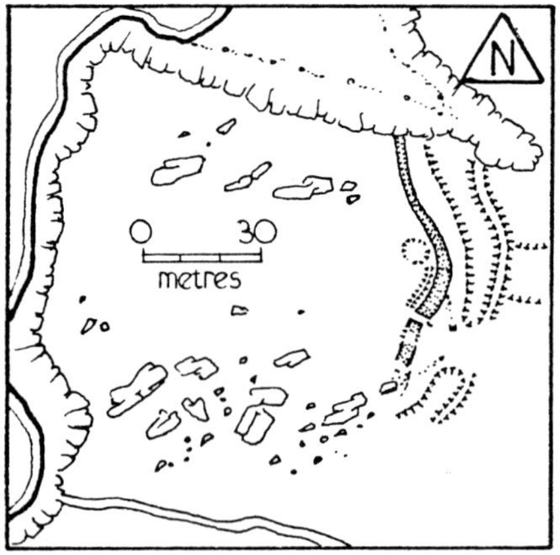

Maen Castle (28)

29 **Mên-an-Tol, holed stone,** Morvah.

SW 426349.

Reached by signposted track on NE side of Penzance-Morvah road at Bosullow Common, opposite turning to Chûn Castle.

This mysterious and famous monument, assumed to be Bronze Age, is of unknown purpose, although oracular and healing powers have been ascribed to it. It is a wheel-shaped slab 1.3m across, set on edge, and pierced by a round hole 51cm in diameter. It is flanked by two small upright stones 1.2m high, at least one of which has been moved during the past couple of centuries, and there is a third, recumbent stone. It should not be assumed to have been part of a dismantled chamber tomb.

Mên-an-Tol (29)

Above and below: *Mên Scryfa (30)*

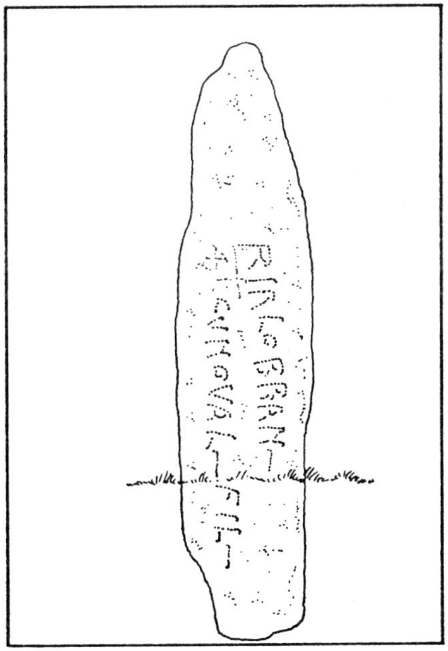

30 **Mên Scryfa, inscribed stone,** Morvah.

SW 427353.

The stone stands in a field on the north side of the track, 300m beyond the Mên-an-tol (Site 29).

The northern face of this stone, which stands 1.8m tall, is clearly inscribed to the memory of RIALOBRAN-CVNOVAL-FIL- (Rialobran, son of Cunoval). These names, in modern Cornish *Ryalvran* and *Kenwal*, mean respectively 'Royal Raven' and 'Famous Chieftain', so the stone almost certainly commemorates local royalty of the sixth century AD, the date ascribed to the style of lettering used.

31 **Merry Maidens, stone circle,** Lamorna.

SW 433245.

In a field on S side of the B3315, ¾ mile SW of the Lamorna valley.

Apparently complete, this beautiful Bronze Age site is a true circle, 23.8m across, consisting of nineteen stones ranging in height from 0.8m to 1.4m. The stones were graded so that the tallest are on the south-west, the smallest directly opposite. The gap facing east may have been a ritual entrance, although it is possible that it results from a missing stone. The circle was restored in the 1860s when three fallen stones were re-erected. In the immediate vicinity are a number of outlying menhirs: pairs at the Pipers (Site 35) to the north-east and Boscawen-rôs to the south-west, and a fine single stone, the Fiddler or Gûn Rith stone, which is clearly visible to the west. A number of barrows and holed stones occur nearby. The circle is also known as the Rosemodress circle and as *Dons Meyn* (Cornish for 'stone dance').

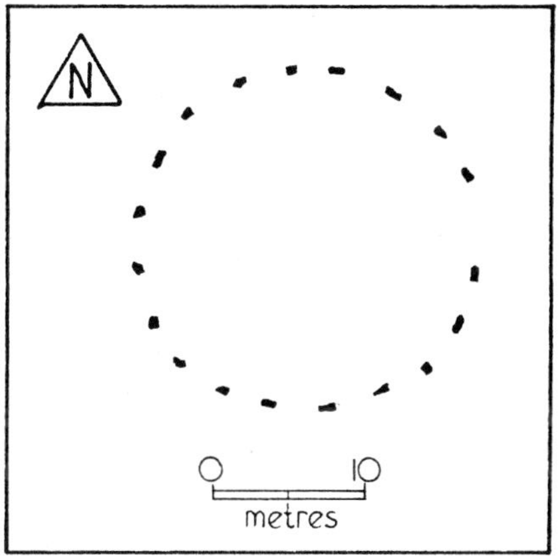

Above and below: *The Merry Maidens (31)*

32 **Mulfra Quoit, Penwith chamb tomb,** Newmill.

SW 452354.

Reached by footpath to the summit of Mulfr Hill leading off W side of Penzance-Gurnard Head road 1 mile N of Newmill.

This partially ruined but impressive neolithi tomb near the summit of Mulfra Hill originall stood within a mound 11m across, which i now barely traceable. Three slabs 1.7m high remain of the four that formed the sides of a closed chamber. The fourth has been missing for at least three centuries. The 2.9m square capstone slipped long ago and now leans sharply against the chamber. The monument must once have borne a close resemblance to Chûn Quoit (Site 21). Dr Borlase dug within the chamber in 1749 and found a pit 0.5m deep containing 'black, greasy loam'.

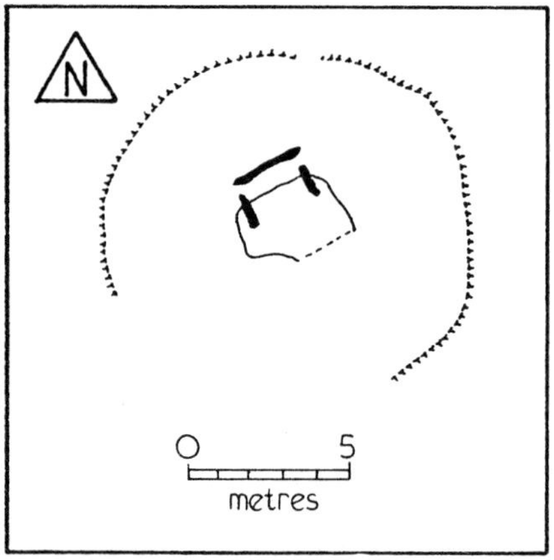

Mulfra Quoit (32)

Pendeen Vau (33)

33 **Pendeen Vau, fogou,** Pendeen.

SW 384355.

Lane marked 'To the Lighthouse' leads NW from the B3306 at Portheras Cross, Pendeen. Track to Pendeen Manor Farm leaves E side of lane ½ mile NW of Pendeen. Permission to visit and torch required.

This superb Iron Age fogou lies in the farmyard behind the ancient Pendeen Manor, birthplace of the eighteenth-century 'Father of Cornish Archaeology', Dr William Borlase. Opening in the side of a huge, ancient stone hedge, the fogou descends steeply underground, then levels and turns sharply to the left. This passage, lined and roofed with stone, is 17.2m long. At the angle of the passage is the tiny opening into a remarkable chamber 7.3m long, 1.5m wide and 1.2m high, semi-circular in section and cut entirely from the natural rab (granite clay) with no supporting stonework. It is in perfect condition.

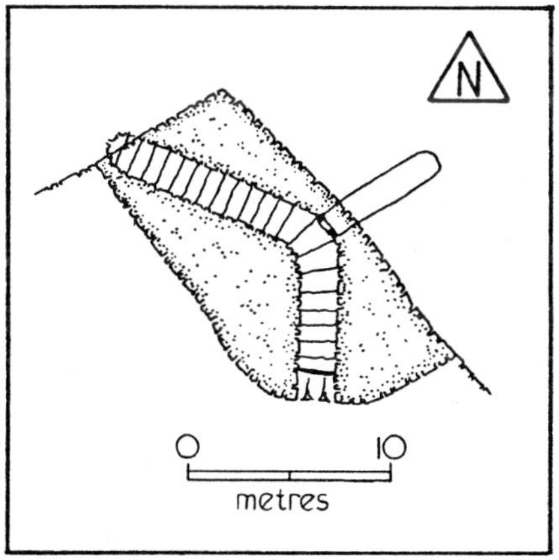

Pendeen Vau (33)

34 **Pennance, Scillonian chamber tomb,** Zennor.

SW 448376.

Visible from SW side of the B3306, 1 mile W of Zennor.

This fine neolithic tomb is 7.9m in diameter and 1.8m high, retained by a kerb of heavy stones. The partially choked chamber, facing south-east, is 4.0m long, 1.4m wide and 0.8m high. It is roofed by five capstones: there may originally have been six or seven. The tomb is known locally as the 'Giant's Craw', (Cornish *crow* – hut).

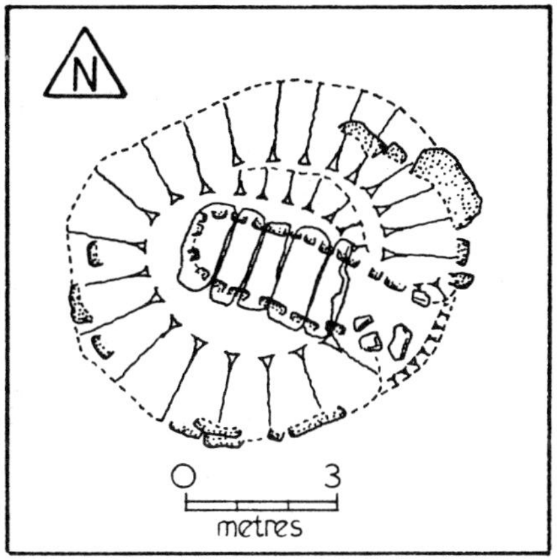

Pennance (34)

35 **The Pipers, menhirs,** Lamorna.

SW 435248 and 435247.

Visible on W side of the B3315 behind Boleigh Farm.

The north-east Piper, that nearest to Boleigh Farm, is, at 4.6m, the tallest Bronze Age menhir in Cornwall. Its neighbour, 99m to the south-west, is the second tallest at 4.1m. A line drawn from one to the other and continued south-west would touch the north-west quadrant of the Merry Maidens stone circle which is not visible from either of the stones.

36 **Porthmeor, courtyard house settlement**, Porthmeor.

SW 434371.

Permission required for access to Porthmeor Farm on the B3306, ½ mile W of Gurnard's Head Hotel at Treen.

In the Late Iron Age this was an open settlement of round houses within their field system. In the second century AD the main body of the settlement was surrounded by an oval wall, still 2.4m high in places, and three courtyard houses were built within on four artificial terraces. Just outside the enclosure, to the south-west, are the ruins of a further courtyard house and an above-ground fogou which runs around the outside of its one surviving room. This fogou is a curved passage 12.8m long, the inner 7.3m of which was roofed by corbelling, the rest by stone lintels. The whole roof is now missing, but the corbelled structure is still evident. The fogou walls survive to a height of 1.7m and it is 1.5m wide. Like the Carn Euny fogou (Site 16), it was furnished with underfloor drainage. The settlement was excavated from 1933 to 1939.

Porthmeor (36)

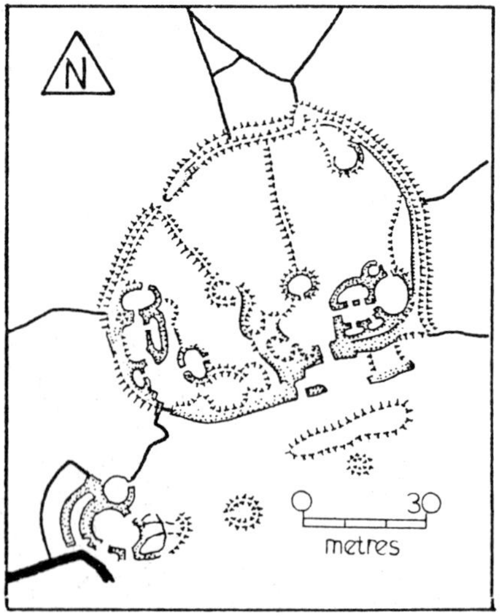

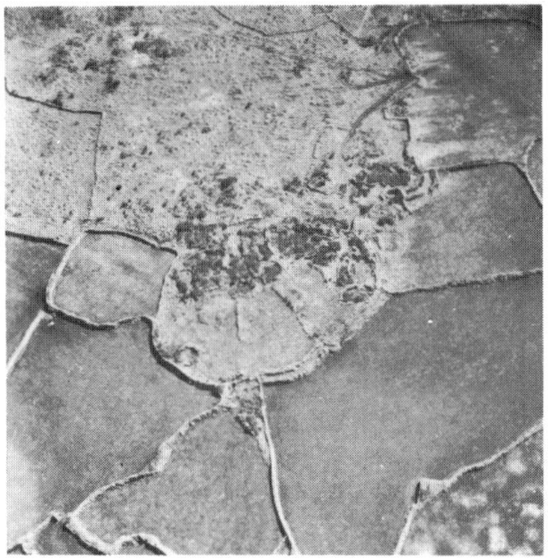

Porthmeor (36)

37 **St Hilary, Roman milestone,** St Hilary.

SW 551313.

The stone is within St Hilary parish church.

This fine stone, 1.3m high, has ten horizontal lines of inscription reading: IMP CAES FLAV VAL CONSTANTINO PIO NOB CAES DIVI CONSTANTI PII AUG FILIO (In the reign of the Emperor Flavius Valerius Constantinus, pious, noble Caesar, son of the divine Constantius Pius Augustus). The Emperor Constantinus is better known as Constantine the Great, and the stone is dated to AD 306-8. In the churchyard is an Early Christian stone inscribed NOTI NOTI (presumably 'Notus son of Notus'). It is 1.9m high.

St Hilary Roman milestone (37)

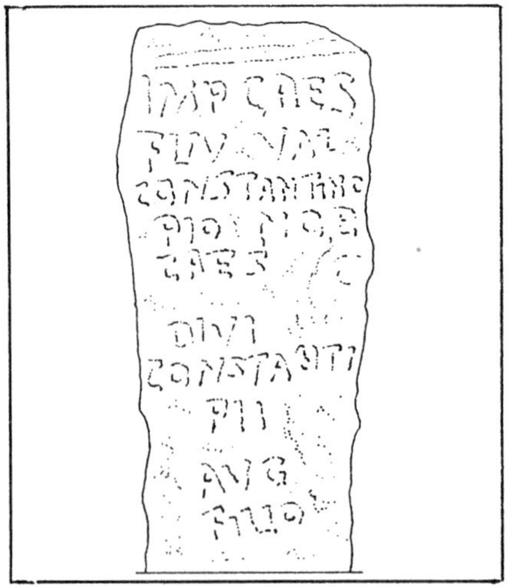

38 **The Selus Stone, inscribed stone,** St Just.

SW 372315.

The stone stands in the north aisle of St Just church.

This stone, 1.6m high, carries two inscriptions. The first is a late form of the Chi-Rho monogram (the first two letters of Christ in the Greek alphabet) surrounded by a simple incised border. The second, on an adjacent side of the stone, dates from the fifth or sixth century AD and reads: SELVS IC IACIT (Selus lies here). Some believe that Selus is Selyf (later Selevan and St Levan), brother of Yestin (St Just) and son of Gerent, High King of Dumnonia.

The Selus Stone (38)

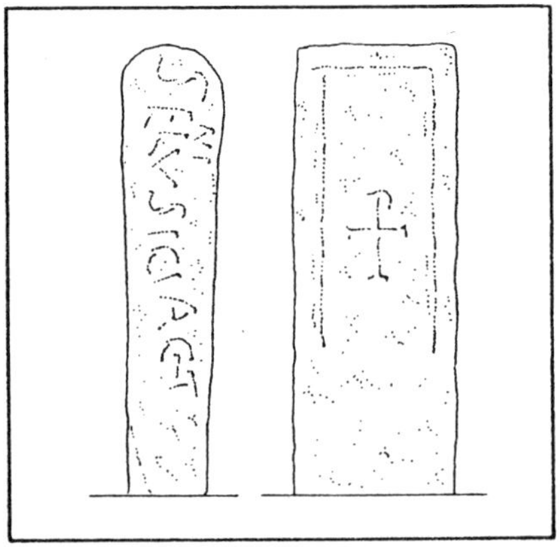

39 **Sperris and Wicca, round house settlements**, Zennor.

SW 473384 and 473385.

Footpath to the sites ascends hill on S side of the B3306, 1 mile E of Zennor.

Sperris Croft lies at the very top of the ridge and consists of seven round houses strung out in a line. Excavated in 1939, two of the huts have smaller rooms attached. Wicca Round lies 150m to the north. Excavated in 1956-7, it has three ruinous huts arranged in a close triangle and set in the midst of an extensive field system. Both settlements date from the Late Bronze Age/Early Iron Age transition.

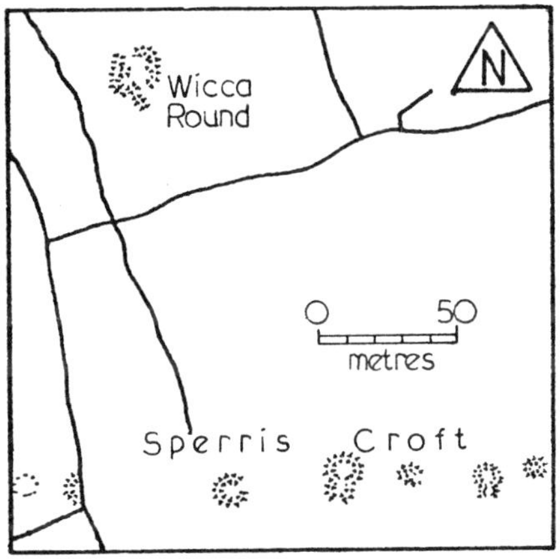

Sperris and Wicca (39)

40 **Treen Common, embanked stone circle**, Treen.

SW 444366.

By W side of Penzance-Gurnard's Head road, 1 mile S of Treen.

A curious monument consisting of an irregular, elliptical ring of fourteen upright and numerous fallen and displaced stones, the greater diameter of which is 33m. The stones, from 0.3m to 1.4m high, stand in a low bank of earth and rubble, similar to the Welsh circle of Penmenmawr. There is still some doubt concerning the true identity of the site; as it stands within a large field system it may be seen as the remains of an Iron Age / Romano-British settlement enclosure or 'round', rather than as a Bronze Age stone circle.

Treen Common (40)

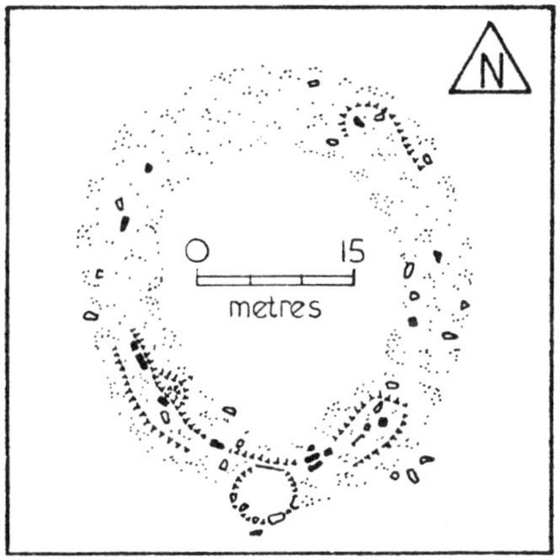

41 **Treen, Scillonian chamber tombs**, Treen.

SW 438371.

On W side of Penzance-Gurnard's Head road 200m S of its junction with B3306.

There are four mounds here, two so mutilated that it is now impossible to tell whether they ever held chambers. However, two neolithic tombs of Scillonian type survive. The south tomb, 7.6m across, is well preserved, containing a chamber 4.0m long and 0.9m high, roofed by three partly exposed capstones. A fragment of kerb, two courses high, survives on the south-east side. Its neighbour, 60m to the north, is 6.0m in diameter but only the inner end of its chamber and one capstone surivive. The chamber of this tomb faces south-west; that of the south tomb faces north-west.

Top right: *Treen tombs (41)*
Above right: *Treen tombs: north cairn (41)*
Right: *Treen tombs: south cairn (41)*

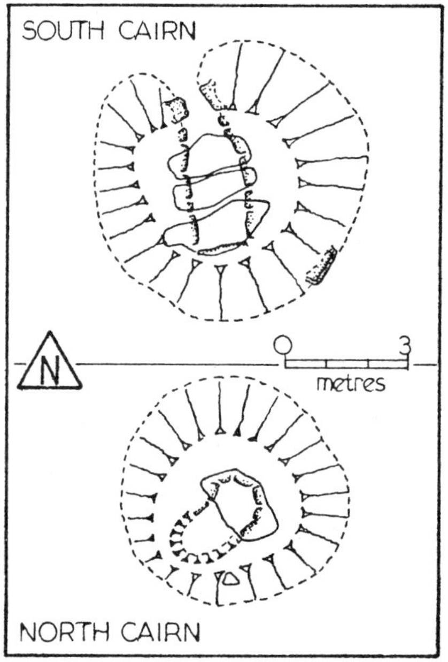

42 Tregeseal, stone circle, St Just.

SW 387324.

Best reached by footpath leading E from the B3306 at Carnyorth, 1 mile N of St Just.

The surviving circle, with diameters of 21.7m and 21.1m, appears to have been the easternmost of three circles in a line, similar to the Hurlers, Caradon. The site of the western circle was found by aerial photography; the central one was mostly dismantled in 1905, the damage being completed in 1961. It was 23.5m across but all that remains are four stones, still *in situ* but incorporated into the field wall. Only one of these is now visible. The eastern circle has been much mutilated and restored, and probably bears little resemblance to its original form. Nineteen stones are present, all but one erect; their heights vary from 0.8m to 1.5m. 300m to the north-east, beside a footpath, are the two largest of a group of round barrows. The bigger of the two, on the west side of the path, contains the ruins of a neolithic Scillonian chamber tomb. A little further on are six holed stones, presumably Bronze Age. Four of these are in a line, with two outliers to the west and to the north.

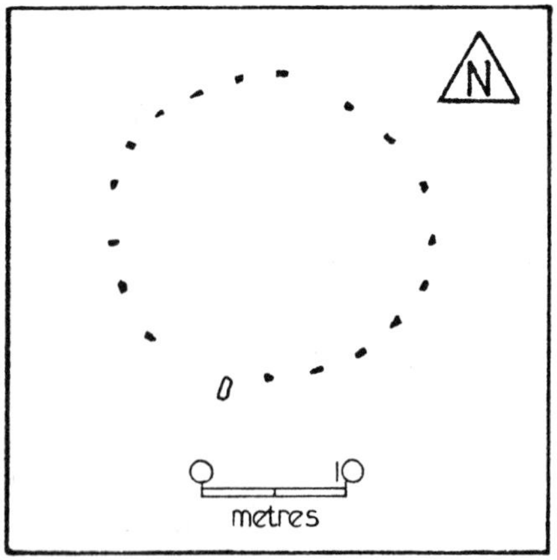

Tregeseal (42)

Tregiffian (43)

43 Tregiffian, Scillonian chamber tomb, Lamorna.

SW 430244. DE.

On grass verge of S side of the B3315, just W of the Merry Maidens stone circle (Site 31).

This important neolithic tomb was about 12m in diameter before the road cut it in half. Part of a polygonal kerb remains from a second phase reconstruction. The chamber is 4.3m long and 1.2m wide, with three large capstones in place and a further one fallen. A remarkable stone covered with artificial cup-marks is now in the County Museum, Truro; a cast replica remains on site, beside the closed-off entrance to the chamber. Finds included cremated bone fragments and a complete urn 38cm high, all apparently from the second phase use of the site. A radio-carbon date of 1540 bc was returned, calibrated to 1900 BC.

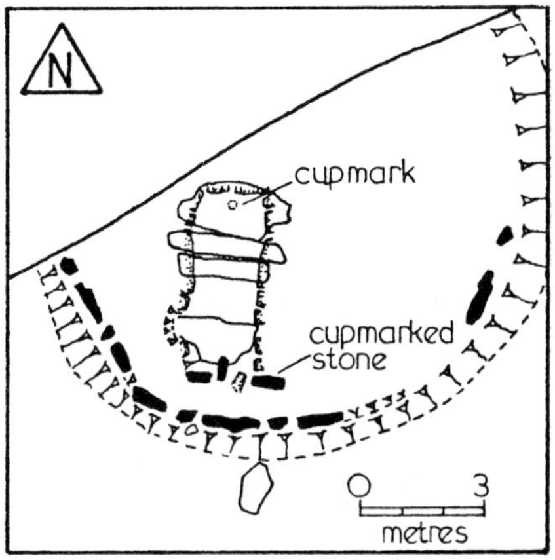

Tregiffian (43)

44 **Trencrom Castle, tor enclosure,** Lelant.

SW 518362. NT.

Reached by lanes NW from the A3074 near its junction with the A30. There is a small car park on the south side of the hill.

Finds of neolithic axes on the slopes of the hill indicate that this hilltop was occupied during that era, and it may be that the massive wall surrounding the flattish summit originated then. It is recognized, however, that the wall as it appears today is probably Iron Age. It is up to 2.5m high on its external side and makes full use of the many natural outcrops. There is no external ditch owing to the sudden steepness of the hillsides. The fort is pear-shaped in plan, 137m from north to south, by 91m, and there is a pair of fine entrances, complete with gate-jambs, on the east and west sides. A number of round house foundations can be traced in the interior; as many as sixteen have been counted. Surface pottery shows that Iron Age occupation dated from about 200 BC, and that the site was in use well into the Dark Ages – possibly as late as the eighth or ninth century AD.

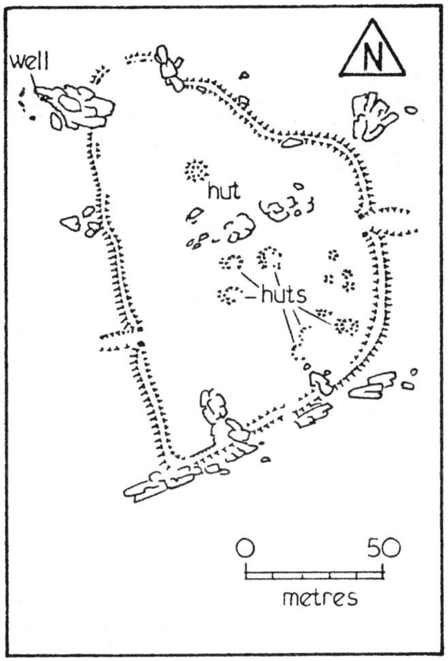

Trencrom Castle (44)

45 **Treryn Dinas, cliff castle,** Treen.

SW 397222. NT.

Footpath S from car-park at Treen.

This magnificent headland was defended by one of Cornwall's finest Iron Age cliff castles. The outer defence is a deep ditch fronting a colossal earth rampart 6.5m high and 275m long. 60m beyond this are two slighter ramparts and ditches. The outermost of these reaches a height of 2.0m, and the outer edge of its ditch has a faint counterscarp. The inner bank, originally stone-faced, makes use of a low ridge. The fourth and final line of defence is another deep ditch, backed by a heavy masonry wall, crossing the extremely narrow neck of the headland's tip. The inturned entrance retains its gate jambs, and behind it lie traces of two round houses. The appearance of the site suggests that there were two or three phases of construction.

Treryn Dinas (45)

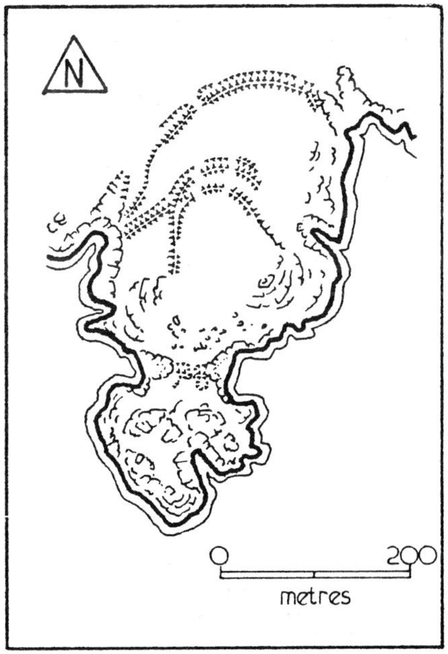

Trencrom Castle (44)

Treryn Dinas (45)

46 **Tresvennack, menhir,** Drift.

SW 442279.

Footpath S from Tresvennack Farm on road between the A30 at Lower Drift and the B3315 at Chywoone Grove.

3.5m tall and gracefully shaped, this fine Bronze Age stone is set 1.2m into the ground. Two magnificent urns, one very large and containing bones, were found near its foot in 1840, hidden beneath a stone slab. These are on view in the Penlee Museum, Penzance.

47 **Try, menhir,** Newmill.

SW 460350.

200m S of Trye Farm, off E side of Penzance–Gurnard's Head road 1 mile N of Newmill.

This elegant stone is 2.7m tall and triangular in section. Excavations in 1958 and 1962 revealed a perfect stone cist at the foot of the stone, containing a 'handled A' beaker, pot sherds and bones, both burnt and unburnt. Further sherds and flints were scattered about the cist which had once been covered by a small cairn.

48 **Zennor Quoit, Penwith chamber tomb,** Zennor.

SW 469380.

Footpath leads uphill from S side of the B3306, opposite a prominent house ¾ mile E of Zennor.

This great neolithic tomb stands high on a bare, windswept ridge. Five massive upright slabs support an immense capstone, 5.5m by 2.9m by 0.4m thick, partially dismounted due to the collapse of the back support. A further pair of slabs forms an impressive façade to an ante-chamber and false portal. The chamber is 2.4m high and once stood within a stone mound 12.8m in diameter, little of which remains. Various excavations have recovered neolithic and Early Bronze Age pottery, bones, flints and a perforated whetstone which indicated that the site had been in use until at least 1500 bc (1850 BC). The northern façade stone has lost its top, due to the vandalism of a Georgian farmer who wished to break up the Quoit to build a shed, part of which stands close by. Only the intervention of the vicar – one of the Borlase family – saved the monument. A sketch made in 1762 by the vicar's great-grandfather, Dr William Borlase, shows substantial remains of the stone barrow, and the capstone in its original position.

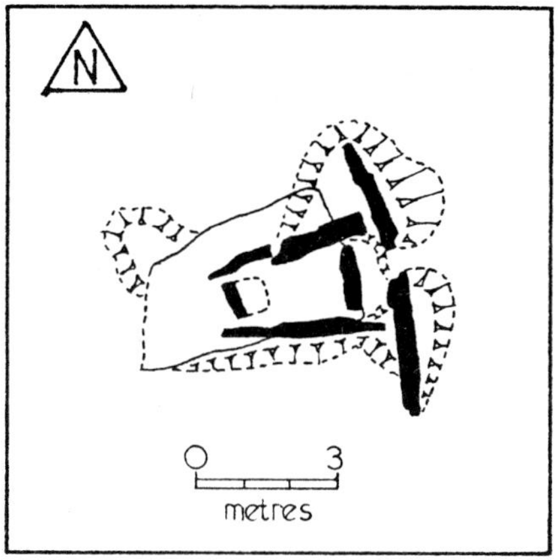

Zennor Quoit (48)

Zennor Quoit (48)

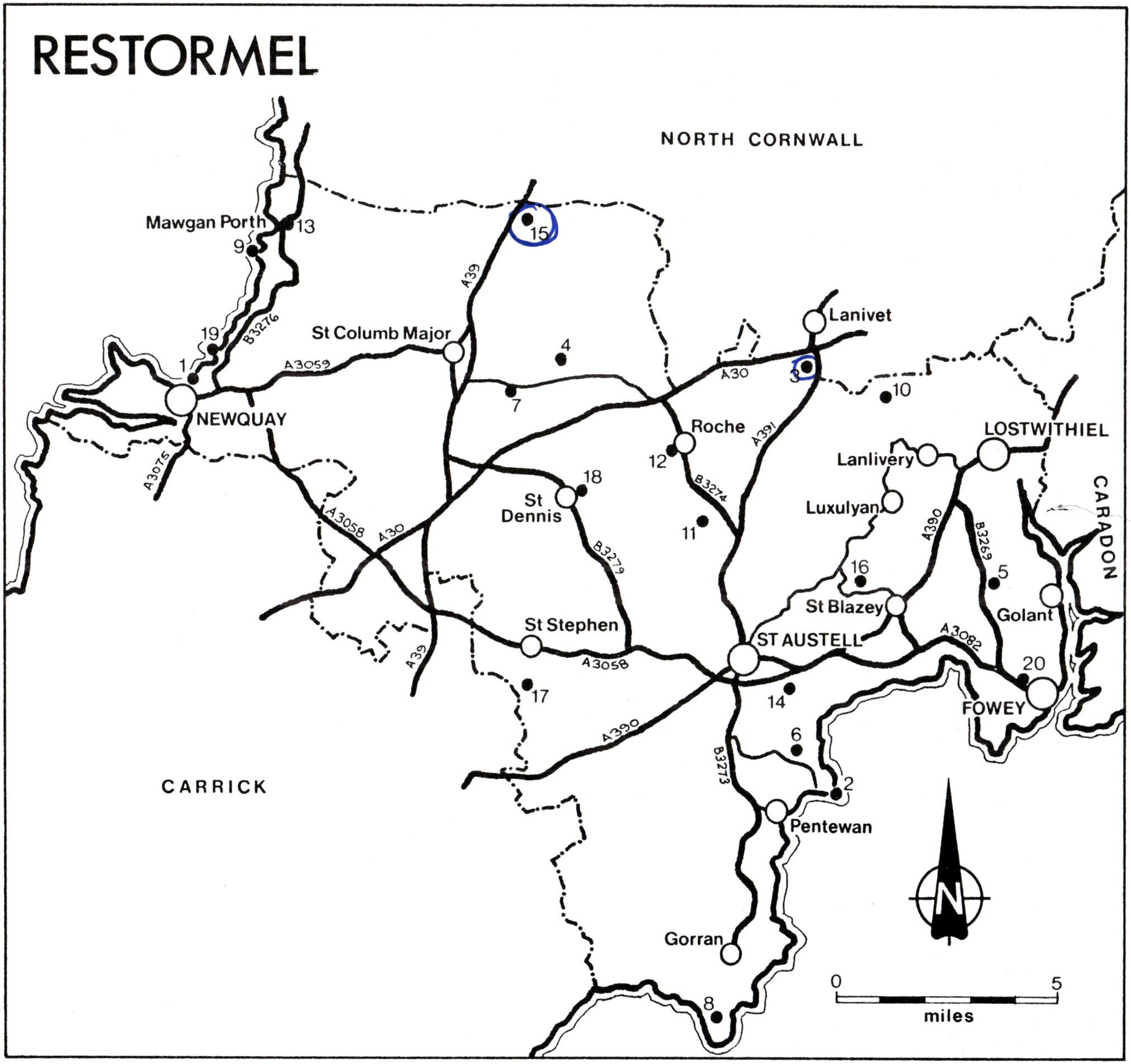
RESTORMEL
NORTH CORNWALL
Mawgan Porth
13
9
15
B3276
19
1
St Columb Major
A3059
A39
4
Lanivet
A30
3
10
NEWQUAY
7
Roche
A391
LOSTWITHIEL
Lanlivery
12
18
St Dennis
B3274
A3075
Luxulyan
CARADON
A3058
A30
11
A390
B3269
B3279
16
5
St Blazey
Golant
St Stephen
ST AUSTELL
A3082
A39
A3058
17
14
20
FOWEY
A390
6
B3273
CARRICK
2
Pentewan
N
Gorran
0
5
miles
8

1 **Barrowfields, round barrow cemetery,** Newquay.

SW 820622.
On seafront at Newquay, in middle of a miniature golf course.

Originally a cemetery of at least eighteen Bronze Age bowl barrows; all except three were destroyed in 1821. The remaining barrows are poorly preserved. Two are very low and the third, although well defined, is no higher than 0.9m.

2 **Black Head, cliff castle,** Pentewan.

SX 039479.
On cliff path between Porthpean and Pentewan.

This headland has three lines of defence across its neck. The outer rampart is slight, and its ditch virtually untraceable. The central bank is set back from it; it is 5.2m high and fronted by a ditch 2.1m deep. The innermost rampart is of similar height. None of these Iron Age defences is so well preserved on the south side of the headland.

Black Head (2)

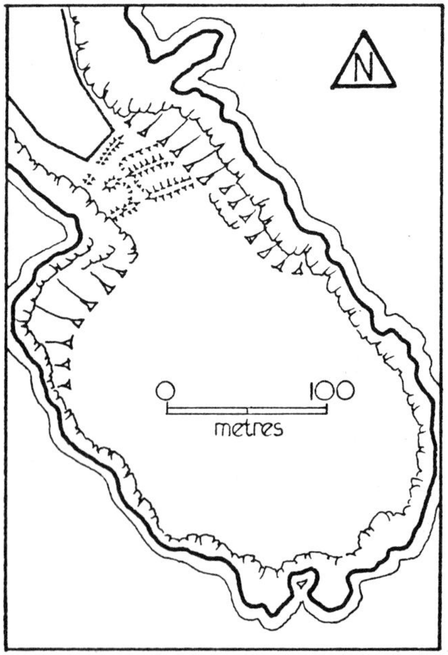

3 **Castilly, henge,** Lanivet.

SX 031627.
Above W side of the A391, just S of its junction with the A30. The site is clearly visible from the A30.

An oval earthwork with a maximum diameter of 66m. The surrounding bank is 1.8m high; the internal ditch is 2.1m deep and 5.5m wide. The flat, featureless central area measures 49m by 29m. The broad opening on the north-west side is the original entrance; the smaller south-eastern gap dates from about the thirteenth century when the site was remodelled for use as a *plen-an-gwary* (medieval amphitheatre). It was adapted again, this time for defensive purposes, during the Civil War. The henge, recognized as such in 1954, was excavated in 1962, but its neolithic origin was not conclusively proved. Sited on a north-facing slope, it lies near the junction of two major prehistoric trackways and was formerly surrounded by several round barrows, few of which remain.

Castilly (3)

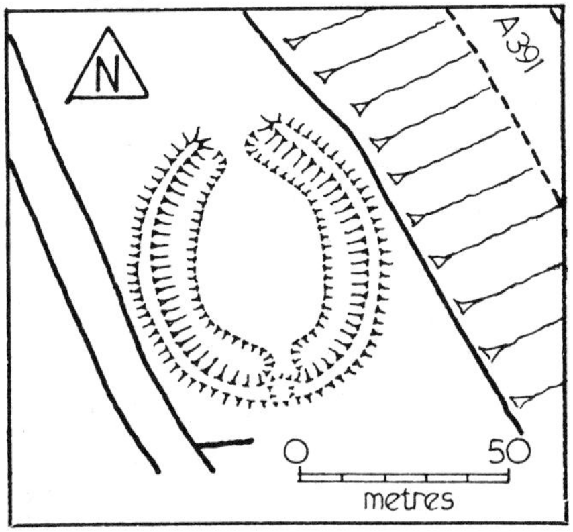

Castilly (3)

4 **Castle-an-dinas, hill fort,** St Columb Major.

SW 946624.
2 miles SE of St Columb Major, and reached by minor road E from the A39. Lane W of Providence leads N to the fort (no unauthorized vehicles).

The first phase of this superb Iron Age fort was a univallate enclosure some 220m in diameter, defined by an insubstantial bank and outer ditch pierced by no less than six entrances. This was later abandoned, and a series of massive defences was thrown up to produce a large and formidable hill fort 260m across. These huge earth ramparts, of unrevetted dump construction, are a prominent feature of the landscape for miles around.

The inner rampart, reaching a height of 7.5m, is fronted by a deep ditch which has a

Castle-an-dinas (4)

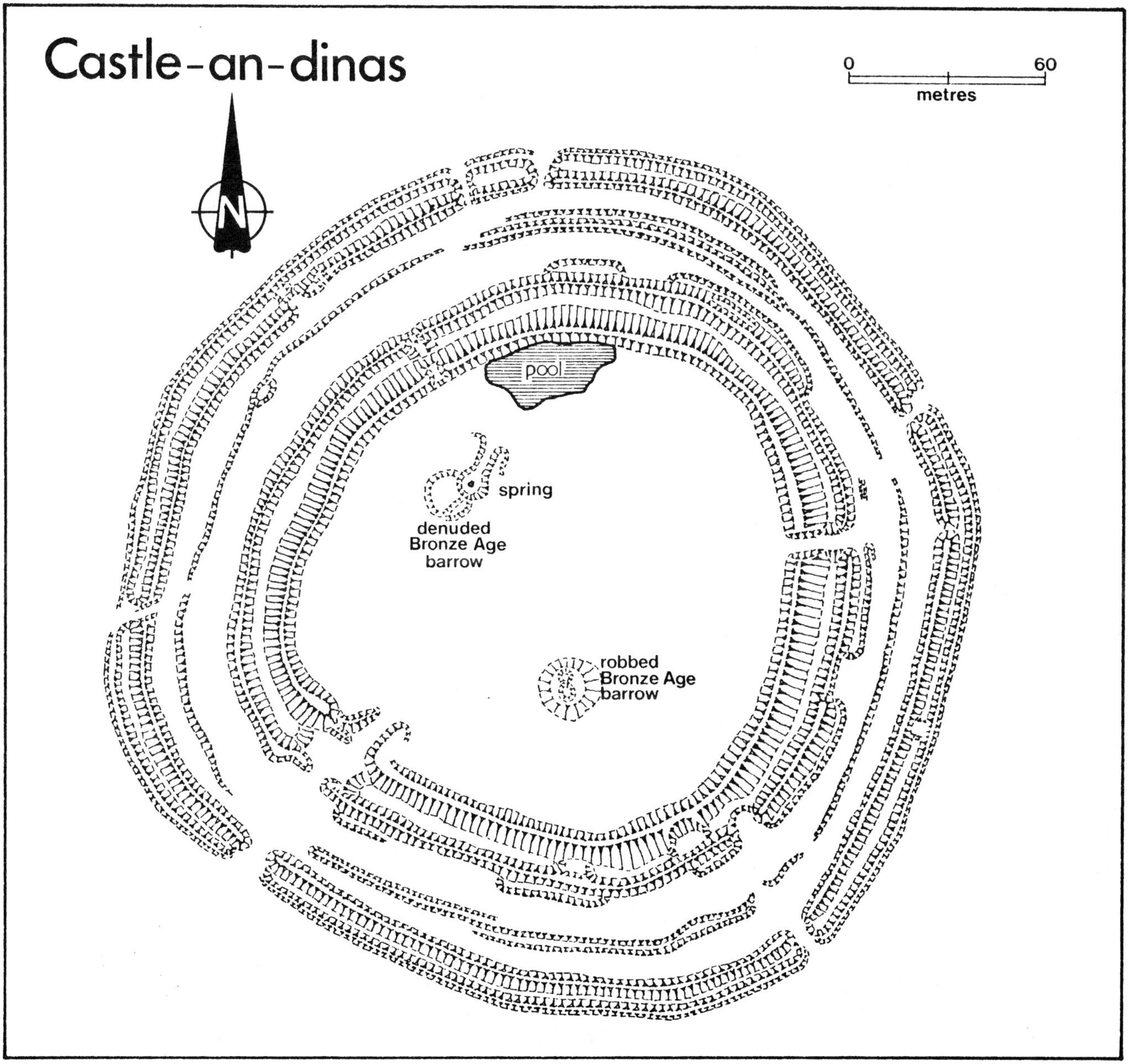

Castle-an-dinas
0
60
metres
N
pool
spring
denuded
Bronze Age
barrow
robbed
Bronze Age
barrow

large bank up to 2.0m high on its outer lip. Despite the remains of a shallow external ditch, this is now interpreted as a counterscarp rather than as a separate rampart. The slight remains of the first phase bank and ditch can be traced between this and the outer rampart, still rising 3.7m above the foot of its lightly counterscarped ditch, which has an average depth of 1.5m. The single entrance is a simple, straight-through affair facing south-west; signs of a cobbled road were found during the 1962-4 excavations. These excavations were small and failed to prove the traditions of occupation extending into post-Roman times. Some signs of Iron Age occupation were found near the spring hollow in the northern interior of the fort, and near the inner entrance. Sling-stones were also found. A slight mound on the south side of the spring hollow may have been a Bronze Age barrow; a second barrow, plundered long ago, can be seen in the southern part of the inner enclosure. It is 17m in diameter and 0.9m high.

5 Castle Dore, hill fort, Golant.

SX 103548.

Beside the B3269, 2¼ miles N of Fowey, on E side of road.

An Iron Age fort with two ramparts. The inner one is as much as 4.6m high externally and is circular, 90m across. For much of its circuit it is closely followed by an outer bank which reaches a height of 5.0m, with an outer ditch originally 3.7m deep but now only partially visible and 1.8m deep. On the east side, this outer bank bulges away from the inner one to form a roughly triangular annexe, through which passes the entrance. The overall dimensions of the fort are 150m by 134m. Excavations in 1936-7 revealed that it was built *c.*200 BC, and that the defences were remodelled *c.*50 BC. The occupants had been wealthy farmers and metalworkers.

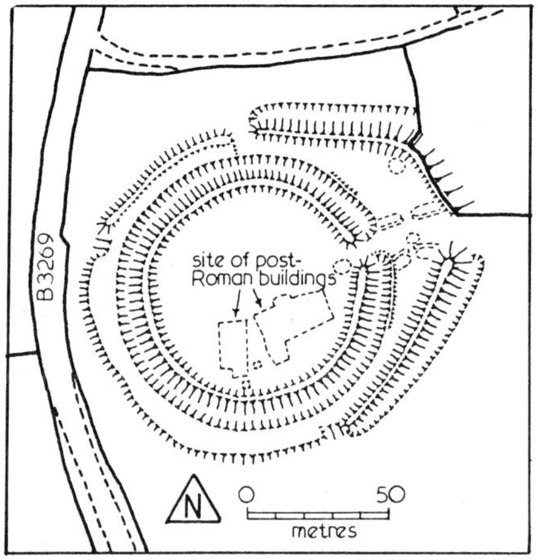

Castle Dore (5)

In the sixth century AD the fort was re-occupied by local royalty and the defences were again remodelled. This may well have been the work of Mark Cynvawr (Marcus Cunomorus), the King Mark of later Arthurian tales whose son Drustans (Tristan) is commemorated on the sixth-century pillar near Fowey (Site 20). A series of post-holes in the inner enclosure of the fort marked out the site of a timber-built 'palace', a hall 27m by 12m with a small annexe at one end. The site of another, smaller hall was also found. To complete its history, Castle Dore was used again during the Civil War.

Castle Dore (5)

6 Castle Gotha, settlement enclosure, St Austell.

SX 028496.

Near E side of minor road due S from St Austell, 1 mile beyond turning to Porthpean.

Only traces remain of most of the single rampart and ditch of this small oval earthwork, although there is a stretch of bank 1.8m high on the south side. The enclosure originally measured 109m from north to south, by 97m; the entrance faced north-east. Excavations showed that it was constructed during the second century BC, with occupation continuing into the second century AD. Huddled against the inside of the rampart were the sites of timber huts which were shown to have been occupied by metalworkers. Pits, hearths and a stone mould for casting penannular brooches were found; so too was an ingot mould embedded in the floor of a hut.

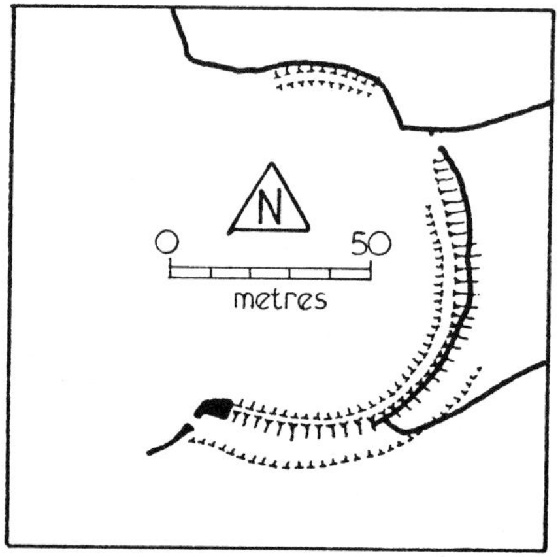

Castle Gotha(6)

7 Devil's Coyt, Penwith chamber tomb, St Columb Major.

SW 923619.

Minor road E from the A39 at SW 912623. Site lies by roadside at Quoit, after ½ mile.

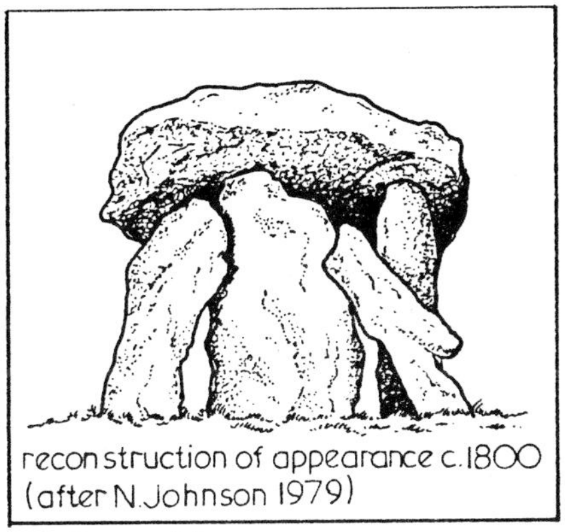

Devil's Coyt(7)

Fragments of this tomb were rediscovered in 1977 by the Cornwall Committee for Rescue Archaeology while pipe-laying was under way. Early reports described a monument similar in appearance to Chûn and Mulfra Quoits, Penwith, with a closed chamber 2.1m by 1.8m by about 2.0m tall, surmounted by a heavy capstone. It was complete until the eighteenth century when the western side stone was removed. After 1840 the quoit partially collapsed, so that one end of the capstone rested on the ground. The northern side stone broke in the fall. Around 1870 the collapsed tomb was broken up and the stones were buried or used to build field walls. The 1977 examination found a number of stones of the same type as those used in the monument, and dowsing revealed what is believed to have been the original capstone. It measures approximately 3.0m by 2.0m, corresponding to the dimensions given in the early reports. This stone and a descriptive plaque were set on the roadside by the Old Cornwall Society. The tomb would have been neolithic.

The Dodman (8)

8 The Dodman, cliff castle, Gorran.

SX 001399. NT.

Best reached by farm track leading S from National Trust car-park at Penare, 1 mile S of Gorran Churchtown.

A large area of this massive headland was defended by a huge earth rampart up to 6.5m high – in an outer ditch of which runs a modern farm track – and a counterscarp bank 1.2m high, its inner face revetted with stone. These earthworks are variously known as the 'Balk' and the 'Hack and Cast'. The position of the original entrance is difficult to determine from the number of modern breaches. Within the defences are the remains of two Bronze Age round barrows; no dwelling sites have yet been located. The name Dodman is derived from the Cornish word *tomen*, a bank or dyke.

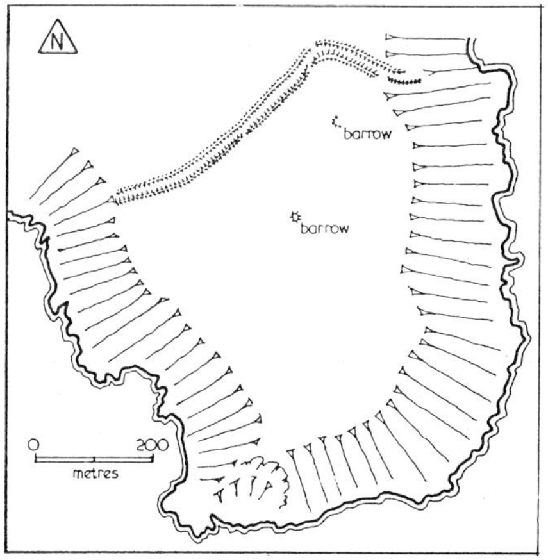

The Dodman (8)

9 Griffin's Point, cliff castle, Mawgan Porth.

SW 842664.

Reached by cliff path S from Mawgan Porth.

The entrance of this Iron Age cliff castle is on the higher, southern side of the headland; three ramparts descend the steep, north-facing slope. The two lower ones are little more than scarped terraces; the inner bank is much stronger, reaching 2.5m in height. Inside the fort are three circular depressions which may represent hut sites.

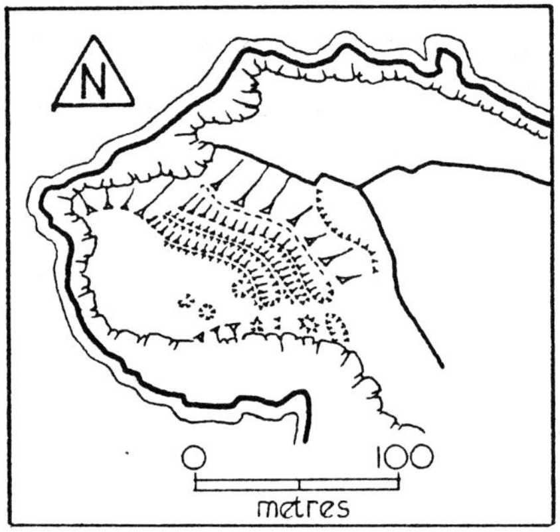

10 Helman Tor, tor enclosure, Lanlivery.

SX 061617.

Reached by minor road NW from Lanlivery, off the A390, 2½ miles N of St Blazey.

The slopes of Helman Tor carry the remains of a field system, among which are the relics of at least one round house. The rocky summit of the hill is enclosed by the battered remnants of an earth and stone wall which utilizes the natural outcrops of rock. This enclosure is long and thin, measuring 170m from north to south, by 60m. It is similar in size and construction to the neolithic village enclosure on Carn Brea, Kerrier, and may be of similar date. No internal structures have yet been identified.

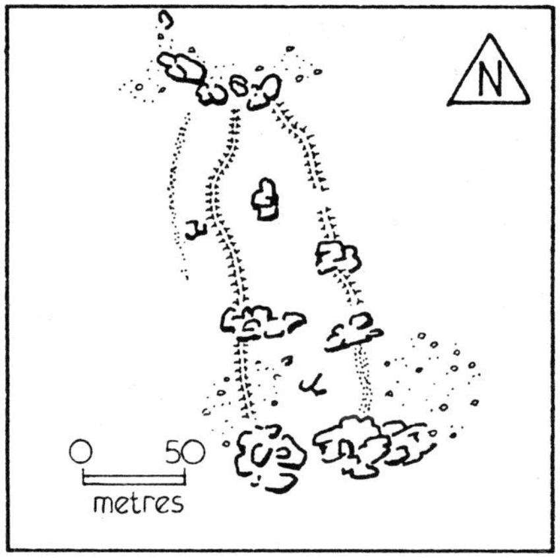

Helman Tor (10)

11 Hensbarrow, round barrow, Roche.

SW 997575.

Accessible by footpath leading SW from the B3274, 1¾ miles SE of Roche.

Sited on the highest natural point (312m) of the china clay country is this exceptionally large cairn, 5.4m high and 36m in diameter. Once used as a beacon, the original Bronze Age cairn may have been enlarged to suit this purpose.

12 The Longstone, menhir, Roche.

SW 986601.

Now set up on a green at Holmleigh Crescent, St Dennis Road, Roche.

This fine Bronze Age menhir was moved to its present position a few years ago as its original site on Longstone Downs (at SW 984561) was to be swallowed by the extension of china clay workings. Excavation found that this broad, pointed slab, 3.2m high, had replaced an earlier stone which, in turn, had taken the place of a wooden post.

The Longstone (12)

13 Mawgan Porth, settlement, Mawgan Porth.

SW 852673.

On E side of the B3276 in centre of village.

This Dark Age settlement, set on the bank of a former tidal estuary, was occupied between AD 850 and AD 1050. There are three clusters of buildings, two of which were excavated in 1950-4, and it is believed that a fourth existed. The stone houses were rectangular, with walls averaging 0.7m thick.

The larger of the two excavated groups consisted of four buildings set around a central courtyard. The group measured 21m by 17m overall. The largest building, on the west side of the courtyard, was an early longhouse with a through passage and partition dividing it into living room and byre, the latter containing drains. The second group, arranged in a similar

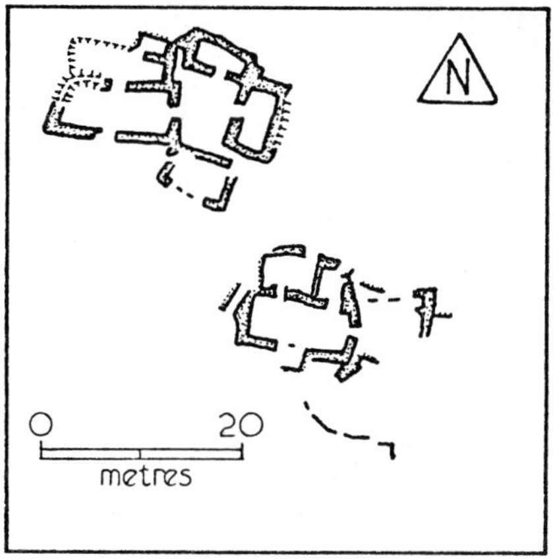

Mawgan Porth (13)

way, was of a later phase. Above the village was a cemetery of slate cists, the western part being set aside for the burial of children. The proportion of child burials was unusually high. The inhabitants of the village were farmers and fishermen who seemed to have existed without the use of metal implements. Among the animals they kept were sheep, goats, horses and oxen as well as dogs, cats and poultry. Some contact with Anglo-Saxons was indicated by a coin from the time of Aethelred II (*c.*AD 1000).

14 **Mount Charles, menhir,** St Austell.

SX 030521.
In grounds of school which fronts on to the A3061 just S of roundabout intersection with the A390.

A Bronze Age menhir, 3.5m tall. The land on which it stands was formerly known as Gwallon Downs, and an extensive cemetery of round barrows, now destroyed, stood close by. The menhir is granite, the nearest source of which is more than a mile away.

15 **Nine Maidens, stone alignment,** St Columb Major.

SW 937676.
3 miles NE of St Columb Major, 300 metres E of the A39.

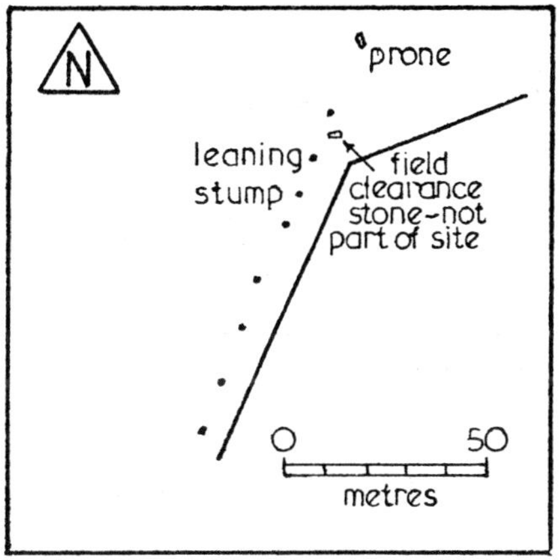

This Bronze Age stone row has nine stones, irregularly spaced, in a line 106m long and aligned from south-west to north-east. Six of the stones are erect and from 1.0m to 1.9m high; a seventh, 1.8m long, is almost down. Another is merely a stump, 0.8m high, and the ninth, the northernmost, is prone and measures 3.0m in length. There are a number of field clearance stones that should not be confused with the alignment which pointed towards an outlying menhir – variously known as 'The Fiddler', 'The Old Man' or 'Magi Stone' – about 500m to the north-east. The menhir was broken up some years ago, but part of it, 1.8m long, still lies on the site at SW 939682. The Nine Maidens was thought to be Cornwall's only stone row, but eight more, all on Bodmin Moor have been discovered recently.

Nine Maidens (15)

16 **Prideaux Castle, hill fort,** St Blazey.

SX 059556.

Reached by footpath off minor road which leads north and west from the A390 at St Blazey.

Situated on a wooded spur, this large multivallate Iron Age fort has two concentric earth ramparts and parts of a third, outermost rampart surviving. The fort is pronouncedly oval, and would originally have had diameters of 235m and 160m. The ramparts range in height from 1.3m to 2.7m, the innermost being the strongest. The ditch surrounding the inner rampart has a counterscarp 1.0m high on its outer lip. The fort appears to have had a staggered entrance: the outer bank is pierced on the north side; the gap through the inner defences faces north-west. An apparent straight-through eastern entrance may be of recent origin.

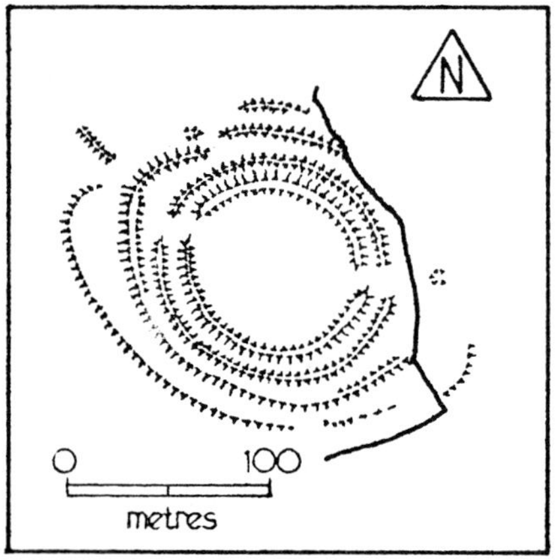

Above: *Prideaux Castle (16)*
Right: *Resugga Castle (17)*
Far right: *St Dennis (18)*

17 **Resugga Castle, hill fort,** St Stephen-in-Brannel.

SW 940510.

Reached by minor road running S from St Stephen. Site lies in fields on E side of road, 2 miles S of village.

This well-preserved Iron Age fort stands on level ground near the brink of a deep valley to the south and west. It is oval with a single rampart 3.0m high surrounded by a ditch up to 1.0m deep. The diameters of the fort are 116m and 100m. The entrance, on the north-west, is approached by a sunken track passing through an isolated length of rampart which was either a protective outwork or the remains of an annexe.

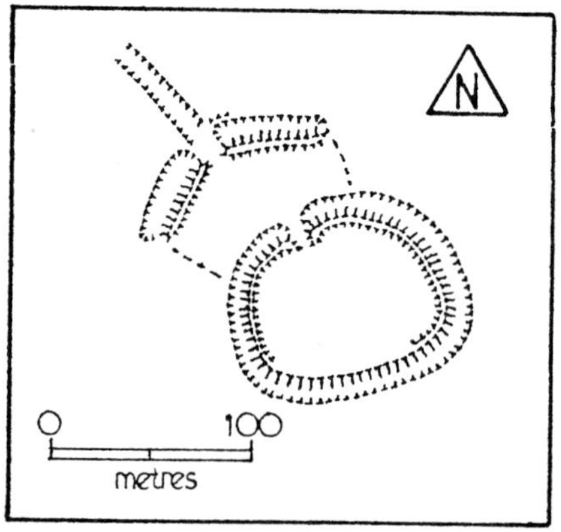

Left: *Prideaux Castle (16)*
Above: *Resugga Castle (17)*

18 **St Dennis, hill fort,** St Dennis.

SW 951583.

St Dennis church (named not after the saint but the dynas *– fort) stands in the centre of this site.*

This strikingly conical hill was formerly surmounted by two Iron Age ramparts defending an area 113m in diameter. The line of the inner bank, which may have been stone-built, is followed by the churchyard wall. Only faint traces of the outer rampart can be seen, on the north and east sides, about 18m beyond the churchyard wall.

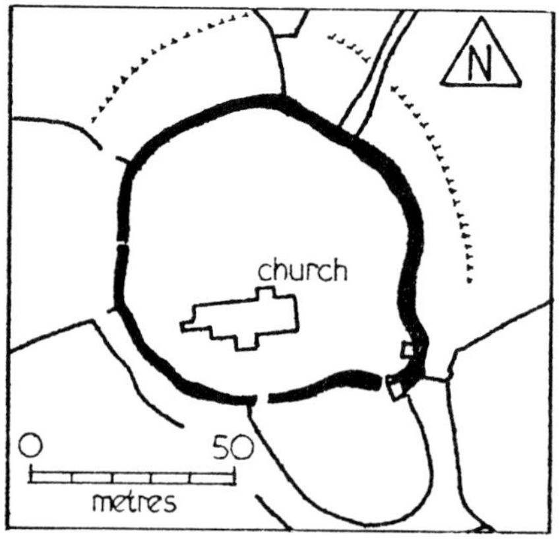

19 **Trevelgue Head, cliff castle,** Newquay.

SW 825631.

Footpath W from the B3276 just N of St Columb Porth.

An outstanding Iron Age cliff castle with no less than six lines of defence. The outermost, adjoining the putting green, is up to 2.2m high and fronted by parts of a deep ditch, one stretch of which is heavily counterscarped. Beyond this are three large and closely spaced ramparts 2.2m, 4.0m and 2.9m high. The ditch fronting the easternmost of these is 1.4m deep. The innermost of the three ramparts sits on the edge of a narrow chasm now crossed by a wooden footbridge. The next rampart, on the far edge of the chasm, is 2.7m high; the entrances through both are recent. The sixth line of defence is a ditch 1.6m deep and an earth rampart 3.5m high. Behind this rampart, and close to the northern cliff, are an L-shaped bank and ditch which may be Roman.

Excavation in 1939 showed that the cliff castle was continuously occupied from the third century BC to the fifth or sixth century AD. Two rows of round houses were found behind the inner rampart. One of these huts was 17.6m in overall diameter, with a stone wall 1.8m thick. Inside were two concentric rings of post holes – the inner having held posts up to 30cm thick – a central hearth. Evidence of contact with the Romans appeared in the form of coins of Vespasian and Trajan. The hut was occupied from *c.*250 BC to AD 150. An iron mine was located under the cliffs on the north side of the headland, and bronze and iron smelting was much in evidence. A bronze horse harness of Iron Age date was discovered.

There are two Bronze Age bowl barrows on the headland: one on the north cliff just within the outer rampart, the other on the highest point of Porth Island, beyond the innermost rampart. These are 21m and 15m across respectively; their heights are 3.7m and 3.0m. Both were opened in the nineteenth century, but nothing is known of their contents.

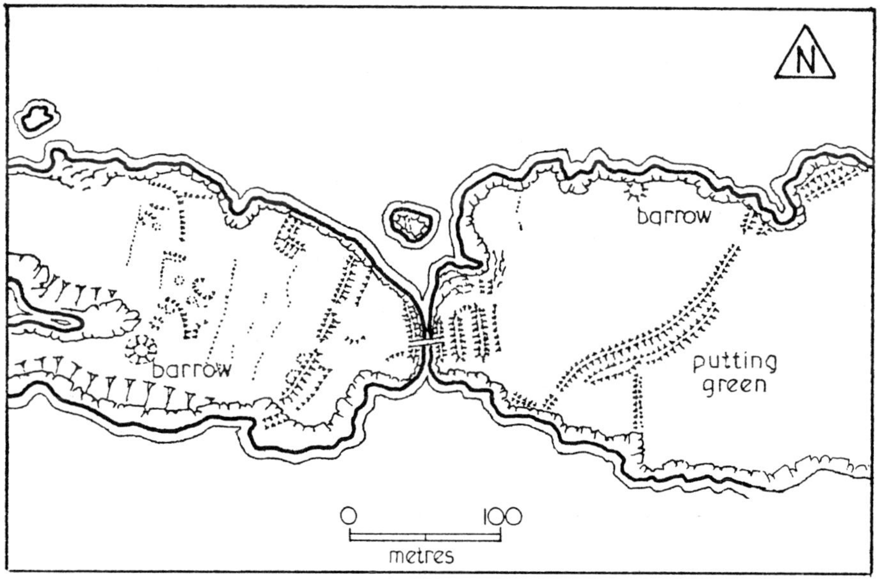

Half a mile north of the cliff castle, on a cliff overlooking Zacry's Islands, are two further bowl barrows which were opened in 1872. The eastern barrow contained a stone cist in which lay a crouched adult skeleton with a stone battleaxe by his hand; the other held a cist containing unburnt human bones. It appeared that a huge funeral pyre had been burning on this cist for several days before the barrow was heaped over it. Finds from these barrows are in the County Museum, Truro.

20 **The Tristan Stone, inscribed stone,** Fowey.

SX 110524.

By roadside at Four Turnings, on the A3082, 1 mile NW of Fowey.

This great pillar stone, 2.7m high and set on a modern plinth, was formerly called the Longstone. Originally it stood closer to Castle Dore (Site 5), 2 miles to the north. High on the back of the stone is a Tau cross, carved in relief; on the front, running vertically down the stone, is a two-line inscription interpreted as: DRVSTANVS HIC IACIT CVNOMORI FILIVS (Drustanus lies here, son of Cunomorus). This has been dated to the sixth century AD. The two names have been equated with the famous Tristan and King Mark of Cornwall; indeed, a ninth century manuscript speaks of 'Marcus, also named Quonomorius' who ruled over both the British and Breton regions of Dumnonia and Domnonée. Unfortunately, the first name of the inscription is now almost illegible.

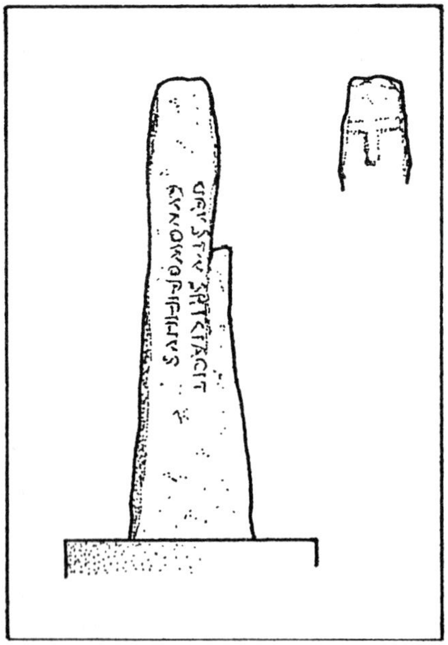

The Tristan Stone (20)

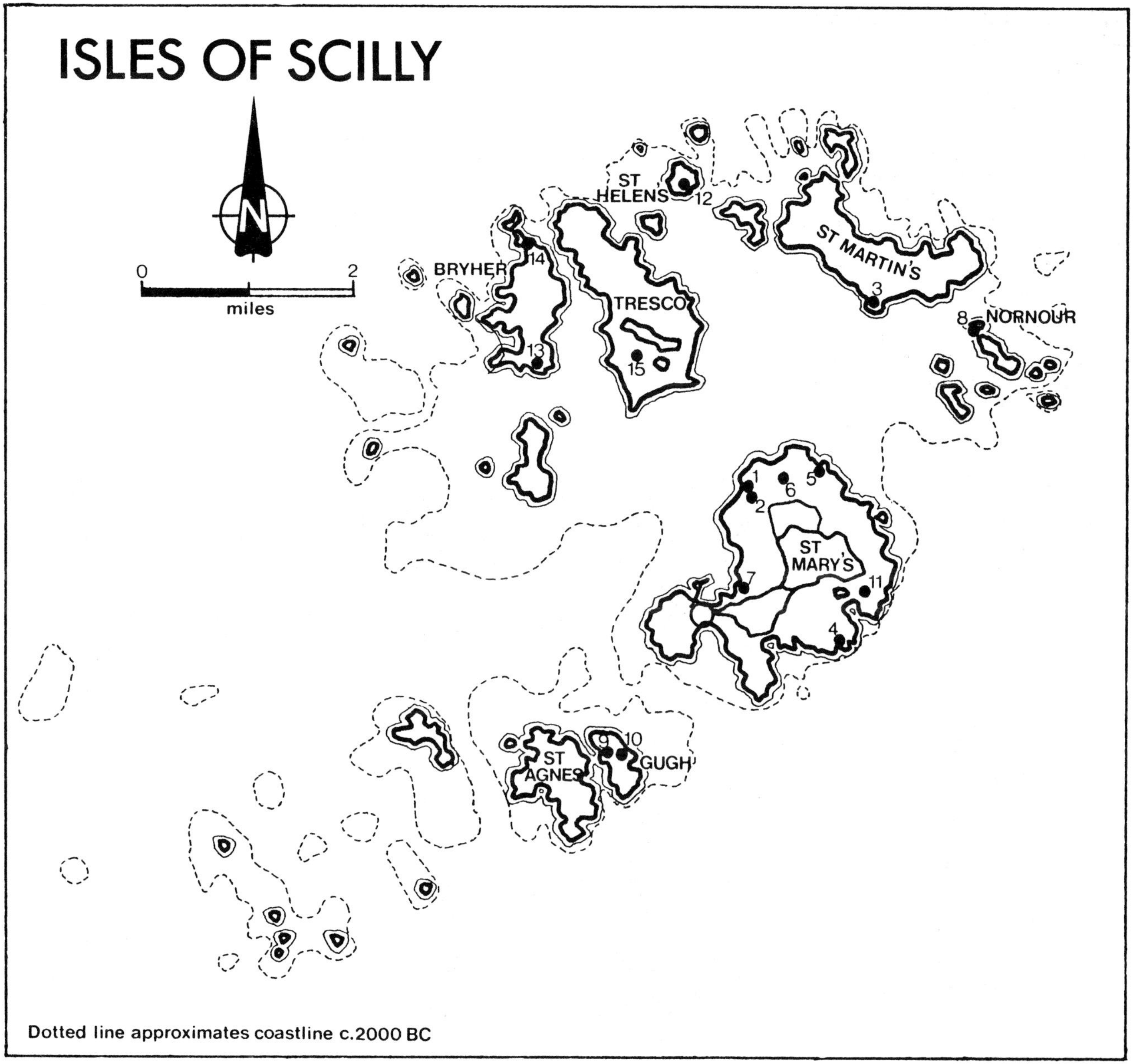
ISLES OF SCILLY
N
0
2
miles
ST HELENS
12
BRYHER
14
TRESCO
15
13
ST MARTIN'S
3
8
NORNOUR
1
2
5
6
ST MARY'S
7
11
4
ST AGNES
9
10
GUGH
Dotted line approximates coastline c.2000 BC

1 Bant's Carn, courtyard house settlement, St. Mary's.

SV 910124. DE.
Beside coastal path near N end of golf course, and well signposted from Macfarland Downs at SV 913126.

Excavated in 1935, and again from 1964-70, this fine little settlement stands on a steep slope among the extensive remains of a terraced field system. A number of conjoined and free-standing huts stand close to an apparent courtyard house of the type otherwise found only in the Penwith peninsula of Cornwall. This building is 26m long by 14m wide, and its walls survive to a height of 1.2m. There was settlement on the site from the Bronze Age to post-Roman times, but the main period of occupation, to which the visible structures belong, was from the second to the fourth centuries AD. The field system, now largely overgrown, covers 2ha, and its lynchets stand as high as 1.5m. There are traces of perhaps half a dozen round houses among these fields some 70m east of the main settlement, and the Bant's Carn entrance grave (Site 2) stands against a lynchet at the top of the slope.

Bant's Carn settlement (1)

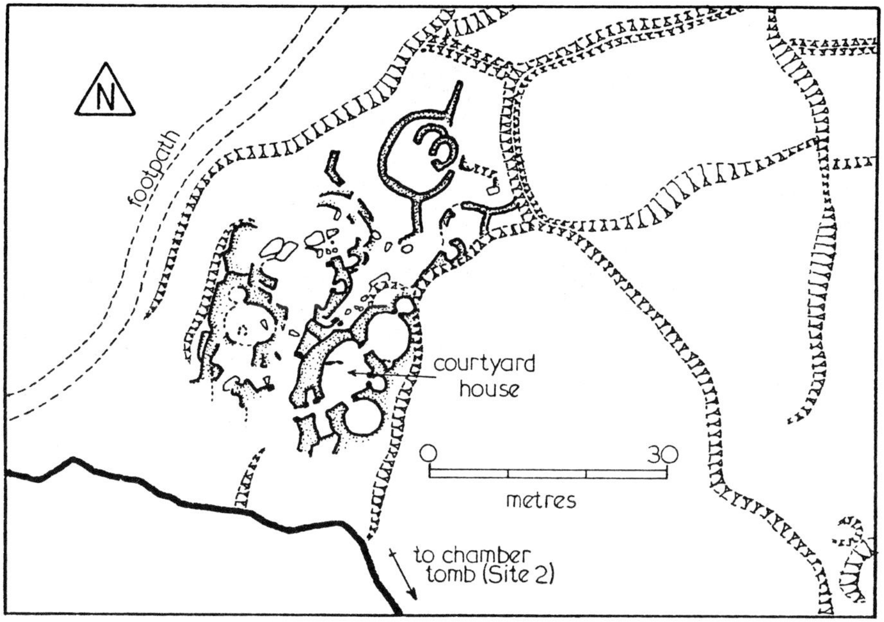

Bant's Carn settlement (1)

2 Bant's Carn, Scillonian chamber tomb, St Mary's.

SV 910123. DE.
See Site 1 for directions.

This round cairn, 11.6m across and 1.8m high, consists of a kerbed inner cairn 8.2m in diameter, surrounded by a low, wide collar also retained by a kerb of granite blocks. An entrance passage 4.6m long passes through the outer collar to the chamber which is 5.2m long, 1.5m wide and 1.5m high, and roofed by four capstones. The chamber entrance, which faces south-east, has stone jambs and its walls are slightly corbelled. Excavations have produced neolithic and Late Bronze Age pottery – the latter from a re-use of the site – cremations and human bones.

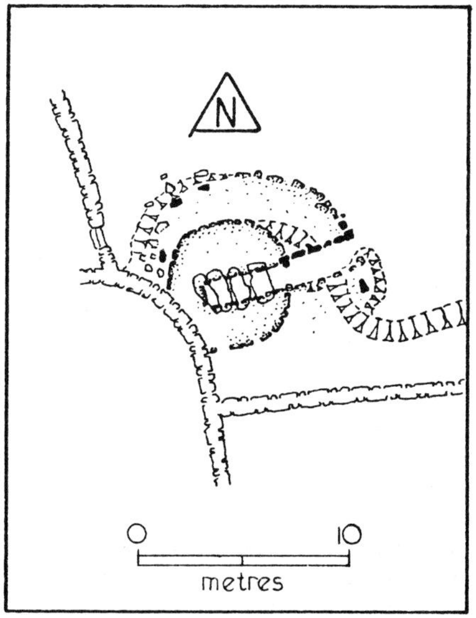

Bant's Carn tomb (2)

Bant's Carn tomb (2)

centre are the remains of what may have been an entrance grave, but its original plan and orientation are impossible to ascertain from surface appearance. The southern mound is 4.5m in diameter and 0.8m high and retains much of its kerb. There is a large natural boulder within the kerb, but no trace remains of any chamber or cist that the barrow may have held. All the barrows are likely to be of late neolithic or Early Bronze Age date.

Cruther's Hill tomb (3)

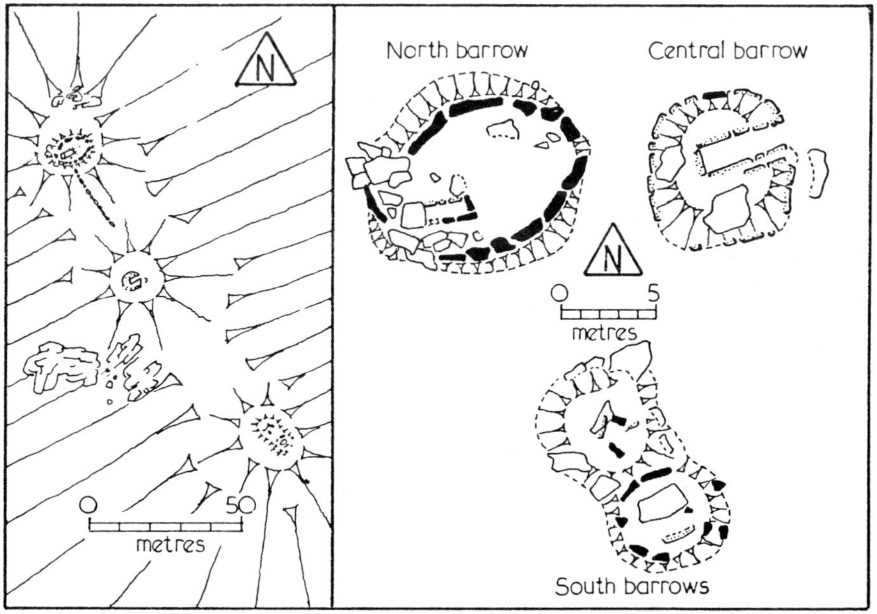

3 **Cruther's Hill, Scillonian chamber tombs**, St Martin's.

SV 930152.
On hilltop above landing quays, S of Higher Town.

Each of the three summits of Cruther's Hill carries barrows. The northern summit has an oval, kerbed mound with diameters of 12m and 8m. It is 0.9m high and incorporates natural outcrops. The chamber, in an off-centre position near the south-western end of the mound, appears rather cist-like despite its length of 3.8m. It is 0.7m wide, with its western end covered by one surviving capstone.

The tomb on the central summit is an unmistakeable entrance grave, 8m in diameter and 1.8m high. It has a massive kerb, broken on the north-east by the entrance to a roofless chamber 4.7m long, 1.2m long and 1.0m deep.

The southern summit bears the remains of two conjoined barrows. The northernmost, 6.5m across, incorporates natural rock. In the

4 Giant's Castle, cliff castle, St Mary's.

SV 925101.
Beside coastal path S of Porth Hellick, and just SE of the airfield.

This small rocky headland, facing into deep water, is protected by four curving lines of defence. The outermost is a low bank up to 1.0m high, fronted by the shallow remnants of an outer ditch and mutilated at its western end by the ruins of a watch-house. The second defence reaches a height of 1.2m and traces of a ditch can be seen near its western end. Behind this is a stone-revetted rampart 1.6m high, utilizing natural outcrops. The innermost line of defence takes advantage of a natural scarp 2.0m high, the top of which has been revetted and built up. A circular depression behind this rampart may be a hut platform. The enclosed area is very small indeed, and is largely occupied by a large granite outcrop. The site is unexcavated, but Early Iron Age pottery was found here during World War II.

Giant's Castle (4)

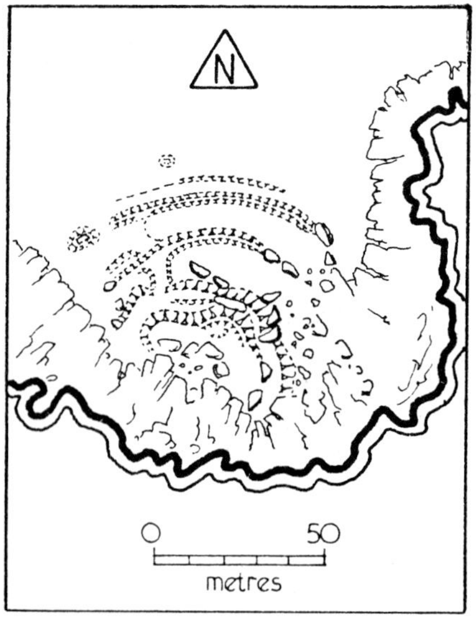

Giant's Castle (4)

5 Innisidgen, Scillonian chamber tombs, St Mary's.

SV 921128 and 922127.
Beside coastal path half-way between Watermill Cove and Bar Point. The tombs are well signposted.

Approaching from the west, following the signposted track from Macfarland Downs, the first tomb is the Lower Innisidgen grave which lies at the foot of a slope, close to the sea. The mound is oval with diameters of 8m and 7m, and part of its retaining kerb remains. The chamber, which lies due north-south, is 0.6m wide at the entrance (facing south), widening to 0.9m, and two of its capstones survive. It has been dated to around 1700bc (2095 BC).

This tomb is but a prelude to the magnificent Innisidgen Carn or 'Giant's Grave' which stands by the path 100m further to the south-east, at the top of the slope near a rocky outcrop. It has a well preserved mound 8.2m across with a complete kerb that survives up to three courses high. This was formerly surrounded by an outer collar, similar to the Bant's Carn site (Site 2), which was about 3m wide. Its outline can just be traced. The chamber, entered from the south-east, is 5.5m long and 1.4m high. It is coffin-shaped, 0.9m wide at the entrance widening to 1.5m, and is roofed by five large capstones. The tomb has so many similarities to the Bant's Carn site that both may have had the same architect. It is likely that this tomb is of about the same date as its neighbour.

Innisidgen tomb (5)

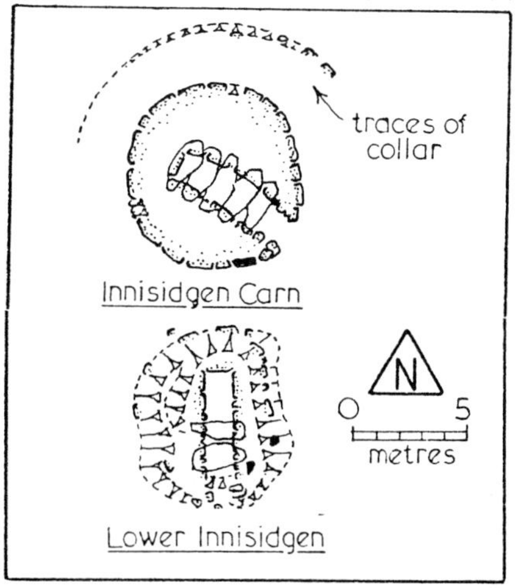

Innisidgen carn (5)

7 Mount Flagon, menhir,
St Mary's.

SV 909109.

The stone stands next to a windmill-shaped daymark adjacent to the incomplete Tudor fort of Harry's Walls, which is signposted from the coast path between Porthloo and Hugh Town.

It is remarkable that this presumably Bronze Age stone was not incorporated in the Tudor fort. It is a massive stone, 2.7m high, set up on a modern base 0.6m high.

Lower Innisidgen tomb (5)

Mount Flagon menhir (7)

6 The Long Rock, menhir,
St Mary's.

SV 914124.

In a grove of trees immediately behind houses at Macfarland Downs.

This Bronze Age stone has an almost mystic appearance, standing in a small clearing in the midst of a pine grove. It is 2.5m tall and leans to the north-east.

The Long Rock (6)

8 Nornour, round house settlement, Nornour.

SV 944148.

On S coast of the uninhabited island of Nornour, which is joined to the uninhabited island of Great Ganilly at low water. Access to either island is difficult, but the site is included because of its importance.

The settlement was discovered in 1962 and excavated in 1968 and from 1969 to '70. Just above present high water mark are a group of round houses founded *c.*1500 BC and occupied continuously into the Roman Iron Age. Eleven buildings, constructed at various times, have been recognized. They measure up to 5.5m in internal diameter and some walls are up to 3.0m thick and stand up to 1.2m high. Evidence was found of cereal crop cultivation, stock-rearing, fishing and the manufacture of pottery and stone tools. It was obvious that the area of dry land then available for agriculture was considerably greater than it is today.

9 Obadiah's Barrow, Scillonian chamber tomb, Gugh.

SV 888085.

Gugh can be reached at low water by a sand spit connecting it to the island of St Agnes (properly 'Agnes'). The site lies on the SW flank of Kittern Hill, 80m NW of the barrow-crowned outcrop of Carn Valla.

Named after one Obadiah Hicks, a former St Agnes farmer, Obadiah's Barrow is the best of about a dozen tombs on this tiny island. Built into the hillslope, it has a stone mound 7.3m in diameter. Its chamber, 5.2m long, 1.5m wide and 1.0m high, is entered by a short, angled passage. Four large capstones remain, two of which have fallen into the chamber. It was excavated in 1901 and remains of inhumation burials, later cremations, and a piece of bronze were found.

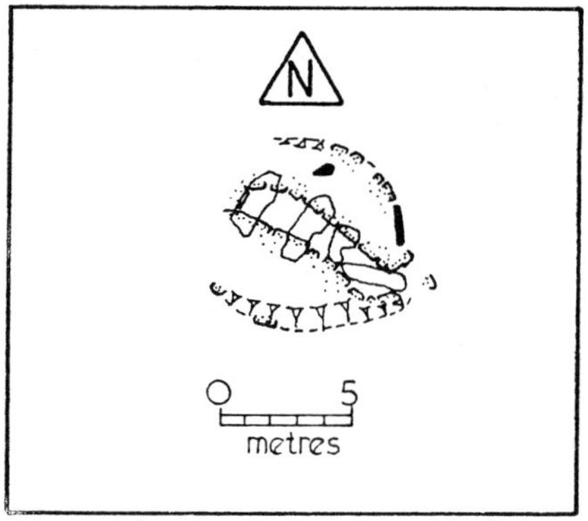

Above and below: *Obadiah's Barrow (9)*

Nornour (8)

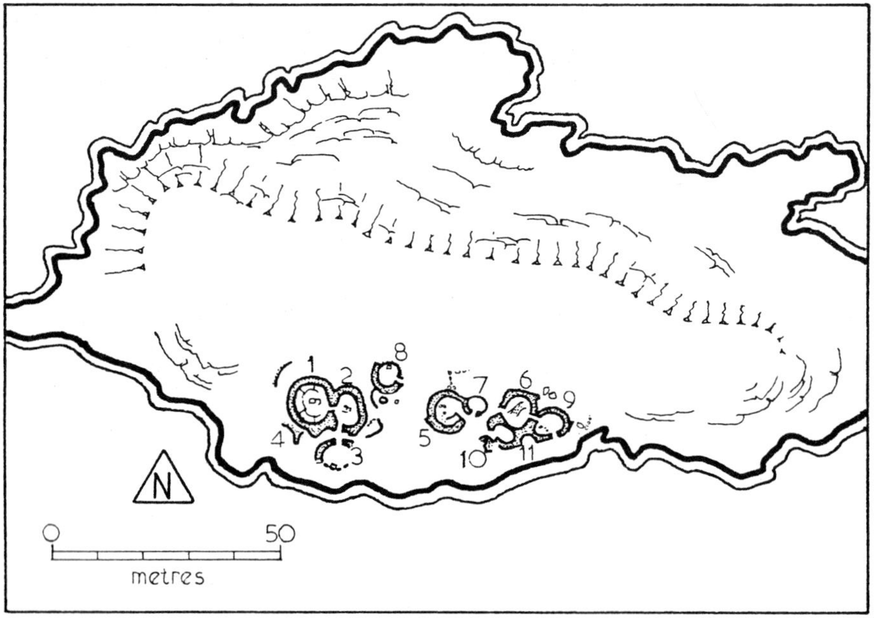

10 The Old Man of Gugh, menhir, Gugh.

SV 891085.
At SE base of Kittern Hill.

This fine Bronze Age standing stone is a bulky, leaning pillar of weathered granite. Its top is 2.4m above the ground, but would be 2.7m if fully upright. The ground around its base has been dug, but nothing was found.

The Old Man of Gugh (10)

11 Porth Hellick Down, Scillonian chamber tomb, St Mary's.

SV 928108. DE.
At N end of Porth Hellick Down, well signposted from Porth Hellick, and from the A3110 at Carn Friars.

This large, impressive tomb has a mound 12.2m in diameter, retained by a well-built kerb up to three courses high. A lower collar which once surrounded it was destroyed during 'restoration' by the then Ministry of Works. A roofless entrance passage 4.3m long and 0.9m wide approaches the chamber at an angle. The chamber itself is 3.7m long, 1.4m wide and 1.1m high, roofed by four capstones. Its entrance is restricted by a single upright slab to a width of 0.6m. Excavated in 1899, the site produced Late Bronze Age pottery, probably from a re-use of the tomb which belongs to the late neolithic/Early Bronze Age. To the south, on the overgrown downs, are a number of ruinous mounds, four of which show remains of chamber tombs.

Porth Hellick Down (11)

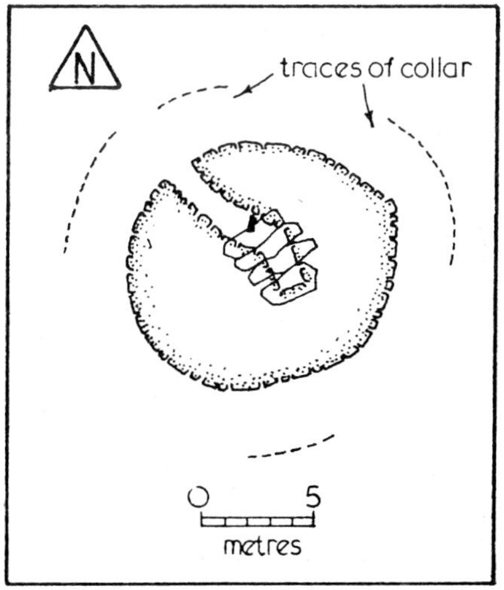

Porth Hellick Down (11)

12 **St Helen's Oratory,** St Helen's.

SV 902169.

On S coast of uninhabited island of St Helen's.

The name St Helen's is recent; the island was formerly St Elidius, named after the traditional founder of this religious site. There are a number of stone-walled enclosures, the largest containing a collection of buildings the most obvious of which is the ruin of a twelfth-century church, in use until the dissolution of the monasteries in the sixteenth century. Immediately west of the church is a circular Romano-British hut with an overall diameter of 5.5m. The oratory, a rectangular structure 7.3m long and 4.6m wide, lies just north of the church. Its wall is 1.2m thick, and a stone altar can still be seen. The oratory possibly dates from the seventh or eighth century AD, and the settlement strongly resembles the seventh century hermitage of Ynys Seiriol, Anglesey.

St Helen's Oratory (12)

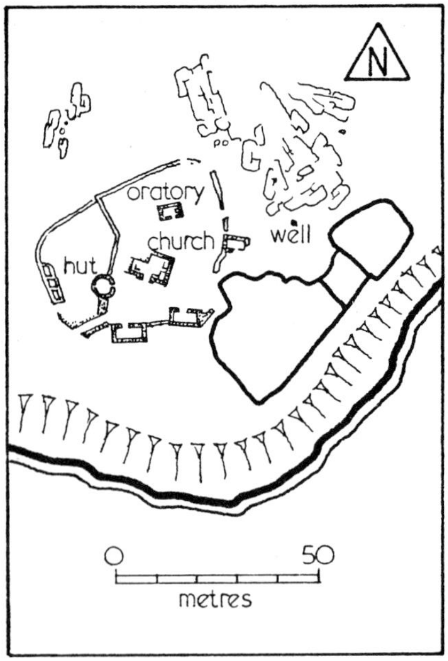

13 **Samson Hill, Scillonian chamber tomb,** Bryher.

SV 878142.

Situated half-way down the S slope of Samson Hill.

There is a sadly ruined tomb on the summit of Samson Hill, but this excellent tomb is situated on a flat ledge on the steep southern face of the hill, directly beneath a high outcrop whence one gains a superb aerial view of the site. 9m in diameter, the denuded mound is retained by a massive kerb still two courses high in places. The chamber (entered from the north-east) is coffin-shaped: 0.8m wide at the entrance, 1.4m in the middle and 1.1m at the distal end. Six capstones, one of which is displaced, still cover much of the somewhat infilled chamber.

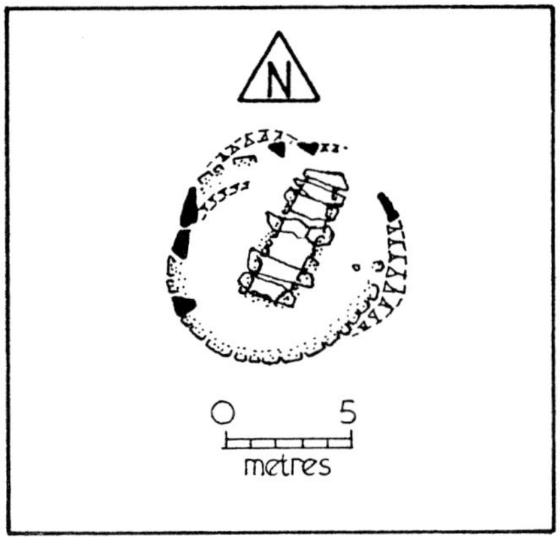

Samson Hill (13)

Samson Hill (13)

14 **Shipman Head, cliff castle,** Bryher.

SV 876161.
On lowest part of headland to N of Shipman Head Down.

The headland faces deep water. The remains of a massive wall across it are the ruins of an Iron Age cliff castle. The tumbled wall, vestiges of whose inner and outer facings are visible, is 5.0m thick and stands to a height of 0.9m. No outer ditch is traceable and the position of the entrance is not obvious. No hut remains have been found yet within this defensive line.

Shipman Head (14)

Shipman Head (14)

15 **Tresco Abbey Gardens, Roman altar,** Tresco.

SV 893143.
At W end of 'Long Walk' within the gardens.

Reputedly found on the site of the 'Pilot's Gig' café in Hugh Town, St Mary's, this unusual find, the only one of its type west of the Tamar, was subsequently taken to Tresco. Carved from granite, it stands 0.8m high and 0.5m square. Panels are picked out on all four sides, two displaying raised carvings of a cleaver and an axe respectively. Any inscription which may have existed is no longer visible.

Built into the foot of the smaller arch in the surviving wall of the old abbey is an Early Christian inscribed stone. Discovered in 1868, the incomplete inscription reads: . . . THI FILI COGVI (. . . thus, son of Coguus). It has been dated to the sixth century.

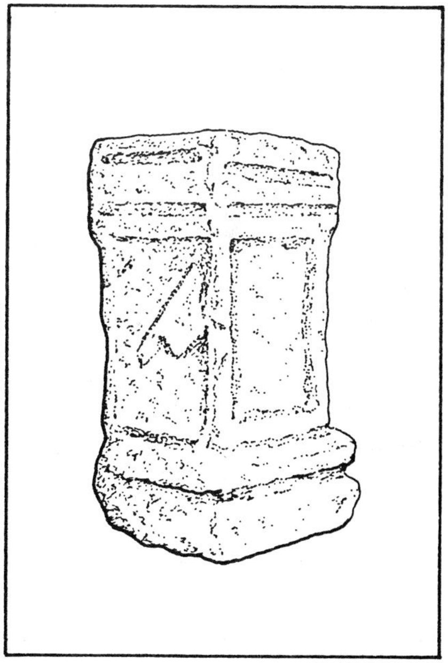

Tresco Abbey altar (15)

Appendix

A selection of radiocarbon and recalibrated dates

The following dates have been produced from organic material, often charcoal, recovered from excavations in Cornwall over the last fifteen years. The radio-carbon (C14) dates are shown in years bc or ad. The calibrated dates, calculated from tree-ring checks on the long-living Bristlecone pine and reproduced here from the tables formulated by Clark (1975), are deemed to represent true years and are indicated by years BC or AD. In my list these dates have been rounded. Sites featured in this book are shown in bold type.

Poldowrian, St Keverne: mesolithic occupation	4500±110bc	5500–5250BC
Poldowrian, St Keverne: neolithic occupation	3230±150bc	4200–3850BC
Carn Brea, Redruth: neolithic occupation	3049±64bc	3900–3750BC
Poldowrian, St Keverne: neolithic occupation	2920±130bc	3850–3600BC
Carn Brea, Redruth: neolithic occupation	2747±60bc	3600–3500BC
Carn Brea, Redruth: neolithic hearth outside settlement enclosure	2611±47bc	3450–3300BC
Poldowrian, St Keverne: charcoal beneath Beaker mound	2050±150bc	2850–2400BC
Poldowrian, St Keverne: lowest layer of Beaker mound	1540±90bc	2000–1800BC
Crig-a-Mennis barrow, Perranporth	1565±90bc	2000–1800BC
Tregiffian, Lamorna: secondary cremation	1539±59bc	2000–1800BC
Watch Hill barrow, St Stephen-in-Brannel	1520±70bc	2000–1800BC
Nornour, Scilly: Period I midden	1310±280bc	2000–1300BC
Gwithian: Layer 5 cremation	1120±103bc	1550–1300BC
Trevisker, St Eval: Bronze Age occupation	1110±95bc	1500–1300BC
Nornour, Scilly: Building 9	1040±100bc	1450–1150BC
Kelly Rounds (Castle Killibury): pre hill fort occupation	930±70bc	1250–1050BC
Kelly Rounds (Castle Killibury): pre hill fort occupation	840±70bc	1100–950BC
Nornour, Scilly: Building 5	740±90bc	1050–850BC
Carn Euny, Sancreed: Phase I occupation	420±70bc	600–425BC
Kelly Rounds (Castle Killibury): hill fort occupation	260±70bc	400–200BC
Trevisker, St Eval: Iron Age occupation	185±90bc	400–100BC
Kelly Rounds (Castle Killibury): hill fort occupation	167±70bc	300–100BC
Carn Euny, Sancreed: Phase 2 occupation	130±80bc	200–1BC
Carn Euny, Sancreed: storage pit, Courtyard House 4	ad90±100	AD50–250
Nornour, Scilly: Building 7	ad110±70	AD90–250
Shortlanesend, settlement enclosure	ad110±70	AD90–250
Shortlanesend, settlement enclosure	ad170±90	AD150–300
Carn Euny, Sancreed: pits dug through extramural road	ad210±70	AD215–300

Bibliography

Ashbee, P., *Ancient Scilly* (David & Charles, 1974).
Barnett, J., *Prehistoric Cornwall: The Ceremonial Sites* (Turnstone Press, 1982).
Borlase, W., *Antiquities Historical and Monumental of the County of Cornwall* (1754; EP Publishing, 1973).
Clark, R.M., 'A calibration curve for radiocarbon dates', *Antiquity* XLIX (1975), pp. 251-66.
Cook, J., *When I set out for Lyonesse: Cornish Walks and Legends*, Alison Hodge, 1984.
Dyer, J., *Southern England: An Archaeological Guide* (Faber, 1973).
Dyer, J., *The Penguin Guide to Prehistoric England and Wales* (Penguin, 1982).
Jenkin, J., *A First History of Cornwall* (Dyllansow Truran, 1984).
Laing, L., *The Archaeology of Late Celtic Britain and Ireland* (Methuen, 1975).
Laing, L. and J., *The Origins of Britain* (Routledge & Kegan Paul, 1980).
Laing, L. and J., *Celtic Britain* (Routledge & Kegan Paul, 1979).
Laing, L. and J., *A Guide to the Dark Age Remains in Britain* (Constable, 1979).
Michell, J., *The Old Stones of Land's End* (Garnstone Press, 1974; Pentacle Books, 1979).
Pearce, S., *The Archaeology of the South West* (Collins, 1981).
Pearce, S., *The Kingdom of Dumnonia* (Lodenek Press, 1978).
Pevsner, N., *The Buildings of England: Cornwall* (Penguin, 2nd edn., 1970).
Russell, V., *West Penwith Survey* (Cornwall Archaeological Society, 1971).
Russell, V., *Isles of Scilly Survey* (Institute of Cornish Studies and Isles of Scilly Museum, 1980).
Thomas, A.C., *Exploration of a Drowned Landscape: Archaeology and History of the Isles of Scilly* (Batsford, 1985).
Thomas, A.C., Pool, P.A.S., Weatherhill, C., *The Principal Antiquities of the Land's End District* (Cornwall Archaeological Society, 16th edn., 1980).
Weatherhill, C., *Belerion: Ancient Sites of Land's End* (Alison Hodge, 1981).
Woolf, C., *An Introduction to the Archaeology of Cornwall* (Bradford Barton, 1970).
Cornish Archaeology, the annual journal of the Cornwall Archaeological Society.

Museums to visit

Camborne: Public Library and Museum, Cross Street.
Camelford: North Cornwall Museum and Gallery, The Clease.
Helston: Town Museum, The Butter Market, Church Street.
Isles of Scilly: Isles of Scilly Museum, Church Street, Hugh Town, St Mary's.
Penzance: Penzance Natural History and Antiquarian Museum, Penlee House, Penlee Park, Morrab Road.
Truro: County Museum, Royal Institution of Cornwall, River Street.
Zennor: Wayside Museum, Old Millhouse.

Index of Sites

Page references in bold type indicate illustrations.